TOWARDS
TOMORROW

TOWARDS
TOMORROW

The Autobiography of
FENNER BROCKWAY

Hart-Davis, MacGibbon   London

Granada Publishing Limited
First published in Great Britain 1977 by Hart-Davis, MacGibbon Ltd
Frogmore, St Albans, Hertfordshire AL2 2NF and
3 Upper James Street, London W1R 4BP

ISBN 0 246 10847 9

Printed in Great Britain by Richard Clay (The Chaucer Press), Ltd.,
Bungay, Suffolk

ACKNOWLEDGEMENTS

Thanks are due to Messrs George Allen and Unwin for permission to repeat much that was in my books, *Inside the Left* and *Outside the Right*, and to the Society of Authors for permission to print the playlet by George Bernard Shaw. I am indebted to Joan Hymans for cooperation in correcting the proofs and to Mabel Eyles for typing my manuscript.

For permission to reproduce the following photographs thanks are due to: *Keystone Press* for 'F.B. greets Jawaharlal Nehru on his visit to Tilak House' and 'Fascist slogans daubed on the author's house'; *Romano Cagnoni (Report)* for 'With Anne Kerr and Sydney Silverman at a CND demonstration' and 'F.B. at a feeding centre at Nguru, Biafra'; *Press Association* for 'In the ceremonial fur cloak of a chief of the Kikuyu'; *Universal Pictorial and Press Agency* for 'A group family photograph'; *Society of Authors* for 'A postcard from Bernard Shaw'; and *Slough Observer* for 'Clem Attlee presenting F.B. with a briefcase'.

CONTENTS

*To my children, grandchildren
and great-grandchildren and to
the coming generations who will
build the New World*

CHAPTER ONE

BOYHOOD

Towards Tomorrow. I have had difficulty in selecting a title for these mem-oirs, but, looking back, I think perhaps these two words express the motive of the better part of a life which also has regrets. The Tomorrow of which I have dreamed remains distant. I tell this story not only as history, but in the hope that the failures, the few successes, may help those who follow. They will achieve.

For three generations my family – grandparents, parents, uncle, aunt, sister – were Christian missionaries in Madagascar, India, China. I was born in Calcutta on 1 November 1888, but spent my early childhood at Berham-pur, a small Bengali township on the banks of a tributary of the Ganges. Although I was there only four years my memories are vivid. We lived within a walled compound, balconied house at its centre, the servants' hutted quarters far back, the river across a sanded road, our little steamboat, *Jessie*, anchored among its weeds. I had a pet chicken and remember when it was eaten by a jackal I was comforted by another under a wastepaper basket by my tub-bath.

I seem to have been a healthily mischievous baby. In his life of my mother, *Frances E. Brockway*, James Brown quotes a letter from her describing how at morning prayers, when the servants prostrated themselves on the floor, her one-year-old grabbed their hair. One of the servants later gave a less refined account saying I toddled round pinching their upraised sari-thin bottoms. My mother told me I preferred making mud pies with the Indian servants' children to going to parties at the homes of the European élite. A shape of things to come?

At four I was sent to England because India's climate was unsuitable for a growing child. I was placed under the care of my maternal grandparents at Rangemore near Burton upon Trent. My grandfather was estate manager for Lord Burton, the head of Bass & Company; there were high iron gates to his private grounds, a treelined drive, a magnificent mansion, a small zoo with caged animals. Beyond were woods and fields and tenant farms with fox hunting and pheasant shooting in season. My grandfather supervised all this.

The family – there were two daughters, Kate and Eva, in their early twenties – lived in a beautiful thatched cottage in a hollow of the woods. One looked down from a lofty road to a green carpet, cottage beyond, firs and beeches all about it. In tall trees peacocks sheltered at night, shrieking at dawn, the glowing tails of the males upright as they flirted on the lawn by day. I saw the Burton family at Church on Sunday mornings, the service never beginning before they took their places in the front pew. Lady Burton came once to the cottage to see the strange little boy from India who could speak Bengali. I disappointed her; I had entirely forgotten my Indian tongue on the three-week journey from Bombay on the P & O liner. For the moment I thought I remembered. 'ABCD' I said, pleased with myself, knowing they were not English words.

My grandparents were conventional supporters of the Establishment. The daughters were more lively, both engaged, talking about their love affairs in a concocted language to which I soon caught on, giving myself away by laughing at one of their stories. I do not know how I came to rebel against this ultra bourgeois atmosphere, or at what age. One Sunday morning I refused to go to Church, insisting that as my parents were Nonconformists I should be allowed to go to chapel. I was kept in bed where I sang lustily 'Dare to be a Daniel'. After that I was allowed to go to Chapel with one of the servants.

Two years later my parents came home on furlough and brought with them my sister Nora, two years younger. We went on a long summer holiday to Pitlochry in Scotland and there I was sent to school for the first time. Scottish schools were voluntarily comprehensive even then, all children, boys and girls, attending whatever their background. Punishment was by strokes on the hand from a broad black strap called a tawse. The headmaster took our infants class, and a procession of children were brought in during the day to be chastised. I lost my heart to a little fair-haired girl who was a repeated offender. I remember crying at home, my mother comforting me, a little amused at my first love affair. My Rangemore grandfather sent us money for picnics and I have colourful memories of lovely places, Dunkeld, Aberfeldy, the Pass of Killiecrankie, the Falls of Tummel. I have a more fearful memory. Near Pitlochry a rushing rivulet fell over a perpendicular rocky cliff, the Black Spout. I fell in the water some yards above the fall and was swept on but clung to a boulder. I can still see the anguished face of my father as he held out his stick to draw me to the bank.

The missionary vocation is open to philosophic criticism (though it did great service in education and health), but there is also a domestic objection. Except for furloughs I hardly knew my father. I admired him from a distance, but there was little relationship of parent to son. Affection grew on his retirement when for a time he stayed in our home. He was superbly tolerant and kind. With my mother association was closer. She was prevented from returning to India because she became pregnant and, except for school, I was with her; afterwards she came home with heart trouble and for six beautiful months she was everything to me. She died at the early age of forty-two. I am afraid the absence of a home with parents affected my later life.

At eight years of age I went to the School for the Sons of Missionaries, (SSM) at Blackheath where I stayed until I was sixteen. My sister Nora went to a similar school for missionaries' daughters, Walthamstow Hall, at Seven-oaks. Both were in fact charity schools, maintained by donations from sympathisers, but the Boards of Governors set out to run them on Public School lines. At Blackheath we had prefects who had the power to beat boys, we had fags, and on public occasions (always on Sundays) we wore Eton suits. Educationally, for me at least, the school was a washout. I learned little and was the worst behaved boy. We were caned if given more than one hundred 'order marks' in a week and I established a school record by achieving the target fourteen times in one term. The punishment became of little inconvenience to me. I got a boy in my dormitory to beat me with a slipper every night on thighs and bottom and they became as tough as leather. I created my own interests, many of them reprehensible. Four of us arranged to creep downstairs at 2 am each morning to finish the master's supper, usually stewed fruit, biscuits and cheese. On those night adventures we were interested in more than the left-over food. We would go down to the playground in our pyjamas to swing round the giant stride. We would go to the aviary and take pigeons back to the dormitory, and boys and masters would wonder in the morning light how they got in. We were never caught.

I have referred to the Governors of the school. Their chairman was Edward Unwin, founder of the printing firm and later of the publishers who bear his name. He was an impressive, grandfatherly figure, devoted to the welfare of the boys. He invited some of us to spend holidays at his large-gardened home in a Kentish suburb, Shortlands, where we had a marvellous time. My parents were so grateful that they decided to name my younger sister

Phyllis Unwin Brockway, reversing their decision only when they realised that her initials would be PUB.

The school adventures I have described were only mischievous, but on Sunday evenings we sometimes did things for which we would have been taken to a juvenile court if we had been caught by the police. When left alone to write letters, four of us would sneak out and rob orchards from the large houses in Blackheath Park. On one occasion an incident occurred which has remained a nightmare recollection. Finding an unoccupied house we broke in and climbed to its flat roof; a boy threw an apple to me, I stepped back to catch it, swayed on the gutter, managed to fall forward. Ever since I have been unable to stand heights. That frightening incident still sometimes comes back to me as I go to sleep.

My interests in school were not only mischievous. I loved games and sport. We were only ninety boys, but we turned out a Rugby international year after year. Before my time there was Gillespie of Scotland; among my fellows, Sibree of England and Fahmy of Wales; afterwards the great Gracie, perhaps the greater Liddel of Scotland (the latter won an Olympic medal as well) and one of the Smiths of England. Why were we so good? I think it was because of a unique ball game which, except during the hot summer months, the whole school played every minute of the day when we were not in class. The game was incredibly fast and we became expert in side-stepping and seizing an opening. Rugby became my religion. When I was about to leave at the end of the summer term in my sixteenth year, the headmaster asked me what I intended to do. 'Learn shorthand, become a journalist,' I said. 'Stay on and play rugby for us and we will pay for your course in shorthand,' he responded. I accepted and henceforth travelled to Pitman's college in Southampton Row each day. By accepting this bribe I suppose I became a professional.

Two afternoons a week were devoted to sport. When we were not playing, my chum, Harold Hills, and I explored the near-by countryside, keen on wildlife, fields and woods, an early indication of a later obsession and inspiration. Sometimes our interest was not Nature but strawberry plantations. One afternoon we were back late and, under reprimand by a master, I held the inside of my hat towards him; it was stained with red juice. That meant a caning for both of us. Harold aimed to be a surgeon and once operated on a pet pigeon which had a blocked throat, using gas from a burner as anaesthetic. He claimed the operation successful, but the bird died three days later. We remained friends after our school days, as I shall tell.

It is said journalists are born. My devotion seems to have been instinctive. About two years before I left school, I started a weekly magazine which I read to the assembled boys after 'prep'. It was a success at first but soon few listened. I turned to journalism for the local papers. To one weekly I contributed a series of profiles of church services and their parsons. The editor thought I was a master at the school. Pride, however, led me to my fall. I wrote an account of our annual sports day; the headmaster wrote one as well and my report appeared. Not satisfied with that, I pinned mine on the school notice board (reserved for official announcements) and added my initials. That brought a caning and the prohibition of all further journalism for the local papers.

My school successes were two: I won an essay prize, the subject 'Country or Town?'; I compromised by favouring a garden city. No one in later life believes that I also got a prize for singing. I had a good soprano voice, so good that I was chosen to sing 'Wings to Fly me Over' on prize day. It was a disaster. As I sang I noticed many in the audience were smiling, finding it difficult indeed not to laugh. My grandmother's face was in deep distress. I looked down. My stiff front to the Eton suit was descending between waistcoat and trouser tops, more and more evident. I did not sing the second verse, taking refuge behind the piano.

We had distinguished speakers on prize days – on this particular occasion it was Augustine Birrell, Minister of Education. He had a reputation for humour but began his speech by saying he could not compete with me in making the audience laugh. Another speaker I remember was Lady Aberdeen – she was a huge woman who laughed uproariously at the thought of a joke before she told it. The particular joke this day was to describe the trick by which she rescued two boys at our school from slavery in Egypt. She invited them on board her ship and then declined to hand them back on the ground that they were on British territory. Their name was Fahmy, perhaps related to Egypt's Foreign Secretary of the seventies. The elder of them was my school fag, later becoming the Welsh Rugby international.

The Boer War started my interest in politics. At the beginning I was all patriotic, wearing buttons with generals' portraits – White and Buller – on my chest, but before the end, captivated by Lloyd George, I became pro-Boer, joining the Young Liberals, whose Secretary if I remember rightly was Aubrey Smith in Edinburgh. After the war, the Reformers' Year Book became my bible, with photographs of Lloyd George and Winston Churchill as my pin-ups. I travelled to the old Queen's Hall to hear John Morley speak and fell for Churchill as, in lisping voice exuding his rich personality, he moved the vote of thanks. Back to school, I stood in front of a mirror trying to reproduce on my forehead his two deep lines. I began to publish pamphlets, neatly written and bound, for distribution among a few adherents.

Chinese labour in South Africa and Church teaching in schools were among the wrongs which I confidently exposed.

In my last year at school I broke into politics publicly by working for Liberal candidates for the London County Council and for David Williamson, the Liberal, in a Parliamentary by-election in neighbouring Dulwich. Boys slept in the headmaster's house ten minutes away as well as in the school building. I was among the former; seniors were allowed to arrive either at 8 pm or, with the excuse of studying, at 10 pm. I used to leave at eight, proceed to the Liberal Committee Rooms, distribute leaflets or canvass and return at ten. Dulwich, further away, was more difficult. I arranged with another boy to let me in, but one night he fell asleep. My gentle tapping disturbed the headmaster who was outraged by the time, nearly midnight. He was a Liberal and did not cane me, though I had five hundred lines to write.

A third interest, perhaps strange in a schoolboy, was pigeon breeding. We had school pets, among them pigeons which we bought from a deaf old man in a scruffy little shop in Deptford. Each cost a shilling when fledglings, but on one visit he insisted on half a crown for an unusually upstanding red-feathered bird. 'It's a real racing pigeon,' he said and I bought it. Happy, as I named her, grew up magnificently. I cycled to Chislehurst with her and she was back home before I was. I took her to Sevenoaks when visiting my sister, and she flew back safely. Then I heard of the Blackheath Flying Club and joined it, sending Happy in their basket by train to Hastings. Again she came back. The great day came – the Club organised a race from Boulogne in France. I entered Happy – and she won. How vividly I remember that Saturday afternoon, seeing her descend, grasping her, hurrying away to the Club Rooms in Blackheath Village to register her arrival, learning that she was first. I was presented with a silver medal. When I left school, I sold Happy to a club member for £5 – a lot of money in those days.

I must jump seventy years. A few days ago Happy fell just outside my window – not *my* Happy of course, but her very image, a beautiful red homing pigeon; she had bruised a leg on a near-by wire. Under the wing, as I expected, I found the name of her Racing Club in the Midlands. I phoned, learned that the bird was racing from Europe and that she was one of their most valuable possessions. 'Happy the Second' became a close friend, strutting on my newspaper-covered table, eating out of my hand. The day came, three weeks later, when she circled in the air and flew straight north. The club secretary phoned an hour later that she had arrived and added that they could never race her from the south again; she would always visit me en route. 'Happy the Second' now races from Scandinavia.

A fourth interest developed which I still cannot explain. On Sunday evenings religious boys held a prayer meeting led by a prefect named Haile, for whom I had respect because he was our rugger captain. We did a deal; he would lend me his watch, wanted because I was to go orchard robbing, and I would attend the prayer meeting the following Sunday. At the time a religious revival was taking place in South Wales, under the evangelism of a young Evan Roberts. Its emotionalism captured our boys and when I attended the prayer meeting it was in full command. Even I, sinner though I was, could not resist it. Boys stood and confessed their misdeeds, crying. I was converted and my life was redirected.

An epidemic of chicken pox had recently broken out at school. I was among those confined to a dormitory and boys used to get into bed together, no doubt practising some form of homosexuality. I was not attracted, but I had masturbated, and with my religious conversion this became a heinous sin. The headmaster had distributed among us a booklet by a Methodist minister named Bisseker, the head of the West Central Mission, which painted an appalling picture of the effect of masturbation: we were destined to insanity. Haile and I led a crusade among the boys against masturbation and against homosexuality though we knew little about it. I had a deeply religious period. Except for that frightening booklet, I never had any sex education. My first distorted knowledge of the facts of life came from the stable boy at Rangemore when I was about eight. I took my sister into a lavatory and explained my amazing discovery to her. I told poor Nora that her tummy would have to be opened for the baby to be born.

I may have given a wrong impression of my school. I was most of the time a misfit and it was doubtless a much better place for others, but I cannot avoid the feeling that it was wrongly conceived. It was a closed community of boys who were denied family life because their parents were abroad and who needed more than most the warmth and help of some adult friendship. We did not get it, and I am not sure that in a boarding school we could have got it. Our only contact with adults was with masters, and the atmosphere was 'them' and 'us'. One master succeeded in overcoming this obstacle: our language and literature teacher, Sidney Moore – subsequently headmaster of Saltcoats School in Yorkshire – who made every boy feel he was a friend. He was the one person (except for Lloyd George and Winston Churchill) to whom I looked up in my schooldays.

CHAPTER TWO

TEENAGER

My father married again and was now in charge of the multi-racial Union Chapel in Calcutta. He appointed the husband of one of my Rangemore aunts as my guardian, a dental consultant living at Muswell Hill in North London. I found him distant and bourgeois, though I liked Aunt Eva and their toddler son, Wilfred. I left school at the end of 1905 and spent the Christmas holidays playing rugby for various clubs, including the emerging Saracens and the Blackheath reserves. I applied to join Blackheath but soon appreciated that I could not afford the cost of its social life, remarking bitterly, though optimistically, that if I had been born in proletarian Wales, I would have become an international.

My first job was as a junior on the *Quiver*, a monthly magazine published by Cassells with offices in Ludgate Hill. Its editor was David Williamson, the Liberal candidate at Dulwich for whom I had worked in that last year at school. In addition to editing the *Quiver* he was the brilliant writer of Parliamentary sketches which appeared on the front page of the *Daily News* over the initials PWW. When I now applied to him he gave me a job at fifteen shillings a week. It ended disastrously. He requested me to count the words of three articles. Not knowing the device of calculating each page by averaging the words in a line (and not bright enough to think of it), I had finished only one article when he demanded answers. I noticed a figure on the top page of the first article and saw it was almost exactly my calculation. On the top pages of the other two there were also figures; I reported numbers approximating closely to them. Very angry, not with me but with the authors, my too trusting editor returned the offending articles only to receive replies that they were within fifty words of the length specified. I got the sack – my first job had lasted three weeks.

My uncle summoned me to discuss my future. It was a dramatic interview, more decisive than either of us anticipated. He offered to send me to Oxford University (a generous gesture) on the understanding that I would follow the family tradition by becoming a minister of religion. I told him I had no such intention. 'What do you propose to become?' he asked. 'A journalist.' He laughed. 'You are not clever enough. You'll be spongeing on me for the rest of your life,' he commented. I lost my temper and spoke hotly. Dismissed, I borrowed eighteen shillings from his son's nurse, packed my bag and left, never to return. Subsequently my only contact with the family was through secret lunches with my Aunt Eva when later I got jobs in London. My father was characteristically tolerant about my break with my guardian, regretting but saying I must live my own life, and wishing me well.

I went to distant Quaker relatives at Rusthall, near Tunbridge Wells, whilst I sought employment. The General Election came in 1906 and I got a job as Liberal sub-agent. Two memories remain – the first is of the fear of her landlord by the woman from whom I hired a committee room. She walked half a mile to pay the rent so that he would not see the Liberal posters on her wall. The second recollection is of a hugh red-tied driver of a traction engine. He regarded both Tories and Liberals as capitalist exploiters and, after I had argued with him, prophesied that I would be a Socialist within a year. (He proved right.) The Liberal, a Mr Hedges, won the seat, the only time a Tory has not been returned for the constituency. I cannot describe our elation. I was among the hundreds who dragged the victor in triumph in an open carriage from Tunbridge Wells to Tonbridge. Perhaps more important for my future was work which I did for the *Tunbridge Wells Advertiser*. I was particularly proud of an article which I wrote about that memorable night procession to Tonbridge. I sent a copy to my father and it appeared in India's leading paper, the Calcutta *Statesman*.

I suppose an incident at a public school's camp to which I went whilst at Blackheath eased the way for my next job. The Rev. W. B. Selbie, Head of Mansfield College, Oxford, was the chaplain and I had found him in distress after bathing because the boys had hidden his clothes. I recovered them for him. I now reminded him of the incident in applying for a job as a junior on the *Examiner*, the organ of the Congregational denomination, of which he was editor, and I was appointed. I was still nominally a Christian and joined Whitfield's Church in Tottenham Court Road, the politically-minded minister of which, the Rev. Silvester Horne, got me digs in Camden Town together with four others, including my school chum, Harold Hills, now a medical student.

Our landlady was a vast, deaf woman helped by a half-witted servant who used to stand on her head on the stairs to welcome a lodger. We paid six shillings a week for bed and living room, buying our own food, biscuits and cocoa at night and a bacon-and-egg breakfast (for me egg only, I had become a vegetarian). We took it in turn to shop at the Co-op and woe to anyone who spent more than five shillings each a week. My wage was eighteen shillings which left me a shilling a day for bus fare and a midday meal. One day each week I would go to a vegetarian restaurant in St Bride's Street where I got a plentiful meal of left-overs for sixpence. On alternate days I bought two bananas in the street.

We were a mixed lot: a fair-haired Norwegian spiritualist, who claimed that he wrote in Arab script 'under possession'; a building craftsman from the Midlands; a young schoolmaster, paid monthly, and who, having advanced his board, got drunk and spent nights with prostitutes for a week; and Harold Hills, philosophic agnostic, studious, with a sly sense of humour. Our evening discussions were a tremendous education, destroying my theology and speeding me towards Socialism. We took Republican *Reynolds News* on Sunday and Robert Blatchford's *Clarion* on Thursday. We read hugely – Wells, Shaw, Galsworthy, Samuel Butler, Carpenter, among British writers, and the Americans, Dreiser, Sinclair Lewis, Mark Twain, Jack London and Upton Sinclair. My growing interest in Socialism led me to go back to Bellamy, William Morris and even the Levellers. I could not master Marx, satisfying myself with Hyndman's summary of *Das Kapital*, rejecting its materialism. On Sunday afternoons we went to Silvester Horne's men's meeting at Whitfields where he always had 'The Man of the Week' as speaker, very often a Socialist. An additional reason for our attendance was the fact that for sixpence we could eat as much as we liked at a high tea.

A word about Silvester Horne. I have never known a speaker who could so arouse an audience to white heat of enthusiasm or indignation in a few sentences. He was as much a politician as a parson and became Liberal MP for an East Anglian constituency. He was not a success in the House of Commons being too addicted to rhetoric. When finally I resigned from the church because of my growing Humanist and Socialist views, he sent me a most understanding letter. His son, Kenneth Horne, of TV fame, often reminded me of him in gestures and voice. Whitfields gave me my start in free-lance journalism. Silvester Horne told me that the motor busmen on the Vanguard service, the largest in London, were meeting at midnight in the chapel hall to discuss a strike. I was the only journalist who knew about it and when the decision to stop work was made I wrote thirteen reports and went to Fleet Street in the early hours to deliver them. How proud I was to see the posters of the evening papers announcing my story! I made £30, a fortune, and the *Daily News* gave me an assignment to cover the rest of the strike.

I am not sure whether it was the *DN* or the *Tribune*, a wonderful quality daily which alas had only a short life, which sent me to interview Keir Hardie, the father and founder of the Labour Movement. It was a turning point in my life. Hardie had rooms in an Elizabethan house in Neville's Court just north of Fleet Street. The Court was surrounded by office buildings, but in Elizabethan times it must have been a village, with a narrow alley where one could touch both sides with outstretched arms, a chapel, the squire's mansion and rows of picturesque cottages fronted by gardens. Hardie opened the door to me. He was like a granite statue, clothed in tweed grey, his figure firm and square, his domed head of grey hair erect, his stern features a carving of struggle and strength. He took me to his living room crowded with old furniture, sat me down and walked from wall to wall, pipe alternately in hand and mouth, whilst I put my allotted questions. Hardie had a healthy scepticism of journalists and was not forthcoming, but when he had replied to my last question he said, 'Young man, if you will put away your pencil and notebook I will talk to you.'

He did, for an hour, telling me how he had gone down the mine as a boy, wished to be a journalist (he laughed), taught himself shorthand with a pin on a slate, organised the first miners' union at this pit of virtual slavery; and how he was nominated as Liberal Parliamentary candidate but turned down because he was a working man. He told me of his formation of the Scottish Labour Party, how he became a Socialist after meeting European miners' leaders, how he initiated the Independent Labour Party in 1893 and was elected to Parliament for West Ham. He had been walking to and fro, but now looked directly in my face from a seat a few feet away, eager that I should understand. He described how he worked to win the Trade Union Movement to political independence and his gratification when Labour was returned as a group in 1906, and then, his voice warming, explained what Socialism meant to him, his confidence in its triumph, and his belief that by international action the workers of Europe would prevent war. I cannot convey the depth of his ringing Scottish accent as he declared his faith. I went to him a Young Liberal. I left him a Young Socialist.

My first political activity, however, was in the suffragette movement. My introduction was not encouraging. I had written to the Pankhursts offering my services as a journalist. They must have been impressed by my letter because they invited me to Clements Inn and Emmeline Pankhurst, Christabel, and Annie Kenney received me. Their faces dropped when they saw my youthfulness – and gave me envelopes to address. But personal association maintained my interest. I had at that time an explosive friend, Wilfred Spinks, who led a women's strike in East London. It was unofficial and the strike failed, but he swore that we would get every girl work elsewhere at the wage they demanded, and he succeeded, but only by pawning his furniture and living at a common lodging house on a few pence a night. Wilfred had a sister, Jessie, who was a suffragette. We became friends and I participated in the 'Bloody Friday' raid on Parliament when hundreds of women were arrested attempting to force their way into the House of Commons. I used to meet her at the gate of Holloway Prison when she was periodically freed under the Cat and Mouse Act, which released hunger strikers when near death and re-imprisoned them when they recovered. Jessie adopted the name Vera Wentworth for suffragette purposes and became notorious for accosting Asquith, Lloyd George and Winston Churchill. My sympathy with suffragette methods decreased when they took to arson, setting alight the contents of letter boxes. I lost contact with Vera.

The Pankhursts and Annie Kenney had begun as devoted Socialists. Dr Pankhurst, Emmeline's husband, was the first ILP Parliamentary candidate for a Manchester constituency, and Annie, a Lancashire millworker, had been an enthusiast in her local ILP. When they boycotted other politics for the women's cause, their appeal was mostly to the middle class and from this Sylvia, younger daughter, revolted. She adored Keir Hardie – early, because of his Socialism. It was whispered that they were lovers, and certainly they loved. One evening at the House of Commons Hardie asked me to his rooms at Neville's Court for a cup of tea (he was a teetotaller, and did not drink coffee) and Sylvia arrived; he embraced her and took her on his knee. I was astonished because I had never seen Keir unbent and warm. Even at social gatherings he was stern, relaxing only to sing 'Annie Laurie' and then solemnly reminding us that it had been sung outside prison for the Chicago martyrs, working-class rebels, on the eve of their execution. But here he was stroking Sylvia's hair and laughing with her. I was glad – Hardie had become human. It was the reaction of a father in his late fifties to a daughter in her twenties, and probably it was that; they would hardly have been so open in their affection if they had anything to hide. I do not know, but why should we worry? They were happy, they harmed no one, Hardie influenced Sylvia, she comforted him when war came. Hardie inspired Sylvia. She devoted herself to arousing working women in East London to their rights, linking the vote with Socialism. She started a nursery school for under-fives and, whilst I was in prison during the war, my daughter Audrey was one of her resident pupils. Sylvia was the best of the Pankhursts.

I forget how I came to transfer from the *Examiner* to the *Christian Com-*

monwealth, but it exactly represented my developing attitude to life. The *CC* became the organ of the Rev. R. J. Campbell's New Theology, a rational interpretation of Christianity, rejecting the virgin birth, supernatural miracles, the physical resurrection and the unique divinity of Jesus. R. J. Campbell also became a Socialist, generously recognising in a debate (I think with R. C. K. Ensor) that he had been converted by his opponent. He was ethereal in appearance with white hair rising in tufts on each side of his head. We published a sermon by him each week and one of my duties was to take a verbatim note of the prayer which accompanied it, collecting the text of the sermon from him in the vestry afterwards. I was a little put off on these occasions by the adulation for him of women members of his congregation and his evident appreciation of it, but I admired the courage with which he challenged orthodoxy. I was distressed to hear afterwards that he had reverted to the creed and become a clergyman in the Church of England.

Except for my membership of the Progressive League, devoted to R. J. Campbell's New Theology and ethical Socialism, I did not join the Socialist movement until a few months later and then accidentally and temporarily. I enrolled in the Marxist Social Democratic Federation. I was unaware of theoretical differences and after hearing Herbert Burrows, who spoke with persuasive humanity, at a meeting in Regent's Park, I succumbed to the appeal of an attractive actress to join up. The branch, twelve or so strong, met in a room above a shop in Prince of Wales Road, Camden, and I became uneasy at the first meeting because of sectarian opposition to the Labour Party affiliating with the Socialist International. Shortly afterwards I was shocked by a gross speech by Harry Quelch and in 1907 transferred to the ILP. On the same day I identified myself with the whole Labour movement by joining my local Cooperative store and the local branch of the trade union for clerks. It was not until 1910 that I became a member of my present Union, the National Union of Journalists, of which I believe I am the longest paid up member.

Our lodgings in Camden Town ended – I forget why – and Harold Hills and I became residents of a settlement near the Angel, Islington – Claremont Mission run by Congregationalists. The poverty of the surrounding slum made my Socialism a passion. Most men were workless or only working three days a week; there was no unemployment benefit. Hungry children had no free meals at school. Most women were doing sweated home work in their vermin-infested rooms, making artificial flowers and cardboard boxes or putting the pricks in toothbrushes (I came to think brushing one's teeth an overrated hygienic exercise). I visited a smelly room where three women lived, slept and worked; they were putting together cardboard boxes. One died. When I went a second time the two women were still working with the body of the third in a coffin on the table. To stop work would have meant no food, no candle light.

I acknowledge that I did little work for the settlement. I had joined the ILP and nearly all my activity outside working hours was devoted to Socialist propaganda. But soon came crisis – I was adopted as a candidate for the Finsbury Borough Council. I am not sure that the nomination was legal because I was not twenty-one on nomination day, only on the actual day of the election. The announcement of my candidature was made the occasion by the settlement authorities to sever my association with it. The reverend superintendent explained that it would be embarrassing to have a resident who was a Socialist candidate. It may be that the real reason was my inactivity, but that was the bald explanation given.

There followed a memorable association. I went to live with Alfred Harvey Smith, the Secretary of the ILP, his sisters and other youngsters. We occupied a large house in Myddelton Square and lived for our Socialism. To us it was a way of life – friendliness to everyone, utter equality, no thought of personal careers, never any idea of making money or becoming rich. We devoted ourselves to the ILP, published a monthly paper, rented a shop in Goswell Road and converted it into a hall. We had meetings every Sunday night with well-known speakers, and with singing accompanied by a small orchestra. Henry Slesser (later Lord Justice Slesser) of the Fabian Society taught us theory in a study class.

Bernard Shaw spoke one evening and he inspired a philosophy which has remained mine through life. His subject was 'How to achieve the Superman', arguing that the Superman would come only by natural selection which was inhibited by the class structure of society. 'He might well be born by the mating of the Archbishop of Canterbury and a charwoman at Lambeth Palace', he said, 'but our class snobbery would never permit that marriage of destiny.' Such an alliance would not now be so inconceivable as it was then; but Shaw set us all buzzing with excitement. I can see him now, tall, straight-backed, a little red in hair and beard, arms crossed on chest, pouring out his challenging words in a torrent which drowned us. It was not so much his speech which influenced me as his answer to a question which I put. 'We are youngsters,' I said, 'what are we to do with our lives?' Quick as a flash came the reply: 'Find out what the life force is making for and make for it too.' These words directed my thinking and feeling all through subsequent life. The life force – the creative element in life which is making for good. Sometimes in great moments of beauty one can feel it, linking oneself with all that has been and is and will be, and then working within it and

with it for a harmony in life which expresses it. This realisation of oneness
with a universal life had come to me in the deep silences of Nature; eyes
to the horizon over the sea, standing beneath a towering mountain, sitting
by a woodland stream, watching the sun rise or set amidst coloured sky and
cloud. The consciousness of universal identity uplifted me sometimes for days
and became my religion. The spiritual experience came first. Shaw gave it
an objective meaning.

Our ILP was continuously active in agitation. Unemployment was rife.
My first speech was at an unemployed demonstration outside Finsbury Town
Hall. The Liberal Government was doing nothing in the way of social reform
and the Labour Party, for the first time a distinct group in the House of
Commons, was winning by-election after by-election. Among the victors
was irrepressible Victor Grayson at Colne Valley. We were thrilled when
he pressed the unemployment issue to the point of suspension in the Commons, but disillusioned when Keir Hardie told us he was drunk on a second
occasion.

Our little community at Myddelton Square began to attract young Socialists all over London. Dora Lansbury came and her boy friend, Ernest
Thurtle, who afterwards became MP for Shoreditch, and Reginald Sorensen,
then a young Free Church minister in Walthamstow, afterwards MP and a
Minister in the House of Lords. J. R. Clynes, not so young, lived with us
when elected to Parliament, reserved but one of us in tolerant spirit. A
bright young New Zealander named Thorne, who was a full-time propagandist on a Clarion van, stayed with us when in London. He afterwards
became a Minister in a Labour Government in New Zealand. We were
unlike youth of today in our sexual correctness, though we mostly married
each other subsequently. Reginald Sorensen married Muriel, one of Alfred's
sisters and, as I shall tell, I married another sister, Lilla. Alfred's eldest
sister, Violet, looked after us, cooking, cleaning; she married an uncle-in-
law of mine, a continual visitor.

Our dynamic community broke up when Alfred emigrated to Canada,
becoming in time a Socialist Member of the British Columbia Legislative
Council. Alfred and I were great chums. We went on holiday to Hungary
together and were shown round Budapest by an idealistic, utopian Socialist
– Giörgu Lukäcz – who later, quite out of character, became the ruthless
dictator of the Communist revolution in Hungary. I got into hot water about
this visit. I wrote critically in the *Christian Commonwealth* of the régime.
The consequence was a violent attack on me in the Hungarian Legislature
and a decision to refuse visas in future.

Life was good for me on the *Christian Commonwealth*. The editor was

Albert Dawson who believed in R. J. Campbell's New Theology but who was also a hard-headed business man who understood how the tide of progressive opinion was running towards Humanism and Socialism. He gave me a free hand and used me a lot. My biggest contribution was a weekly front page interview with top radical thinkers. They included H. G. Wells, Bernard Shaw, Granville Barker, Israel Zangwill, Sybil Thorndike and Henry Holliday. Granville Barker was the most difficult. He put his feet on the mantelpiece and in answer to my first question rattled away at two hundred words a minute for half an hour. My shorthand was not equal to that. He laughed, and explained he was reciting a lecture. Fortunately he had a typescript. Henry Holliday was the artist who painted *Dante and Beatrice*. I went to see him often in his Hampstead home. He designed a wonderful headquarters for the Labour Movement which never got beyond the drawing board. I took the subjects of my interviews to be photographed by one of our Myddelton Square associates, Lena Connell. Shaw fell for her and allowed her to take eighty photographs of him which made her reputation. Otherwise, my main duty was to make contact with the rising Socialist leaders. Philip Snowden wrote regularly for us. Our office boy became a life-long friend and a person of distinction. He was a little cockney lad with bent head and inquisitive mind, Clement J. Bundock, revered by Fleet Street in the 1930s as the best secretary-negotiator the National Union of Journalists ever had. About him I have much to tell.

An interview for the paper with W. C. Anderson led to my next move. He was an important figure in the ILP and invited me to become assistant editor of its organ, the *Labour Leader*. Anderson, as I shall indicate later, was one of the ablest men British Socialism ever attracted. He had a good mind, was a brilliant orator and a practical administrator. Our Finsbury ILP invited him to become our Parliamentary candidate and I am still amused by the memory of my visit to him to make the request. It was 10 am, but not too early to get him out of bed. As we talked Mary Macarthur, the pioneer woman trade union organiser, came in. Unaware that I was there she was in négligée, her hair dishevelled. I did not know that Mary, whom he later married, was his girlfriend.

The *Labour Leader* was published in Manchester. I packed my bag, and for the first time went North.

CHAPTER THREE

EDITOR AT TWENTY-FOUR

The office of the *Labour Leader* was in a drab building beside the Irwell, a brown sewer-like river, dividing Manchester from Salford. But within the doors I got a real ILP welcome and the manager, Edgar Whitely, found good lodgings for me. The editor J. S. Mills was a little distant but quietly reassuring. That first evening I was invited to tea in the home of Dick Wallhead, the prince of ILP propagandists. Dick had the appearance of Disraeli but was more dynamic if less academic. I was soon to learn how he could captivate a crowd. I was with him at an open-air meeting at Blackburn where he prophesied a depression. 'Look,' he said, shading his eyes with one hand, the other pointing over the crowd, 'I see the threatening clouds approaching.' The whole audience turned round to see. Wallhead followed Keir Hardie as MP for Merthyr Tydfil in South Wales and was bitterly disappointed when MacDonald did not give him a place in the first Labour government, but he was probably a better speaker than administrator. Dick's daughter Muriel was employed in the *Labour Leader* office, dark haired, bright-eyed, with her father's engaging personality. We became close friends. Later Muriel was MP for North Bradford as Mrs Wallhead Nichol.

After a year, when twenty-four, I was appointed acting editor of the *Labour Leader* with W. C. Anderson contributing editorial notes. In fact, he wrote little and I was promoted to editor a year later. I immediately telegraphed to Clem Bundock, the junior on the *Christian Commonwealth*, to join me and, disliking the sooty environment of Manchester, we found lodgings in Red Row in the Derbyshire village of Mellor. Red Row stood high like a bastion, primitive, with a line of waterless lavatories for eight cottages. It looked down upon a deep valley with the ruins of one of the first cotton mills, and a river and a lake with wooded hills rising beyond. Our landlady, stocky, black-dressed Mrs Saint, was a mother to us. We travelled by train from Manchester to the last Cheshire town, Marple, and then had a long climb which we never tired of.

The *Labour Leader* went to press, unusually for a weekly, on a Monday night and whilst it was printing Clem and I had the extraordinary privilege of two press tickets at Miss Horniman's pioneering Gaiety Theatre. We saw plays by Ibsen, Shaw, Barrie, Galsworthy, St John Irvine snd other contemporary playwrights with Sybil Thorndike, Lewis Casson, Esme Percy, Milton Rosmer, Miles Malleson, and others taking leads, the most educative experience of my life. A remarkable thing happened to Clem. He had been a shy cockney lad, embarrassed in the presence of others, particularly girls. Shaw's *Man and Superman* had the effect on him of a religious conversion. He determined to speak English like Jack Tanner, to challenge girls, to look everyone in the face and to speak his mind. And he did it in an amazingly short time. When later he became Secretary of the National Union of Journalists he was a master of Victorian oratory. No one would have believed he had been the diffident cockney I first knew.

As editor of the ILP paper I was invited as observer to the meetings of the National Council of the party. Sometimes the Council met in a third-rate hotel across the Irwell Bridge, sometimes at a second-rate hotel in Fetter Lane in London; there was still a puritanical sense among Socialists eschewing luxury. To mix with the great ones was an awesome experience. With Hardie, my political father, and Anderson, a political uncle, I was at ease, but Ramsay MacDonald and Philip Snowden were another matter. Neither was forthcoming – MacDonald, aristocratically lofty, distantly handsome; Snowden, his left leg partially paralysed, thin-lipped, intimidating. They did not hide their distrust of each other. At a meeting it seemed that MacDonald had only to take one line for Snowden to take the opposite. MacDonald was imperious, Snowden sarcastic. Hardie was impatient of their mutual bitterness; Anderson, cool and philosophic, smilingly dismissed it. There were other interesting members of the Council – Fred Jowett, despite his working-class origin looking like a professor, withdrawn, a fundamentalist, estimating, rarely intervening; Bruce Glasier, idealistic, eyes seeking heaven for inspiration; T. D. Benson, treasurer, estate agent, Socialist against his own interests, father of George Benson who became an MP; Egerton Wake, impressive in figure and features, pragmatic, eventually going to Transport House to organise the Labour Party; R. C. Wallhead, whom I have already described.

I was distressed when I first entered these exalted circles by the personal antagonisms, particularly the anger shown towards Victor Grayson, short-lived star of Socialism. Victor had been a student at the Unitarian Theological College in Manchester, climbing through his bedroom window late at night after travelling all over the North to Socialist meetings. He was selected as candidate for Colne Valley against the National Council's nomination of Bruce Glasier, much to the anger of Hardie and others. He was a combination of idealist and sensualist – blue idealistic eyes, thick sensual mouth. His oratory was evangelical, enlivened by humour, winning devotees; but he succumbed to drink, perhaps because of his frustrations in the House of Commons and of his disillusionment with his more accommodating Labour colleagues. After a time he became impossible, failing to appear at meeting after meeting. I remember waiting for him at Victoria Station, Manchester, whilst thousands crowded the Free Trade Hall expecting him. He never arrived. The last time I saw him he was down and out, occupying with his actress wife a room in a side street off Theobalds Road in London – the room furnished only with a bed, one chair, a sugar box for a table. I was among those with Margaret Bondfield who raised money to send him and his wife to New Zealand. His end was a complete mystery. He returned to England early in the First World War to join the Forces, was seen to go to Liverpool to embark, and was never heard of afterwards. But in Colne Valley, as I found when taking meetings there, he remained a loved legend. Grayson had considerable support in the ILP. Indeed, he carried a resolution at the annual conference in 1909 defeating the National Council and leading to the temporary resignation of Hardie, MacDonald, Snowden, Glasier and Benson.

Divisions in the Party had arisen before I went to Manchester and extended far beyond a dislike of Victor Grayson. They went back to the time when Keir Hardie was succeeded as Chairman of the Parliamentary Party by Arthur Henderson and G. N. Barnes. Barnes was a Trades Unionist and opposed subsidies for housing on the ground that lower rents would deter demands for higher wages. This was theoretically the Trades Union view of State aid for some time; Trades Unionists opposed family allowances when first urged by the ILP. Differences came to a head when Ramsay MacDonald became the Parliamentary leader. MacDonald urged a policy of not pressing divisions when they threatened the defeat of the Liberal Government, but there was a minority, led by Hardie, Snowden and Jowett, who were opposed to what they regarded as the acceptance of a manoeuvre by Lloyd George to make Labour a junior partner. Jowett was the first to advocate that the Party should vote on the merits of issues irrespective of the fate of administrations. My sympathies were generally with the minority.

I listened to all these controversies, fought out with a bitterness almost reaching ferocity. In the *Labour Leader* I had to live above the battle, but, despite my editorial neutrality, I was drawn in. One day early in the spring of 1914 Keir Hardie met me at the House of Commons and took me aside with grave face. He said he had just come from a meeting of the Parliamentary group and had heard from MacDonald the 'incredible proposal' that Labour should enter into an alliance with the Liberal Party at the coming General Election. He put his hand on my shoulder and said, 'Laddie, we must kill this at the ILP Conference; you must do it.'

I so revered Keir Hardie that I prepared a speech with great care. We met at Bradford and it was a special occasion, the Coming of Age Conference of the Party, with Hardie in the chair honouring his part in its foundation. He called on me early in the debate. I recounted, one by one, the occasions under MacDonald's leadership when the Parliamentary Party had compromised in order not to endanger the continuation of the Liberal Government in office and argued that the logic of this approach was an alliance. MacDonald was scathing in his reply, challenging anyone to quote from the minutes of the Parliamentary Party any reference to an alliance. He was emotionally disturbed and withdrew from the conference because of sudden illness. Then came sensation. Philip Snowden endorsed everything I had said and told us MacDonald had asked that his proposal for an alliance should not be minuted. The Conference endorsed Jowett's 'Votes on Merit' resolution largely as a reaction to this debate. I had the temerity to accept nomination for the National Council of the Party. Thanks no doubt to Snowden's speech I was defeated by only five votes by W. C. Anderson.

I walked with Hardie that evening to the public demonstration in crowded St George's Hall. I was never more proud than when he said to me, 'Fenner, you did it.' Hardie was in an exalted mood – I have never heard him speak more inspiringly. There was a large children's choir on the platform to whom he turned and made a moving appeal. 'Love flowers, love animals, love your companions, love your fathers and mothers, love all human beings, whatever their race and colour,' he cried. 'Hate injustice, hate cruelty. We old ones have failed but you can succeed. If these were my last words, boys and girls, I would say to you live for that better day.' Unknown to all of us, they were the last words children were to hear from him. They were his last words for most of those present.

Earlier I have written of my identification with the Suffragette Movement and told how I broke with it when methods of arson were adopted. In the ILP there was a great controversy whether we should insist on votes for women on the same terms that men enjoyed or stand out for votes for all men and women. The Liberal Government introduced a Bill to extend the suffrage to men only. Hardie, Snowden and George Lansbury held that the Party should vote against it on the ground that women had been betrayed. MacDonald urged that we should support the extension of the male franchise as an instalment towards adult suffrage. I agreed with Hardie and Lansbury because it seemed to me that the principle of sex equality was important for all aspects of life. When the Party came to Hardie's view, the Women Suffragists (rejecting violence in contrast with the Suffragettes) entered into a political alliance with us. I was made the ILP liaison contact with the National Union of Women's Suffrage Societies and was invited by them to speak at their vast Albert Hall demonstration. The planning was spectacular – the speakers marched in procession the whole length of the hall through the standing applauding audience, Mrs Fawcett, who was to preside, leading. I was at the end and was so young that the stewards thought I was a press messenger and stopped me stepping on to the platform. Mrs Fawcett rescued me.

A theme of my speech was that women, if they had the vote, would serve the cause of peace. It was ironical that Lloyd George, when he gave the vote to women in 1919 (though even then not on the same terms as men) declared that they deserved it for their war service and this was widely accepted as the explanation of their success in 1919. I regarded this as a myth. I believed they would have won the vote earlier and on better terms if there had been no war. If the General Election due in 1915 had taken place there is little doubt that the supporters of women's suffrage would have been in a majority in the House of Commons.

My opposite number as liaison for the Suffragists was Margaret Robertson. I came to admire her very much; she was brilliant both as organiser and speaker and I saw a big future for her in the ILP which she joined under my influence. There was irony in the denial of this hope. In 1913 I took a holiday in the French Alps with Harold Hills. Margaret was staying over the next range by Lake Orta in Italy and I wanted to visit her, but Harold at first scorned what he termed my infatuation. Reluctantly he agreed, but on the condition that we stayed only three days. The three days over, Harold suggested that we should remain for the rest of the holiday – and less than a month after returning to England he announced that he and Margaret were engaged to be married. I congratulated them, but I never forgave Harold for diverting her from politics. She became a dutiful doctor's wife.

I undertook propaganda over a large part of Britain. In those days, speakers never thought of staying in hotels – we lived with the comrades, however restricted the accommodation. I remember sleeping with a miner after he had had his bath in a tub in a Durham cottage, his wife insisting on a made-up bed on chairs. I was startled at supper in Paisley to see a curtain on the wall pulled back to reveal two children sitting up in a bunker bed within the wall. My favourite hosts were the Townleys at Blackburn, mill workers. Socialism was their life. I encouraged them to become full-time workers for the cause: Annie organiser of the women's section of the Labour Party in Bristol, Ernest the *Daily Herald* circulation manager in South Wales. Another Blackburn friend was Philip Snowden's agent, George Shepherd; one of Clem Attlee's boldest actions, when he became Prime Minister, was to make this splendid proletarian a Peer of the Realm. Let me leap ahead in time temporarily. In the 1970s, when in the Lords I was criticising official Labour policy voiced by Lord Malcolm Shepherd, son of my Blackburn friend, I assured the House of my goodwill towards him by saying that I had held him in my arms before he was one year old. 'Pity you didn't drop him,' exclaimed a Tory Lord.

Many times I spoke to the Socialist Society at Manchester University, two of whose members, Ellen Wilkinson and Walton Newbold, became prominent in politics. Newbold, son of Quakers, began by linking his Socialism with religion in a quixotic way. Dressing himself in friar's robes he set out on a bicycle to convert Lancashire, but gave up at his first stop; he would never tell me if the rumour was true that he had been ducked in a pond. Ellen and Walton became engaged, but their engagement ended dramatically at an ILP summer school at Barrow House on the banks of Derwentwater. I glimpsed Ellen in bathing dress drying her long red hair, calm and quiet, whilst Walton gesticulated beside her in angry protest. Suddenly he leapt beserk to the terrace where tea was prepared, throwing chairs and tables to the ground, smashing crockery, restrained after much damage by the strong arms of W. C. Anderson. Newbold settled down to become a serious research worker, one of the first to expose the armaments industry. Intoxicated by the Russian revolution he joined the Communist Party and became MP for Motherwell, one of four Communists who have been in the Commons. Ellen, everyone knows, had a successful Parliamentary career, famous for leading the Hunger Marchers from her northern constituency of Jarrow to Westminster. Both Walton and Ellen died early.

Soon after I became editor of the *Labour Leader*, Clem and I were joined on the staff and in our lodgings by a young Welsh cartoonist J. B. Nicholas. We became famous for a three-man show. It was opened by a short Bernard Shaw speech from Clem, audacious and humorous, Nicholas would sketch caricatures of politicians, giving the drawing to the first member of the audience who recognised it, and I would conclude more seriously. This performance almost rivalled the popularity of 'Casey and Dolly'. Casey was Walter Hampson, first violinist in the Hallé Orchestra, who, with Dolly,

The author, aged a little under one year, with his mother

The author's family, September 1897: his mother, his sisters Phyllis and Nora, his father, himself

the pianist, toured the country adding propaganda comments to the music. He could be very funny, writing a weekly article for the *Labour Leader* which I nearly always had to cut because it was too blue. There was no one to censor his speeches.

Travelling about the country I was able to meet Socialist personalities beyond the inner circle of the ILP leadership. I loved Robert Smillie, the Scottish miners' leader, a friend in personal approach to everyone who belonged to the working class, contemptuous of privilege and unearned wealth which he regarded as robbery, convincing in his simple statement of Socialism – 'the best of life to those who give to life'. At Sheffield I met Edward Carpenter again. He had come to our Myddelton Square community in London, endearing us to him by his outflowing cordiality. I had tea with him in his cottage near Sheffield and was again captivated by his charm, almost feminine in smile and eyes. To many of us as youngsters Edward Carpenter's *Towards Democracy* was a bible. It is indicative of the differences between the generations that young Socialists today, including my own daughters, are untouched by it.

I will conclude this chapter on a very personal note. Lilla Harvey Smith had joined her brother as a teacher in British Columbia. In our Myddelton Square days she was studying at Avery Hill College, staying with us during the holidays. She was the loveliest of the sisters, fair-haired, laughing, and I was attracted to her. My custom was to go round the room and kiss the girls goodnight – there were five of them. On one occasion Lilla was missing, but she waylaid me on the stairs. 'I hate that kissing routine,' she explained. This incident kept on recurring to me after she had left for Canada, and later when I went to Manchester, without warning, she suddenly reappeared. I was sitting in the Saints' kitchen, idly chatting, when the door opened. There was Lilla. With firm step she walked round three sides of the table and embraced me. We married a month later, on the eve of the war, and lived in a newly-built house within a stone's throw of Red Row.

CHAPTER FOUR

THE WAR

The First World War, unlike the Second, came relatively suddenly and unexpectedly. A week before its outbreak I was speaking at an open-air meeting outside the park gates at Oldham. I warned of the danger of war. The audience was impatient. 'Ireland,' they shouted. 'What about Carson?' The Home Rule issue was in everyone's mind – Sir Edward Carson was threatening armed resistance in Ulster. No one was prepared to listen to the danger of a Serbian assassination and Austrian–Russian–German involvement. A week later I was speaking on Sunday night at Great Harwood, near Blackburn. The danger of war was now understood. The local Congregational minister joined me on the platform to protest. I travelled back to Blackburn and in the windows of the *Northern Telegraph* there was the first news of the fighting. A small crowd was reading, bewildered.

In the *Labour Leader*, printed the next day, I committed the ILP to opposition to the war. I did so without the opportunity of consultation, but I had no doubt what the Party attitude would be; all were anti-militarist, anti-war. We ran a slogan across the top of the paper: 'German Socialists are our Comrades Still' and the front page was devoted to a black type manifesto denouncing the war as imperialist. The following Sunday, the National Council of the ILP met in the dismal pub by the Irwell. The members were overwhelmingly against the war, only two dissenting. Keir Hardie had prepared a manifesto, argumentative, verbose. The Council adopted instead an inspiring draft by W. C. Anderson. Its ringing words concluded:

We are told that International Socialism is dead, that all our hopes and ideals are wrecked by fire and pestilence and European war. It is not true. Out of the darkness and the depth we hail our working-class comrades of every land, across the roar of guns we send sympathy and greeting to the German Socialists. They have laboured unceasingly to promote good relations with Britain as we with Germany. They are no enemies of ours but faithful friends. In forcing this appalling crime upon the nations it is the rulers, the diplomats, the militarists who have sealed their doom. In tears and blood and bitterness the great democracy will be born. With steadfast faith, we greet the future; our cause is holy and imperishable and the labour of our hands has not been in vain. Long live freedom and equality, long live International Socialism!

We were all worried by Hardie's appearance – he was broken. He believed that the workers would stop the war by international action. He had just returned from Switzerland where the leaders of all the Socialist Parties had declared their solidarity. Earlier he had urged the Socialist International without success but with encouraging support to organise a general strike across the frontiers if governments declared war. Now the same Socialist leaders, with a few brave exceptions, were supporting their governments. It destroyed Hardie's faith and hope. At that meeting he drooped in his chair, sick in body and spirit.

In the Commons, MacDonald made a speech denouncing the secret diplomacy of Sir Edward Grey, the Foreign Secretary, who had committed Britain to war without the knowledge of the Cabinet. MacDonald had reservations, but his speech infuriated the patriots, including Labour members in the Commons and he had to resign his leadership. From then on, Mac-Donald was the chief villain of the piece and accordingly became the hero of the ILP. The attacks on him took the most vicious and indecent form. I recollect the horror I felt when Horatio Bottomley's *John Bull* published his birth certificate to reveal that he was an illegitimate child – much more reprehensible in 1915 than in the 1970s. MacDonald told me the fortuitous circumstances in which he learned of this revelation. He was travelling to speak at York, and the only fellow passenger in the carriage left *John Bull* on the seat when he got out at Doncaster. MacDonald picked it up and read.

Ramsay MacDonald was a born leader, with a commanding personality and a magnificent presence; the most handsome man in public life. He was a great orator whose deep, resonant voice and sweeping gestures added to the force of his words. In his vehemence, however, he sometimes perpetrated startling malapropisms and I remember him calling on delegates at an ILP conference to 'work by day and propagate by night'. On another occasion, at a time when long underwear was in fashion, he told trade unionists planning to recruit women members: 'Gentlemen, we must grasp our sisters by the scruff of the neck and force them into combinations.'

He received great help from his wife, a Socialist in the truest sense. Margaret, although of the Gladstone family, contrasted with Ramsay's aristocratic appearance and demeanour. She cared nothing for dress and might have passed for a working-class woman in the days before Marks & Spencer cheap mass-produced clothes. Margaret Bondfield once told me how horrified she was when the wife of the Labour leader turned up with a deputation to 10 Downing Street wearing her blouse back to front.

Snowden was away in Canada and declined to commit himself abroad. I met him at Liverpool and travelled with him to Blackburn, his constituency. He was utterly against the war, more forthright than MacDonald had been. I interviewed him for the *Labour Leader* and never have I written more appreciatively.

Opposition to the war was not easy. We persisted with our meetings which were often broken up. At Bolton I stood against a wall with flying stones denting it and had to be protected by stalwart comrades to the station. At a meeting of my own branch at Marple, Clem Bundock and I were viciously attacked and saved from being thrown in the river by the police, honourably impartial, closing the iron gates of a private estate where we took refuge. Perhaps more frightening was an assault made on me on the canal bank at Marple. Five young toughs beat me up, kicked me as I lay in the mud and began to drag me to the canal's edge. Fortunately they heard the steps of someone approaching and fled.

The ILP was not alone in opposing the war. An encouraging number of Liberal politicians and intellectuals joined us, including C. P. Trevelyan, who had resigned from the Government, and Arthur Ponsonby, who had once been a page at Buckingham Palace. The intellectuals began to write for the *Labour Leader*, Lowes Dickenson, Vernon Lee, Gilbert Cannan, Edward Garnett, E. D. Morel and H. N. Brailsford. Our circulation rose progressively from 40,000 to 80,000.

We all waited on the word of Bernard Shaw. He wrote a supplement to the *New Statesman* in which he scathingly attacked the diplomacy which led to the war and all its moral pretensions, but came down nevertheless in support of British arms: we were in and must fight our way out. H. G. Wells from the first was ferociously pro-British. He sent frequent protests to the *Labour Leader*. I can still see his letters, neatly written with little stringed balloons of corrections and additions. One week two letters came. I dealt with one and asked Clem to answer the other. He did so in the spirited tones he had developed. Amusingly Wells refused to believe that 'Clement J. Bundock' was not me. He should have observed the different styles.

We had the support of many who had been active in the Women's Movement, including Mrs H. M. Swanwick, Catherine Marshall and Miss Courteney. I was sent by the Marple branch of the National Union of Women

Suffrage Societies to the conference which decided their attitude to the war. The majority, led by Eleanor Rathbone, later MP for the Northern Universities, took the same line as the Pankhurst suffragettes (except Sylvia) of support for British arms. My memory is of Eleanor Rathbone, the personification of physical force, flaming eyes below bushy black eyebrows, face red, her arms waving with pugilistic fervour.

The intellectuals, brought together by the charisma of Ramsay MacDonald and the organising skill of E. D. Morel, formed the Union of Democratic Control to divert controversy from the rights and wrongs of the war to the peace which should follow. They insisted on no territorial gains and no indemnities. E. D. Morel was bitterly attacked by the Press as pro-German. He had written a book, *Ten Years of Secret Diplomacy*, which was a blistering exposure of British foreign policy before the war, and in his speeches he tended, more than MacDonald liked, to put what he regarded as reasonable in the German case. He was a large handsome man rivalling MacDonald in commanding appearance. I spoke with him at a meeting in Manchester when he moved the audience almost to tears by describing how he had dedicated his life to peace when watching his children playing on the lawn in his garden and thinking of the fate which would come to them if wars continued.

I was invited to Glasgow to speak in the Metropole Theatre where the ILP had crowded Sunday demonstrations. Before the meeting I had a revealing discussion with our remarkable group of Clydeside leaders: James Maxton, John Wheatley, Manny Shinwell, P. J. Dollan, David Kirkwood and Campbell Stephen. They invited John Maclean to come too and his influence over the others struck me as extraordinary. 'Maclean next to Burns is the greatest,' wrote the Scottish poet, Hugh MacDiarmid. He was not a member of the ILP but he had taught most of the group their Socialism in Marxist study classes. My visit revealed that opposition to the war in Scotland was based not on 'Thou shalt not kill' but on working-class wrongs and international working-class solidarity. The leaders – Maclean, Maxton, Shinwell, Kirkwood – deliberately courted imprisonment and deportation not as conscientious objectors but for sedition in urging strikes and boycotts. They were living in a different world from the English pacifist opposition to the war. Thousands of workers marched in procession through the streets singing Maxton's song:

> O I'm Henry Dubb
> And I won't go to war
> Because I don't know
> What they're all fighting for

To hell with the Kaiser
To hell with the Tsar
To hell with Lord Derby
And also GR

I work at munitions
I'm a slave down at Weir's
If I leave my job
They'll give me two years

To hell with the sheriff
To hell with his crew
To hell with Lloyd George
And Henderson too

I don't like the factor
His rent I won't pay
Three cheers for John Wheatley
I'm striking today

To hell with the landlord
I'm not one to grouse
But to hell both with him
And his bloody old house.

In Glasgow I also met two revered Socialists whose personalities were
more akin to English pacifism. The first was George Archibald, a dedicated
humanitarian whom I was later to join in the House of Lords. The second
was Sir Hugh Roberton, the creator and conductor of the famous Orpheus
Choir, a gentle and cultured soul. He revered the humanism of James Maxton, as he revealed many years later in his moving funeral oration.

Maxton was imprisoned in Calton gaol, Edinburgh. A thief doing three
months asked why he was sentenced for a year. 'Sedition,' Jimmy replied.
'Ah,' said the thief, 'they're always hard on sex.' One of Maxton's visitors
was Sissie McCullam, active with him in the Socialist Teachers' Society.
Despite the presence of a warder, he proposed to her, warning that he might
spend most of his life in prison. They became engaged and married when he
was released. Sissie was frail, and he was convinced she died from the long
strain of caring night and day for their seriously ill infant son. Many years
later he referred to this in a speech in the Commons when pleading for

action to end preventable infant mortality. 'I saw only one case,' he said, 'and that made a mark on me I shall never lose. I saw a mother struggling with the last ounce of her strength to save an infant life, and in saving it she lost her own.' Friends said that Maxton, despite his genius for fun, did not smile for two years after his wife's death. It was a book by P. G. Wodehouse which brought renewal.

We had surprisingly little interference from the Government. Once the *Labour Leader* offices were raided by the police and the Public Prosecutor brought an action under the Defence of the Realm Act (DORA) for the destruction of the edition on the unexpected ground of an imaginative article by Isabel Sloan on the theme of two dying soldiers, British and German, realising that their lives had been the same, the same loves enjoyed, the same wrongs suffered. I had a good time in the witness box. Experience at open-air meetings had taught me how to deal with hecklers and I scored repeatedly during the cross-examination by Sir William Cobbett. He became irritated and I retorted to misrepresentation vigorously, whereupon the magistrate remarked that we both appeared to be losing our tempers. The Court found there was nothing to justify destruction of the copies which had been seized. Our smiles can be imagined when police vans arrived to return them.

On another occasion the ILP bookshops in Manchester and London were raided, the police taking away lorry loads of anti-war literature. Among the books confiscated was an anti-armaments play I had written, *The Devil's Business*. In Manchester the police returned the copies as unobjectionable; in London I was invited to the Mansion House to show cause why the seized copies should not be destroyed. I lost the case, but my solicitor advised that I should appeal. When I wrote to friends asking them to contribute to the cost, Bernard Shaw refused, saying that, 'Of all useless ways of wasting money the most useless is trying to fight the Government on its own ground in the Law Courts.' Other friends, however. contributed and I did appeal. Shaw proved right: I lost. The ludicrous position then arose that the play could be bought in Manchester but not in London.

Only once was the *Labour Leader* censored. The police arrived just before the paper was going to press and took away page proofs. Clem and I accompanied them to the Salford Police Station praying that they would cut something; we knew that we would get publicity if blank spaces appeared and I am afraid on this occasion we thought more of circulation than civil rights. They fastened on a letter from Clive Bell which they held might prejudice recruiting. Out it must go. Then they found an advertisement of a book by Bell; if his brief letter was prejudicial what would be the effect of a whole book? They ordered the deletion of the advertisement. I took the suppressed items to Mr Scott of the *Manchester Guardian* and he wrote a strong leading article. The national press added to the publicity. We had to print a second edition.

Herbert Morrison first came on the national scene during the war. He was the paid secretary of the strong ILP branch in Bermondsey of which pacifist Dr Salter was the leader. Morrison was passionately anti-war and he contributed short pieces to the *Labour Leader* which were so challenging that I printed them in black type in a panel on the opening page. The attention of the Government was drawn to them and a Minister gave a warning word to Philip Snowden who asked me to suggest to Herbert that he should soften his comments. Even then, however, I had to edit them. Morrison became a conscientious objector, accepting alternative service at a Quaker's fruit farm and he married the daughter of his employer. In later years he did a great service to the London he loved as a leader of the LCC, but when he became a Minister and subsequently a Peer no one would have believed his youthful record.

It was good to know that in Germany (as indeed in Russia and Serbia) there were Socialists opposing the war. I wrote to them through neutral countries and one morning came a bulky envelope from Sweden which contained warm responses from Clara Zetkin, Karl Liebknecht and Rosa Luxemburg. Clara Zetkin was the leader of the Women's Section of the German Social Democrats and it was encouraging to learn from her that the ILP stand against the war was known in Germany. She wrote:

Moved by the same Socialist feelings, thousands upon thousands in Germany as in other countries stretch out their hands towards you, dear friends and comrades in Great Britain, saying from the depths of their hearts – 'We thank you.' We stand with you as you stand with us against Imperialism and for Socialism. You have preserved the honour of the International. Your attitude is a lofty example of faith and strength in the present, a hope and moral for the future.

Wrote Liebknecht:

It is the duty of every Socialist to be a prophet of international brotherhood, realising that every word he speaks of Socialism and peace, every action he performs for these ideals, inflames similar words and actions in other countries, until the flames of the desire for peace shall flare high over all Europe.

Wrote Rosa Luxemburg:

From this war the rank and file will return to our old flag of International Socialism, only with a more vehement determination not to betray it again at the next Imperialist orgy, but to defend it unitedly against their criminal intrigues, their infamous lies and their miserable phrases and to establish it victoriously on the ruins of the bloody Imperialism.

Karl Liebknecht and Rosa Luxemburg were assassinated at the end of the war, either by militarist Prussians or 'patriotic' Social Democrats. I had profound admiration for them, particularly for Rosa. She was a sensitive person as her letters from prison showed, but she was above everything both a political philosopher and a far-seeing pragmatist. All history might have been different if Lenin had accepted her proposals for democracy following the Soviet Revolution. Since then Rosa has always been my political heroine. When I visited Berlin after the war I stood in silent homage before the Eden Hotel where Karl and Rosa were murdered.

The ILP and the anti-war Socialists of Europe did their utmost to establish common action. We took the initiative early in 1914, but when a year later a conference was held in the mountain village of Zimmerwald in Switzerland our delegates were refused passports. At this conference the subsequent division between Socialists and Communists emerged. Lenin denounced the 'peace by negotiation' policy of the ILP and of many anti-war parties, arguing that any treaty negotiated by capitalist governments would sow the seeds of future wars and that the correct policy was to end hostilities by social revolution.

In September 1915 Keir Hardie died. I will probably be misunderstood if I say that it might have been better if he had died a little earlier. He had been absolutely uncompromising in his opposition to the war, but to the distress of many of us in his last days he wrote to the newspaper in his constituency, Merthyr Tydfil, supporting commitment to the Forces. MacDonald had written the same to a meeting in Leicester but that was not in conflict with the moderate line he had taken from the first. Hardie on the other hand had held that war was murder and had advocated complete resistance. Those of us who revered him were disappointed, but this could not affect our homage to him and for all he had done for Socialism and peace. I could not attend the cremation service in Scotland because I was preparing a memorial supplement to the *Labour Leader*, but I heard from those who were there that it was not worthy of him. Hardie was a sincere Christian, indeed he said in his later years that if he had his life over again he would have become a minister of religion. It was therefore appropriate that a minister – I believe a relative – should conduct the service, but Bruce Glaiser felt the tribute paid was inadequate and rose to supplement it. Unhappily as he uttered his first words the coffin moved through the cremation door, a sad farewell.

I spoke at a crowded memorial meeting in London, but an absurd incident nearly wrecked the solemnity of the occasion. It was a stormy day and the rain left a streak down my trouser leg. As soon as I rose to speak a child's voice pierced the silence: 'Look, Mum, he's wet his trousers!' There was muffled laughter and I hesitated with distressed embarrassment, but only for a moment. Devotion to Hardie fired me, and the audience responded with an emotion which could be felt. I can now write sixty years later that I admired Hardie more deeply than any man I have known in my life. The beauty of Nature gave me my spiritual inspiration, Bernard Shaw gave it direction, Keir Hardie gave it implementation. We have not had another like Hardie.

CHAPTER FIVE

IN PRISON

So far opposition to the war had been political. With the prospect of compulsory military service, it became a personal test. As early as 1914 my wife suggested that an organisation be formed of young men determined to refuse war service and, with my ready concurrence as editor she wrote a letter to the *Labour Leader*. The response was surprisingly large and we formed a provisional committee, representative of those who had replied, to establish the No-Conscription Fellowship. Clifford Allen, an ILP student at Cambridge, became chairman and among its members were Barrett Brown, a Quaker (afterwards Principal of Ruskin College, Oxford); Morgan Jones and James Hudson, afterwards Labour MPs; and C. H. Norman, an official shorthand writer at the Law Courts. My wife acted as secretary for a time, but soon the membership became too large and an office was opened in London.

Among all the men I have known, Clifford Allen (later Lord Hurtwood) was unique in his magnetic quality. He was frail in appearance, slight with bent shoulders, his features of classical beauty, a total impression almost feminine; at the same time his voice was rich and deep, he was confident and masterly in decision, and he had a genius for organisation. Barrett Brown had a boyish mischievousness. Morgan Jones, a school teacher, was reserved despite his Welshness. James Hudson was a pugilistic pacifist, and C. H. Norman was a sensationalist already known for his exposure of war scandals. The only member of our committee above conscription age was appropriately the treasurer, Edward Grubb, a Quaker, a scholar and a saint.

In November 1915 we held our first delegate conference representing branches which had been formed all over the country. Lord Derby was already preparing for conscription, inviting prospective recruits to a test rewarded by khaki armlets. Young women were presenting white feathers to men who were not so specified; I had a collection which I spread like a fan. Our conference received a storm of abuse from the Press, which described us as 'the save-their-skins-brigade'; nevertheless, the effect of publicity was greatly to strengthen our organisation.

The NCF became an extraordinarily efficient underground movement. We prepared a code so that when we telegraphed that a meeting would be held at Manchester it would be at Newcastle. When the National Labour Press, owned by the ILP, was dismantled by the police for running off our journal, the *Tribunal*, we bought a small press and housed it every week at a different address. In fact the *Tribunal* appeared uninterruptedly during the war despite all the efforts of Scotland Yard to suppress it. I liked the story of how Violet Tyrrell, who had been a suffragette, smuggled a supply to the Embankment during a raid on the office, and asked an obliging policeman if he would look after the bundle while she went to the toilet; instead she phoned a supporter for a car and the policeman helped to load it. The *Tribunal* appeared with the imprint of Joan Beauchamp as publisher. She was arrested and imprisoned for contempt of court for refusing to name the printer. That was the spirit of our women. The police came to the office to arrest Bernard Boothroyd, afterwards celebrated as the humorous writer 'Yaffle'; he was dressed as a charming young lady and handed them cups of tea.

Our second conference was held at Devonshire House, then the headquarters of the Society of Friends, a vast dim building which we crowded out. On the way to the conference I saw a *John Bull* poster. 'Take Him to the Tower'. Someone handed me a copy; it demanded that I be taken to the Tower of London and shot! A group of jingoes incited sailors to attack the building. Two or three succeeded in climbing the locked gates but were bewildered when, instead of fists, friendly hands were extended to them. Allen, who was in the chair, inspired a unique method of demonstrating approval as an alternative to the noisy cheering which would have provoked the threatening crowd outside. When Philip Snowden and Dr John Clifford (the famous non-conformist leader) spoke they were received with thousands of fluttering handkerchiefs.

The NCF under Clifford Allen attracted brilliant associates, among them Bertrand Russell, a tutor of Allen at Cambridge, dismissed from his professional post because of his activities on our behalf. He was shy when he came to offer his services and one's first memory of him was of a simple modesty, soon accompanied by twinkle-eyed humour, becoming an irrepressible Puck. Another valuable associate was Catherine Marshall, the pacifist suffragist, who became our political secretary and was so efficient in record keeping that the War Office used to phone her to learn in what camp particular boys were. The Minister wanted the information to answer questions in the House of Commons, not knowing that Catherine had planted them.

I never joined Allen's social circle, which was both academic and Bohemian. He and Bertrand Russell were close friends, and, with Catherine Marshall, he frequently joined Bertie at the country house of Lady Ottoline Morrell at Garsington. Lady Ottoline had been Russell's mistress, and these weekend parties were probably gay and uninhibited. I was not invited because I was not of their world – I was still puritanical and not an intellectual, without university experience, regarded as a provincial innocent which I suppose I was. I do not know how far the relations between Catherine and Allen went. She was much the older but was clearly in love with him, and he had admiration and affection for her – not, I felt, passion. Any intimate association was ended when Allen after the war married his Rome art student. Catherine was upset when the newly-weds made their home at Friday Street, the lovely Surrey valley, near a farm where she and Allen had spent weekends, and even took overlooking lodgings to remind Allen by her presence of their past. Catherine soon recovered her equanimity and became active in peace and freedom movements with which I was associated. I went to see her in a Hampstead hospital just before she died, and to the end she was deeply concerned about the oppressions in the world.

Resistance to conscription extended to anti-militarists from allied countries. Some were Russian Socialists who were not prepared to fight for the Tsarist regime and this brought me into contact with two Bolsheviks subsequently important in Lenin's revolution. The first was Ivan Maisky, who became Soviet Ambassador in Britain, the second Yury Chicherin, afterwards Soviet Commissar for Foreign Affairs. They formed an Anti-Conscription League for Russians with which the NCF cooperated. Maisky was reasonable and quietly competent. Chicherin used to write long indecipherable letters to the *Labour Leader*. When Clem and I saw his envelopes addressed in purple ink we despaired. 'Another letter from Glycerine,' was Clem's comment. Other young men affected were the Irish; how should they resist – physically or by passive refusal to fight? I was in prison before they decided, but I heard how, after a discussion with Catherine Marshall at her Derwentwater home, they were so impressed by the NCF example that they issued instructions for mass non-violent resistance. On the day that compulsory military service was imposed there was a general strike in Ireland and a public declaration that the majority of young men would refuse to answer their call-up papers. Whitehall never dared to apply its conscription across the Irish Channel.

The most dramatic event was the attempt of the military to send thirty-seven objectors to the front in France where refusal to obey orders was punishable by death. On their way to Southampton docks they threw out of the window a message to the NCF and it was providentially picked up by an ILP railwayman. Through her contacts with Sir John Simon and others Catherine Marshall somehow got Asquith to receive a deputation, whilst I took train to Manchester to urge the *Guardian* to protest. I saw H. Side-botham (perhaps forgotten now but once famous as 'A Student of Politics') who wrote a fierce first leader. Asquith telegraphed an order to Southampton forbidding the transference of the men to France, but they had already gone. Seventeen went to Cinder City where they were handcuffed to poles, subjected to 'crucifixion' (ankles and wrists tied to a cross) and put on bread and water diet. Still holding out they were taken to the front where they were told disobedience to orders meant execution. They continued to disobey, were court martialled and paraded before thousands of soldiers to hear their sentences: 'Private——, Number— of the Second Eastern Company NCC, tried by Field Court Martial for disobedience whilst undergoing field punishment. Sentenced to death by being shot, confirmed by General Sir Douglas Haig.' The Commanding Officer paused and then in the silence added, 'and commuted to ten years penal servitude.' The seventeen served their sentences in convict prisons until six months after the armistice.

My interest was inevitably concentrated on the struggle of the objectors but I remained editor of the *Labour Leader* until August 1916. I then obtained leave of absence, partly because I was wanted in London to take on duties as NCF secretary and partly because the Regulations of the Military Service Act exempted editors and I did not feel I could possibly accept exclusion when I had been foremost in mobilising others to resist. Lilla and I moved to London, renting a room in Bryanston Square, putting our baby Audrey to bed in a drawer. Mother and child were evicted by the landlady after police had called to arrest me.

My first imprisonment was for the distribution of a leaflet against the Conscription Act. Under DORA the Government took proceedings against all members of our Committee except Allen, who was due to be charged for failing to obey a call-up notice. We were fined £100 each with the alternative of two months' imprisonment, and when we refused to pay we were taken to Pentonville in a black maria with a thief and two prostitutes – the latter deposited at Holloway en route. Said the thief, 'I'm in for taking things, what you in for?' Replied W. J. Chamberlain (afterwards Press Head at Transport House): 'For giving things away.'

Our cells at Pentonville were 13 feet by 8 feet, and each contained a bed board, a basin for washing, a pot for sanitary purposes, a shelf for toilet articles, a slate and a Bible. During the first week we were kept in solitary confinement, and slept on the bare board. After that we worked for an hour in association and then in our cells sewing mail bags. The daily task was seventy-two feet. At first I could not do ten feet, but before I had finished with prison I could do seventy-two feet in three hours. We were not allowed to speak, but of course we did when out of the warders' hear-ing. On exercise we marched in circles, with five feet between each prisoner; it was extraordinary how one learned to convey words to the person in front without moving one's lips. The one subject of conversation among prisoners generally was whether Sir Roger Casement would be hanged. He had been arrested whilst attempting to reach Ireland to instigate a rebellion. I had admiration for Sir Roger because of his exposure of the appalling con-ditions of the African workers in the Congo and, without supporting his intentions in Ireland, hoped he would be reprieved. His fate became the subject of widespread betting among prisoners, payment to be made in smuggled tobacco. The odds were against his being hanged on the grounds that he was 'one of the nobs'. I have told so often of my sight of Roger Casement on the eve of his execution that I am reluctant to repeat it. Let me just say that I was an arm's length from him as he turned to say farewell to the sunset on his last exercise. I had heard steps and stood on my stool at the cell window a few feet from the door through which he was shepherded by warders. I had a curious feeling of contact with him as his spirit seemed to reach out to the beauty of the sky.

That same night I was released; Clifford Allen's arrest was imminent and the NCF Committee decided that my fine should be paid to enable me to take over. I didn't want to leave – I had felt so much at one with Casement in that brief moment that I wished to remain until the end. When the warder told me to pack up I exclaimed 'damn!' He looked at me with astonishment. 'You're the first bloke I've known,' he said, 'who didn't want to get out of here!' Sentiment on my part? Perhaps.

Two months later I was arrested under the Military Service Act. I had been to the tribunals – unusually to both the Central Tribunal and the revising Pelham Committee – and had been offered exemption if I would do work regarded as of national importance twenty-five miles from our Mellor home. It was a little difficult to dismiss the suggestion of Edmund Harvey, a Quaker MP on the Pelham Committee, that I should regard work for peace as of national importance. I took the view, however, that any duties under the Military Service Act would compromise principle. I ought not to get out of service in the trenches by accepting an alternative at home.

When my shocked landlady reported that the police had been to our lodgings to arrest me I made an appointment with them at the NCF office a week later. Meanwhile, I went into the country to finish a book, *Socialism for Pacifists*. The police kept the appointment, I was taken to Bow Street Police Station for the night, appeared in Court next morning and was handed over to a military escort for Scotland Yard Barracks. I prevailed on my soldier guard to take lunch en route at the Strand Corner House, where we were joined by my wife and NCF colleagues for a gay farewell meal. After a brief stay at Scotland Yard I was taken to the Tower of London (*John Bull*'s wish was partially met!) and locked in a large dungeon where there were twenty or so prisoners, mostly sitting or lying on a sloping wooden platform, which I learned was a communal bed, running the length of the longer wall. Six of the prisoners, still in civilian clothes, were objectors, but almost immediately an escort arrived to take them to camp. From the soldiers I had obscene abuse until the colonel arrived on inspection duty. I declined the order of the sergeant to line up. 'You there,' he shouted, 'fall in, you're in the army now.' I walked within a few feet of the colonel and sat down on the bed. 'I'm sorry, sir,' I said, 'but I'm not prepared to obey any military order.' 'Then you're for the cells.' After the colonel and the sergeant left, the transformation in the attitude of the soldier prisoners stunned me. They gathered round laughing and slapping my back. 'Told the colonel off proper, you did,' one said. When the escort arrived to take me to the regiment to which I had been allotted I was in the middle of a group of soldiers explaining why I was a conshie.

I was to be taken to Chester Castle and my wife travelled to Chester with me. By this time I was on such good terms with the escort that the sergeant insisted on taking her to her lodgings before taking me to the barracks. The Cheshire Regiment did not have a good reputation for its treatment of objectors. The previous week the newspapers had carried reports of how George Beardsworth and Charles Dukes, both subsequently prominent trade union leaders, had been forcibly taken to the drilling ground and kicked, punched, knocked down and thrown over railings until they lay exhausted, bruised and bleeding. I was a little apprehensive.

The next morning I was one of five objectors taken for medical examination. We all declined the order to strip, were placed under arrest and marched to the guard room, another dungeon darker even than that at the

Tower. The communal bed occupied most of the floor space; the atmosphere smelled of urine which leaked from a pail and flowed under the bed. Conditions made me wonder how prisoners existed for years in such places as Chester Castle and the Tower of London in mediaeval times. We were confined here for ten days awaiting court martial but allowed to exercise for one glorious hour a day on the ramparts of the castle. Each morning we were marched to face the colonel who asked the routine question, 'Any complaints?' I described the conditions in the guard room with the result that the floor was levelled from the latrine recess.

An incident then occurred which suggested that the War Office was making a last minute effort to tempt me to compromise. One night I was marched to the Officers' Quarters, welcomed and offered a drink. A senior officer, after casual conversation, assured me that no one was happy about my forthcoming imprisonment and that the authorities wished to avoid it. 'You are an experienced journalist. Why shouldn't you do press work for a department in Whitehall?' I laughed. 'You want me to use my pen for the war when I won't use a gun.' I think the officer saw my point and respected it. He insisted that I should stay the night and at breakfast no reference was made to the conversation the night before.

A few days before my court martial I got a letter from my friend of Manchester Gaiety Theatre days, Miles Malleson, the dramatist and actor. He had joined the army in the enthusiasm of the first days of the war but had thought his way through to a socialist pacifist position (already held by his wife) and had refused to obey orders. Perhaps because the authorities did not want publicity he was not arrested but discharged. An amusing incident arose when I replied congratulating him on his play *Black Hell*, making many references to it. The sergeant who censored our letters came indignantly to me demanding what the bloody hell would people think of the bloody army if we allowed bloody swear words to leave the bloody guard room? I was puzzled. 'Swear words?' 'Yes. There are "hells" all over your letter.' I had forgotten. *Black Hell!*

My court martial was a pantomime. The room was small and few were able to attend except press representatives, but my wife and Bruce Glasier, who came to give me a character reference, squeezed in. The three officers comprising the court were new to the job and knew little about it. I had mastered the volume of complex Military Regulations and, as they turned it over despairingly, guided them to the page and paragraph. After I had proved right a third time the officers accepted my help openly and it became a case of a prisoner conducting his own trial. My defence statement was the Socialist case against the war, afterwards printed as a leaflet with wide distribution in Britain, Canada, Australia and New Zealand. My three fellow objectors and I were sentenced to three months with hard labour.

We were taken by escort to Wormwood Scrubs Prison in London where something like six hundred objectors were already confined. The mere presence of so many was an inspiration. My first conflict with the authorities was on the subject of a vegetarian diet, and I knew there were a number of other vegetarians among our boys. The Medical Officer said that he could only order a change of diet after a serious loss of weight. I petitioned the Home Secretary (my old friend J. R. Clynes) and went on partial hunger strike, eating only skilly, bread and potatoes. It was three months before the Home Office granted a vegetarian diet, but when it came it proved to be more tasty and varied than the regulation diet. The consequence was fantastic. There was a long queue of prisoners at the Governor's Office composed not only of objectors but of hardened criminals, one a man serving a year for bludgeoning his wife with a poker, all claiming that their consciences would not allow them to eat meat.

Soon after going to Scrubs those of us who refused alternative service were transferred to Wandsworth Prison. I was entitled to one visit a month from my wife and she came with baby Audrey, then eighteen months old. We faced each other under the inhuman 'meat safe' conditions, standing in cubicles with thick wire gauze between us. It was so humiliating that it would have been better if they had not come. Lilla was expecting our second child and went to a nursing home run by a friend in Manchester; a few days before the end of my sentence I received a telegram to say that Margaret was born. My one concern now was to manoeuvre a visit to my wife before I was sentenced again, and when the day of discharge came the escort sergeant agreed to travel to Chester via Manchester. I spent the afternoon with Lilla and baby Margaret, arriving as arranged at London Road station for the last train to Chester. My escort turned up just in time, drunk. At Chester it was I who had to escort them to the barracks.

I found a changed attitude in the army. When first conscripted to Chester Castle, soldiers were antagonistic; now they were tolerant, even sympathetic. I was in a more challenging mood. When my sentence of two years' imprisonment with hard labour was read out before a parade of three thousand I stepped forward and in my best Hyde Park voice responded, 'I shall be proud to do it, sir.' The lines of troops seemed to shiver at my audacity. The sergeant kicked me all the way back to the guard room, but that was not the reaction of the ranks.

I was taken to Walton Prison at Liverpool. I entered in a new mood. When first imprisoned I was prepared to accept the punishment, proud to undergo it as a witness to anti-war convictions. Now I had no longer the spiritual exultation of a novice and was not in the temper to accept penalties gladly. I found myself in a hall with sixty other objectors and we developed elaborate plans to overcome the rule which forbade speech and communication. We reversed the morse code and used it for messages to our neighbours by knocking on the wall. Then, by means of a hot-water pipe running from cell to cell, we contrived to communicate with prisoners the length of the hall. From the last cell the pipe lifted to the floor above. Its occupant converted it into a telephone exchange, using cell numbers for identification.

This was only half our plan. We needed to write messages not only between ourselves but to the outside world. With our NCF colleagues outside we arranged that every objector coming into prison should carry pencil leads under the arch of a foot. My wife nearly gave this away – she provided me with indelible leads. At Walton, according to regulations, I stripped and stepped into a bath. The water turned purple. The warder told off the attendant prisoner for adding disinfectant, but fortunately he was one of our boys and accepted the blame. The arch of the foot was also used to smuggle messages out of prison. I wrote a one-act play, *Recruit*, which went out under the feet of departing prisoners; it was actually published whilst I was still in prison.

Now we had the leads, our next move was to produce a prison paper. I became editor of the *Walton Leader*, written neatly on toilet paper, the subscription three sheets from each prisoner. It was quite a creditable journal, including news items from those who had had recent visits, articles, correspondence and cartoons, the last done by Arthur Wragg, who later became well known. One item in the *Walton Leader* might have brought us charges under the Official Secrets Act. An incoming objector brought us a detailed account of the slaughter at Passchendaele written by a deserter who was in the guard room at the same time. The story moved us all deeply. Should we complain of our safe conditions whilst others were facing almost inevitable death? One of our boys even withdrew and joined the army because he could not accept the comparison. It was ironical that whilst the Press outside was not allowed to publish the story a prison paper was able to do so.

A copy of the *Walton Leader* was discovered and I was tried by the Visiting Magistrates. They had no doubt that I produced it and I did not deny it, but they had no evidence. In a normal Court I could not have been found guilty, but they sentenced me to six days on bread and water in the punishment cells. I was taken to a dark basement cell where the furniture consisted of a stool, a chamber pot and a Bible. The second day I became weak and lay on the floor, using the Bible as a pillow, but I found that by the third day I had become adjusted. At night I was permitted to lie on a bed board, which was at least warmer than the stone floor.

Shortly afterwards I got myself into hospital. My teeth were troubling me and I asked for a dentist who was allowed to attend at my expense. I had to cling to the seat of a kitchen chair whilst he levered out a wisdom tooth. Perhaps the severest criticism I can make of the monotony of prison life is that I looked forward to these visits. An improvement in my prison conditions followed. My throat swelled and an eye closed after the extractions and I was detained in hospital. I was still in a cell but there was a bed, mattress, sheets, blankets and I was given library books whenever I asked. When I got well I was kept in hospital for a time as an orderly. The most distressing sight was 'Rotten Row' with cells in which mental cases were confined. Many of the doors were replaced by iron bars, the inmates looking like caged animals. They gibbered idiotically, grinning and masturbating. What on earth were they doing in jail? I asked.

I was in prison when three murderers were executed. The psychological effect on both staff and prisoners was extreme, everyone becoming nervy; prisoners berserk, officers short-tempered. On the day of the executions we were kept in our cells after breakfast instead of going out to exercise or work. The whole place was silent, each of us listening for the steps of the procession to the execution shed and for the striking of the fatal hour which would tell us all was over.

CHAPTER SIX

SOLITARY CONFINEMENT

The time had come for another psychological change. As I have written, at first we accepted imprisonment almost as a privilege. From that we went on to organise disobedience within the system. Now we began to turn to resistance to the system itself. There was a ferment of discussion. Should we disobey orders? Should we continue to work? My own decision was based principally on the silence rule. It seemed to me to be beyond the right of any authority to prohibit such an elementary human attribute as speech. It is true we were defeating the rule by subversive communication, but we accepted its authority and boys were repeatedly put on bread and water when caught talking.

I came to the conclusion that we should openly defy the rule and four others agreed to go with me to the Governor and tell him this. They included three Chester Castle companions and Percy Bartlett, afterwards secretary to George Lansbury on his 'Embassies of Reconciliation' to the War Leaders of Europe. The Governor warned us that our actions might be mutiny, but when we began to speak openly we were not sent to our surprise to the punishment cells but placed in the hall for remand prisoners. A somewhat sinister thing happened there. I had smuggled out an article for the *Manchester Guardian* indicting the prison system. A newcomer in the next cell, talking from window to window, assured me that the article had caused a sensation and that Hilaire Belloc had written supporting my case in the *Sunday Chronicle*; he claimed to have the article with him and read extracts, all in Belloc's unique style. I learned later that my article had passed almost unnoticed and that Belloc had never written to the *Sunday Chronicle*. Without knowing this, however, I became suspicious that my neighbour might be an informer. When he felt he had won my confidence he put a series of questions. Were we proposing to extend resistance to other prisons? How had I got my article to the *Guardian*? Had any warder helped me? My suspicions were strengthened when I noticed that the prison officers made no attempt to stop our talking. I gave nothing away, but I mentally congratulated the Special Branch on their imitation of Hilaire Belloc.

The effect of our defiance of the Silence Rule was felt throughout the prison. All the sixty COs followed our example and disobedience spread to other prisoners. The Governor thought it best to confine the revolt to the COs' hall and the five of us were returned to it. Then for ten momentous days we largely ran our own lives. We elected a representative committee who drew up new prison rules, providing for unrestricted conversation, games during exercise periods, lectures and concerts in the evenings, and periods of silence for reading. It was an exhilarating time. Our liberty was, of course, restricted – once the doors were locked on us we could not get out of our cells – but we had an extraordinary sense of liberation. Our lectures and concerts, delivered through windows with the audience listening at theirs, reached not only our own boys but the inmates of neighbouring halls. The revolution seemed to be extending to the whole prison.

*   *   *

At the end of ten days the five who initiated disobedience were deported to other prisons. I was taken to Lincoln and confined in an empty hall, the one occupied cell. I maintained resistance, including a work strike, and was punished by solitary confinement and one month on bread and water diet (the doctor forbade more); this meant bread and water only for three days and less than the normal diet for three more days. I used to save bread from the latter and got through without too much discomfort. Despite confinement to my cell for most of the time I felt strangely free. Relaxation came in reading. To last a month I selected the longest books from the library list, wonderfully a volume of Shakespeare's plays, but most of the time I had to be content with instalments of Chambers's Encyclopaedia. The Governor allowed me an Esperanto New Testament to replace the Bible and, although I had no knowledge of the international language and little of the Gospels, I found I could soon read it easily; to my regret I have never pursued the study. One got tired of reading. Sometimes moments of frustration came, when I wanted to break windows and storm the door. I wondered then if I would remain sane if this total isolation lasted long. Relief came in an unexpected way.

My cell had the advantage of looking on to a vegetable garden and fruit trees and I feasted eyes on the autumn tints. One day I heard steps outside. I got on my stool. A red-band prisoner (trusted handyman, allowed to go about without warders) signalled me down and a package came hurtling through the one open pane. It contained a note, a pencil and a sheet of paper for reply. The writer was Alastar Macaba, Sinn Fein MP for Sligo, detained in the prison with De Valera, Milroy and sixteen others, detained but allowed freedom of movement within their hall and their exercise ground, as well as food, newspapers and letters from the outside world. The note said: 'We are Irish and can do anything for you – except get you out.' I was asked to indicate my requirements through the 'trustee' who would be outside my window the same time next day.

I asked that my wife and friends should be told I was all right (I was not allowed to write letters or have visits) and I added that I was dying for news. Two days later came the reply. The Sinn Feiners could smuggle out a letter to my wife and would order what newspapers I wanted. I wrote to Lilla and I asked unknown Macaba for the *Manchester Guardian*, the *Labour Leader*, and the *Observer*. Believe it or not, they came. It was the duty of the 'trustee' to clean the latrine in the Sinn Feiners' exercise yard and also in the yard where I walked alone for forty minutes a day. He transferred the papers from one latrine to the other, I tucked them in my trousers (depositing those I had read in exchange), and perused them in a corner of my cell unobservable from the spyhole in the door. This went on for nearly eight months undetected – I was so seemingly isolated from all contact that the warders never troubled to search my cell. Looking back, I think the Sinn Feiners saved my mind. I do not know how I could have stuck long solitary confinement without the relief the papers gave.

Alastar Macaba used to write to me daily. One note indicated that something exciting would happen the following day. I endured it in expectancy and was bitterly disappointed as I got down on my bed board at lights out when nothing had happened. Then, at ten o'clock, whistles began to blow and doors to bang, and orders were loudly shouted. I sensed at once that there had been an escape and jumped on my stool and yelled to two warders peering about with lanterns, 'You won't catch him.' I was as excited as though I had escaped myself. Two days later I heard the details. The Catholic chaplain had momentarily left the master key of the prison on a table in the Sinn Feiners' hall. Milroy had flashed a pencil round it and at Christmas sent a card to friends at Manchester with two sketches. One was marked 'Locked out' and showed a reveller trying to turn a key in his front door. The second, 'Locked in', depicted a prison warder with a large key at his waist, an outline of the master key. The Manchester recipients did not appreciate the significance of the card, but Dublin Sinn Feiners, to whom they forwarded it, were brighter and did.

As I have told, the Sinn Fein detainees were allowed food from outside. From Dublin came a cake containing a key patterned to the outline. It didn't fit. A second cake came with failure again. The third cake contained a file as well as a key and Milroy made it fit. Then, after plans had been completed, De Valera, Milroy and three others let themselves out at five o'clock in the afternoon by the back door of the prison and joined waiting cars which took them to separate ports and they all got back to Ireland. The Lincoln prison had ludicrous security precautions. In front an iron gate was opened for entrants, who were left in an enclosure until second iron gates were unlocked; at the back was one door in a wall.

An exhilarating item of news reached me through the Sinn Feiners. As seems inevitable when prisoners are isolated, rumours spread outside that I was suffering from tuberculosis. The shop stewards in Lincoln's engineering industry heard it, and, amazingly (they were making munitions), they called a one-day stoppage whilst a deputation waited on the prison Governor and Medical Officer who justifiably reassured them. It was a remarkable gesture of solidarity and it was good to know that I was not forgotten.

Meanwhile, momentous events for the world were happening. The Kerensky and Bolshevik revolutions had occurred in Russia. The Socialist parties of Europe had come together at a conference in Stockholm and had decided on common action for peace. Arthur Henderson had been 'left on the mat' by the Cabinet for supporting the conference and had resigned. In Germany the anti-war Socialists were threatening revolt; in Bavaria Kurt Eisner and Ernst Toller (with whom I became friendly later) had succeeded in a Socialist revolution. At Kiel the German navy mutinied. The German front cracked. I learned from a warder on the fatal morning of 11 November that the Germans had been given until eleven o'clock to sign surrender. I was able to tell the time by the line of the sun on the wall and watched fascinated. Then came the sound of Lincoln's hooters announcing that peace had come.

It was more than four months before we were released. That period was darkened for me by the death of W. C. Anderson in the influenza epidemic. He had given me my chance in the Labour movement; in my view he could have become a Labour Prime Minister. In April the prison doors opened for me. My wife met me at King's Cross and we joined our infant daughters in a pacifist community at Standford-le-Hope in Essex. A few weeks later an

OHMS envelope arrived. It contained a War Office intimation that I had been discharged from the Army and that if I ever attempted to join the forces in the future I would be subject to two years imprisonment.

CHAPTER SEVEN

BACK TO WORK

I came out of prison with a partly paralysed leg and it was six months before I was fit to resume work. With the help of MCF friends I was able to convalesce at Scarborough and then at a delightful guest house in Devon built on rocks jutting out to sea. I could not refrain from going to the ILP Conference at Leicester intending to be a silent observer but felt impelled to speak on a motion on the prison system. To many of us the duty to change conditions for prisoners left behind, whatever their offences, was almost a priority. During my convalescence, at the request of Philip Snowden, I wrote a pamphlet, *Prisons as Crime Factories*. I had assumed that I would return as editor of the *Labour Leader* and had a rather sharp exchange of letters with Snowden when I was offered instead a part-time job as London correspondent. I did not know until years later, reading a biography of the Glasiers, that Snowden had it in mind to become editor himself with Mrs Glasier, who during my imprisonment had acted for me, as his assistant. I didn't take the job of London correspondent seriously although it gave me the privilege of a ticket to the Press Gallery in the House of Commons.

Shortly after returning to London I was astonished by a letter which I received from an Australian pacifist enclosing a cheque for £100. He had asked Ramsay MacDonald, Philip Snowden and E. D. Morel whom they thought was the bravest pacifist during the war and two had named me. It was not true. I thought of boys I had met in prison who had no family support and who were not sustained by the political associations I enjoyed. I accepted an invitation to see the donor at his home in Sanderstead. He told me how he had begun life as a boy selling papers on the streets of Sydney and, whilst later he had done well in business, his passion was to save others from the poverty he had experienced and above all to prevent destruction by war. He had now decided to provide an opportunity to someone who would serve peace. When he asked me what I needed most and I replied a house for my family, he took my breath away by saying he would give me £1,000 to buy one. Thus Lilla and I came to live in Keir Cottage at Thorpe Bay.

At the Leicester ILP Conference, Shaperji Saklatvala, the fiery Indian politician, later Communist MP for Battersea, asked me to become organiser for the India League which under the dynamic leadership of Krishna Menon was campaigning for independence. I was attracted as, Indian born, the cause was dear to me but I declined because of unrecovered health. Later I became joint secretary of the British Committee of the Indian National Congress, sharing the post with Syed Hussein, a brilliant young Indian. He had left India in personal distress. He had fallen in love with a daughter of Motilal Nehru, the Congress Party leader, but marriage was barred because he was a Muslim and the Nehrus were Hindus. The daughter afterwards became the distinguished Mrs Pandit, High Commissioner in London, and adviser to her brother, Jawaharlal Nehru, India's Prime Minister after independence. My association with Hussein did not last long because Mahatma Gandhi stopped foreign propaganda, but two events remain in my mind. The first was the visit of Lokomanya Tilak, whom Gandhi called 'the maker of modern India'. Tilak was the first to arouse the Indian people to self-reliance and as early as 1897 was sentenced to eighteen months' imprisonment for sedition. He was a scholar as well as nationalist leader and we gathered together an influential reception committee which did him honour at the House of Commons. The second memory is of Vithal Patel, afterwards Speaker of the Indian Legislative Assembly. He had been commissioned by Gandhi to collect evidence of precedents for non-violent non-cooperation with alien occupations and he asked me to gather information. I did so, and the results were published in Madras in a book under the title *Non-Cooperation in Other Lands*. Gandhi told me later that the book had been of value to him in planning his own campaign.

In my spare time I was active as chairman of the No More War Movement. From Keir Cottage we organised simultaneous demonstrations in nearly all the capitals of the world. They drew enormous crowds and for a time it looked as though a formidable international force for peace would emerge. I spoke at the Berlin demonstration in Max Reinhardt's vast theatre, a spectacular occasion, with Crispien, leading Social Democrat, representing Germany and Jean Longuet, son-in-law of Karl Marx, France. A speaking choir composed of hundreds of men, women and children enacted the horrors of the war years, the misery of the post-war years, and the coming triumph of peace. The climax came in the emotional last scene, when actors and actresses massed on the platform with red banners leading the audience in singing 'The International'.

Walter Ayles, afterwards MP for a Bristol constituency, was treasurer of the No More War Movement. Two women enthusiasts subsequently became well known – Lucy Cox, who married James Middleton, secretary of the Labour Party, and a political figure in her own right, and Dorothy Woodman, companion of Kingsley Martin, famous editor of the *New Statesman*, herself an expert on South East Asia about which she wrote so much. Both were dedicated, dark and engaging.

Complementary to the movement in Britain was the War Resisters International of which also I was made chairman. Its aim was to unite the conscientious objectors of the world and their supporters. The WRI introduced me to many interesting personalities abroad, including Dr Helen Stöcker, leader of what would now be termed 'Women's Lib' in Germany, a large hearty woman; Rajendra Prasad, later President of India, a dedicated Gandhian; and Bart De Ligt, an activist academic, the Dutch author of *The Conquest of Violence*, the textbook of non-violent revolution. Most of all I remember Albert Einstein. With Runham Brown, the devoted secretary, I motored to Oxford to meet him, a friendly, fatherly figure, seeming above current issues by his dedication to eternal truth and yet deeply intrigued by the pacifism in action of the young men of many different countries who accepted severe penalties rather than train for war. 'They are before their time,' he said, 'pioneers of a world in which mankind will have become adult and learned to live beyond the jungle from which we have emerged only a few thousand years – no time at all in evolutionary history.'

A memorable event for peace was the decision of the Labour movement in 1920 to declare a general strike if the Government took hostile measures against Soviet Russia. At the height of a crisis between Poland and Russia, London dockers refused to load munitions for Poland on the *Jolly Roger* and immediately Councils of Action were formed throughout the country. I was one of the ILP delegates to the great Labour Conference which authorised the strike, a deeply impressive occasion. J. H. Thomas, the railwaymen's leader, afterwards regarded as a traitor by the Left, then as revolutionary as anyone, remarked from the chair that the decision was not only a challenge to the Government but to the Constitution, a statement remembered in the 1926 General Strike. The next day the Government said they had never intended hostile action. Few believed them.

Then came an appointment which met my desire, almost an obsession, to do something about prisons. Beatrice Webb invited me to her Millbank home some few hundred yards from the Houses of Parliament. I remember the scene. Mrs Webb, reserved yet inviting response, half-reclining on a legless chair so that her feet stretched forward on the carpet, and bearded

Sidney, more distant, busy with his papers at a desk, occasionally intervening. Beatrice and Sidney had differed politically, probably for the first time,
about the war. Beatrice, anti-war, had joined the ILP and I remember her
at one of our annual conferences, a silent, enquiring observer; Sidney was
pro-war but mainly concerned with achieving Socialism at its end. Beatrice
now explained that her nephew, Stephen Hobhouse, was preparing a report
for the Prison System Enquiry Committee; he was buried under a mountain
of documents and would never finish it. Would I rescue him and the report
by becoming joint secretary and joint editor? Of course I agreed. The office
of the Committee was transferred to our Keir Cottage. I had great admiration for Stephen. When he had broken down in health in prison as a Quaker
objector his mother became prominent in getting together an influential
group to demand the release of those who had served long sentences. He
was still far from well, but worked untiringly. It took about a year to
convert the mass of evidence into a report, *English Prisons Today*, itself a
massive document. Several reforms followed our exposure, including the
abolition of the Silence Rule. I was not satisfied, however. Later I wrote
A New Way With Crime, suggesting methods of dealing with offenders without sending them to prison. Many of these have been adopted.

The chairman of our Committee was Lord Oliver who had been Governor
of Jamaica, author of an admirable book favouring inter-racialism. Besides
Beatrice and Sidney Webb, Bernard Shaw and Margery Fry, expert prison
reformer, were members. I acquired a new knowledge of Shaw. In committee he was not the domineering egoist of public image but, whilst
throwing in explosive remarks and always good fun, was modestly eager to
learn and painstakingly cooperative. When we asked him to write the preface he surprised me by his readiness to take advice. Nevertheless the preface caused a crisis. He concluded that there was only one way to deal with
incurable criminals and that was to put them in a lethal chamber. This
shocked my Quaker co-secretary and he declined to have his name on the
report if the preface appeared. Shaw then offered to rewrite the offending
paragraphs by saying that there were two ways: incurable criminals could
either be put in lethal chambers or be placed under the care of Quakers for
the rest of their lives. Stephen was not appeased and Shaw's preface appeared
in a book by the Webbs on prisons under local government. The Webbs'
book caused me some concern. Sidney asked me to check his manuscript,
written in a large and remarkably clear calligraphy. There were many
mistakes of fact. Apparently it was the custom of the Webbs to employ
students at the London School of Economics to do research. I wondered
how far the other Webb books were reliable.

Our typist came to us in curious circumstances. Before our house was completed, Lilla and the babies and I lived in a tent in the garden. A case was stolen from it and a girl of sixteen was arrested for the theft. The probation officer reported that she had an unhappy background, had run away when her drunken father beat her and had obtained a job as a typist. We went to the court and the magistrate placed the girl on probation under our care. She lived with us and typed our Prison Enquiry chapters. She worked well generally and was happy with our children, but one weekend she disappeared and was arrested for stealing a handbag. This time she was given a Borstal sentence, after which I set her up in lodgings to type manuscripts for authors. It went well for a time, but then she was arrested once more for stealing and sentenced to imprisonment. I thought I had seen the last of her, but when elected to Parliament in 1950, twenty-five years later, I recognised her as a waitress in the tea room. I asked why she had not contacted me on leaving prison and she replied that she was too ashamed; she had gone straight ever since. Perhaps our consideration after all was worth while.

As an ex-prisoner refusing alternative service I was not allowed to vote for five years, but illogically I was allowed to stand for Parliament in 1922. I accepted the candidature at Lancaster where we had a campaign which I think must be unique for its range and quality. Once a month we took the large Ashton Hall and the series of speakers included Ramsay MacDonald, Lord Haldane, Bernard Shaw, Robert Smillie, Maude Royden, J. R. Clynes, Clem Attlee and Philip Snowden. Lord Haldane, brushing aside our differences during the war, offered to come after he had heard me speak at a meeting to raise funds for the Prison System Enquiry. I met Shaw at the station and left him at the Railway Hotel to rest; when I called to take him to the meeting he was brushing his artificial teeth. Lifting a plate in one hand and waving his toothbrush in the other he exclaimed: 'Young man, you are witnessing an historic act. When man made teeth better than God the barrier between barbarism and civilisation was pierced.' Shaw's speech at the Ashton Hall was a flop; he never got going and the audience was bored. He saved it by his last sentence. 'Ladies and Gentlemen,' he declared, his voice vibrant at last, 'you will be able to inform your incredulous grandchildren that you heard Bernard Shaw when he was dull.' There were some in the audience who thought GBS was deliberately dull for the sake of his conclusion, but in fact he was deeply ashamed. He declined to face the ILP members at a social we had arranged after the meeting. I took him to the hotel and put him on the night train to London: 'I shall recover reading my own incomparable writing,' was his last remark. He proposed to correct proofs through the night journey.

CHAPTER EIGHT

ÉLITE IN COMMAND

Meanwhile the ILP was in difficulties. MacDonald, Snowden and most of its MPs had been defeated in the Lloyd George Coupon election at the end of the war and the party had lost its national image. We were acutely divided about international associations; the Vienna Union of anti-war parties had broken up and there was a militant section which wished to join the Third (Communist) International. R. C. Wallhead and Clifford Allen went on a deputation to Moscow and on their return recommended that Lenin's conditions for affiliation should be rejected. This was endorsed by the next annual conference, whereupon there was a split and resignations, including that of Saklatvala. More serious for the status of the ILP was the decision of the Labour Party to open its membership to individual members – previously it was federal and individuals could join only through the ILP or the Fabian Society. For a time I began to doubt whether there was a future for the ILP, particularly since the Labour Party had moved towards the ILP position on peace by denouncing the Versailles Treaty. The success of over one hundred ILP nominees in the General Election of 1922 strengthened still further our identification with the wider Party, and with the election of Ramsay MacDonald as leader the control in Parliament appeared to be in our hands. Why retain a separate ILP?

Clifford Allen ended this defeatism. He believed that the ILP had a great future as an educational and activist force for Socialism and peace. He invited me to his flat in Battersea shortly after his return from the Soviet Union and outlined his views: 'We must do what Russia has done, but by persuasion not force,' he said. I joined a small committee to restate our policy in these terms. Clem Attlee and G. D. H. Cole were members; Attlee had been a major in the war and came out dedicated to 'never again' – at one Labour Party Conference he moved an ILP resolution for unilateral disarmament. He was a man of few words, but they were incisive and decisive. At the following ILP conference Clifford Allen was elected treasurer and proved a wizard at money raising. His control of the purse, his creative ideas, his organising ability and his winning personality made him the directing head of the Party. Inevitably he became chairman.

In December 1922 on the invitation of Allen I became Organising Secretary of the ILP. The Party was booming; in three years the number of branches rose from 521 to 1,028. I came very much under the influence of Allen and his ambitious initiatives. He had a new conception of democracy, rejecting the social democratic view that progress to Socialism should wait consenting opinion. A doctor, he argued, did not await the opinion of others to make a diagnosis and give treatment. Society was sick. Socialists had diagnosed the disease and when they had the opportunity they should proceed with the necessary treatment; the public would have the opportunity to express its opinion of what was done at the subsequent election.

There was one snag in this strategy. We had not decided the necessary treatment for the disease. He therefore got the ILP to appoint a high-powered team to prepare a positive plan for the decisive transformation from capitalism to Socialism. Its members were certainly authoritative. They were J. A. Hobson, leading economist; Frank Wise who had been economic adviser to Lloyd George; the author H. N. Brailsford; and Creech Jones, research officer of the Transport Workers Union. After a year's work they produced a report under the alternative titles, *A Living Incomes Policy* or *Socialism in our Time*. These indicated the double purpose of abolishing poverty and transforming society.

The report was a notable document, extraordinarily relevant as I write fifty years later. It included a national minimum income for all, the socialisation of what Nye Bevan afterwards termed 'the commanding heights of the economy', workers' participation in management, national control of investment and import and export boards to balance foreign exchanges. The rift between MacDonald and the ILP began when he contemptuously dismissed the report, remarking that he had read only its headings in someone else's newspaper when standing in a crowded tube train – but that was enough. The ILP, proletarians and intellectuals alike, received the report enthusiastically; it was to be its bible for ten years.

Allen was not content with this research on fundamental policy. He set up expert committees on all current problems. The Finance Committee included two members who became figures of public dispute. Oswald Mosley, tall, handsome, arrogant, compelling, and Hugh Dalton also an extrovert, loud in speech, a little angular in body and in person but full of ideas and self-confidence. Dalton was often in conflict with Mosley, holding his own aggressively. I was chairman of the Anti-Imperialist and Racial Equality Committee, which included H. N. Brailsford and the novelist Winifred Holtby, who was particularly concerned about South Africa. It

August 1916: Members of the No Conscription Fellowship Council during their trial under the Defence of the Realm Act: front row l. to r., Walter Ayles, W. G. Chamberlain, Clifford Allen, F.B., between Ayles and Chamberlain, J. P. F. Fletcher. All except Allen, who was arrested for refusing military service, were sentenced to one month's imprisonment

On the occasion of his second trial in December 1916 – this time under the Military Service Act – F.B. is handed over to the army at Bow Street

A rare photograph of Ho Chi Minh addressing the French Socialist Conference at Tours in 1920, where F.B. first met him

was largely due to her insistence that we engaged a Scottish trade unionist to go to the Republic to organise African Trade Unions. Allen extended his cultural revolution within the ILP by inviting lecturers of the highest repute to our summer schools. Indeed, the schools became a national forum of political ideas. I am still astonished when I look at the programmes. The lecturers included not only provocative Socialists like Wells, Shaw, Bertrand Russell and George Orwell but others like Walter Elliott, Lord Lothian, Lord Beaverbrook, Sir Harold Nicolson, J. B. Priestley, General Fuller and Liddell Hart.

The changes initiated by Allen included a revolution in the *Labour Leader*. It had been a paper for the Party. Allen decided that it should become a paper for the intelligent public. He changed its name to the *New Leader* and H. N. Brailsford was appointed editor. He produced a unique journal in which the standard of typography and design was as important as its editorial contents. Many issues contained original woodcuts and it always had a nature article emphasising the beauty of the countryside in contrast to the ugliness of industrial existence. An instinct for personal judgement was shown by Allen in appointing a clerk from the staff of the *Daily Citizen* as manager of the *New Leader* (Allen himself had been the director of the *Daily Citizen* before it closed down). Leslie Plummer was extraordinarily successful in circulation boosting and advertisement getting and Beaverbrook kidnapped him for the *Daily Express*, remarking to Allen, 'if you have any more like him let me know'. Plummer (later Sir Leslie) will be remembered for an assignment which was not so successful, though he was little to blame. John Strachey, Minister of Food – he himself began his career under Plummer – was responsible for sending him out on the Groundnuts scheme in Tanganyika during the 1945 Labour Government.

We had a cultural activity unusual for a political party in Britain, 'The Masses Film and Stage Guild'. It was my brain child rather than Allen's and I got Miles Malleson to be director. Arthur Bourchier loaned the Strand Theatre on Sunday evenings and Reginald Stamp, afterwards LCC member responsible for licensing entertainments, organised packed audiences to concerts and plays. We had extraordinary support from playwrights and actors including Ernst Toller, Bernard Shaw, John Galsworthy, John Grierson, Sybil Thorndike, Lewis Casson, Elsa Lanchester and Milton Rosmer. Once a month we took a cinema near Marble Arch for revolutionary films, mostly Russian. Malleson established dramatic societies throughout the country and for a time it looked as though we had intitiated a proletarian cultural revolution. I must add a special word about Ernst Toller. Enthusiastic for working-class culture, he travelled the country to direct our dramatic groups. He was also an enthusiastic political supporter of the ILP. He dramatised for a German film my suspension from Parliament (to be described later).

Allen typically housed our various enterprises in a mansion in Great George Street within a few hundred yards of Big Ben. It flew the Red Flag almost as a challenge to the Union Jack. There was a board room with an Adam fireplace and our offices were decorated under the expert eye of Dick Wallhead; my walls were painted a rare purple-green. On the top floor there was a research department under Ernest Hunter, who was soon to become prominent in ILP controversies and who much later became adviser to the Prime Minister, Clem Attlee.

In the General Election of 1922, not only were MacDonald, Snowden, Jowett and former ILP-ers returned, but also dramatically, the 'Red Clyde-siders' led by Maxton, Wheatley, Shinwell, Buchanan and Stephen. They soon startled Parliament by their militancy, bringing about three expulsions from the House. The Government had cut the allowance for babies' milk and Maxton called them murderers. When he refused to withdraw he was suspended, whereupon Wheatley and Buchanan repeated the charge, and all three were escorted from the Chamber. I used to have tea with them in a Scottish café in Tothill Street, the Thistle. One afternoon Wheatley reported that he had learned confidentially that the suspension was to be lifted the next day, and naughtily proposed that they should exploit this by driving into Palace Yard, the entrance to the House, demanding admission. When their car appeared police stopped them, press photographers enjoying the scene, but the confrontation was interrupted by MPs arriving from the Chamber to report that the House had just agreed to withdraw the exclusion order. Rather unfairly the Press and the public thought that the three rebels had forced the concession – Wheatley was a master of public relations.

Maxton, Campbell Stephen and Buchanan shared rooms, somehow managing without womanly assistance. Stephen cooked, Buchanan washed up, Maxton dusted. They bought a second-hand car for the journey from Battersea to the House. One day in Palace Yard it refused to start, but began unexpectedly to move – they found that Charlie Chaplin and Nancy Astor, who had shown him round the House, were pushing it! This was Maxton's introduction to Chaplin and they became friends; the comedian, as his films indicated, was a social rebel.

In the General Election of December 1923 the Labour Party, though a minority in the Commons, was returned as the largest Party, Ramsay Mac-Donald becoming the first Labour Prime Minister. He rejected the ILP view that he should stand or fall by a Socialist programme, but appointed two ILP representatives to his Cabinet, John Wheatley and Fred Jowett. They both shocked their leader by taking their seals of office at Buckingham Palace without adorning themselves in top hats and morning dress. The Government lasted only nine months, defeated because the Attorney General stopped a prosecution against J. R. Campbell for an allegedly seditious article in the Communist *Weekly Worker*. Its one notable achievement was John Wheatley's Housing Act; he proved himself a masterly front bencher. I remember Jowett's part in the Government for three things. He asked me to his reception at the Ministry of Works and defied custom by inviting the most junior members of his staff, even the messenger boys. My second memory is his inscription added to the Nurse Cavell monument – her last words, 'Patriotism is not enough. I must have no hatred or bitterness for anyone.' Of the third event I am reminded whenever I leave home. Jowett initiated the telephone boxes in our streets, designed by Sir Giles Gilbert Scott.

During the Labour Government I was involved as a candidate in a spectacular by-election in the Abbey Division of Westminster when Winston Churchill intervened as an anti-Socialist. Churchill had left the Liberal Party but had not yet joined the Tories and there were Conservative and Liberal candidates; the Conservative, a Mr Nicholson, better known for his gin than his politics, the Liberal, Scott Duckers, a solicitor, conscientious objector during the war, whose chief grievance in prison appeared to be that he could not wear the pink carnation which always graced his immaculate suit. Churchill inevitably dominated the scene and because of his denunciation of Socialists and all our works the Press paid considerable attention to my candidature. Brendan Bracken was Churchill's agent and ran his campaign like a showman, including a coach and four and a trumpeter. I canvassed in places I never expected to enter; for example, St James's Palace. The Prince of Wales had broken his collarbone hunting and, calling at the front door, I expressed sympathy and asked if I might meet his staff. To my surprise I was invited to the kitchen and the staff gathered. It was a strange place to propagate Socialism, but I was encouraged by the sympathy it received. At one of our school meetings Bernard Shaw strolled in, delivering a torrential speech. He said he had come unannounced because 'nothing would terrify the average Westminster elector more than the prospect of voting with G. Bernard Shaw.'

I have been concerned in election counts on eleven occasions but none has been so dramatic as the one at Caxton Hall. Brendan Bracken came running to Winston Churchill exclaiming, 'You are in by forty-three votes.' Mrs Churchill put her arm over his shoulder and moved to kiss him.

Bracken came leaping back before she could do so and said, 'I'm sorry, sir, you are out by forty-three votes.' Churchill's cigar dropped and he paced Caxton Hall like an angry tiger. The time came for the Returning Officer to announce the votes. Churchill stood by my side. 'Fenner,' he said, 'this Election has been too short. In ten days the machine has defeated ideas. Had it lasted three days more, ideas would have triumphed and either you or I would have been elected.' How Churchillian! He was always considerate to me after that. When in 1929 I was elected to Parliament he sent me a note: 'I hate your politics but you deserve to be here.' The figures at the Westminster Election were Nicholson 8,187, Churchill 8,144, Brockway 6,156, Duckers 291.

The estrangement of the ILP group from the Labour Government caused deep distress to many whose political home had been in the Party. Among them was William Leach, Bradford ILP stalwart, with whose family I had often stayed happily. He came to see me and poured out his heart, recollecting MacDonald's brave stand with the ILP in the World War. With him I left for Westminster, moved, unconvinced but I remember the journey for another reason. I had never believed the story that anyone's hair stood on end when frightened, but in the lift to the tube at King's Cross Leach's hair literally did. To my alarmed questioning he gasped that he was allergic to descending below the surface; we went to the House by bus. Leach was Minister for Aviation and was happy thousands of feet above the earth, yet his nerves went to pieces a few feet below. The human frame is unaccountable.

Despite its rejection of ILP policy we still had a sense of loyalty to the Labour Party. I was one of the crowd who sang 'The Red Flag' in the Central Lobby of the House of Commons in defiance of the Tory–Liberal coalition which defeated the Government in November 1924. Our enthusiasm was damped when during the subsequent election MacDonald did not join in denouncing as a forgery the 'Zinoviev letter' published by the *Daily Mail* which, it was claimed, proved that the Soviet Government was plotting against Britain. The Labour Party went to inevitable defeat and MacDonald's stock fell to zero. It would be difficult to find any informed person now who does not believe that the letter was a forgery.

There was a contradiction in Clifford Allen. He stood for a policy rejected by Ramsay MacDonald and yet he regarded him as the only possible leader of the Labour Party, destined to great achievement. He believed the one hope of acceptance of ILP policy, in some features if not all, was to persuade him. So, whilst the ILP and MacDonald drifted apart, the two leaders lunched together once a week. MacDonald also maintained contact with Ernest Hunter, who was a master of manipulation, and with Mrs Hamilton, also a research worker for us, who later had considerable influence over him when he became Prime Minister.

The crisis for Allen's leadership of the ILP came at the Labour Party Conference at Liverpool in October 1925. There had been growing over the years discontent among working-class members with the middle-class élitists' domination of head office. The revolt was headed by Maxton and Wheatley and the Clydeside group of MPs. They welcomed the 'Socialism in our Time' policy, but felt that it had been placed in cold storage by Allen's loyalty to MacDonald. They saw the ILP becoming a Fabian society of intellectual compromisers rather than a proletarian confrontation with capitalism. The warning had been given at the ILP conference in the Queen's Hall, London, in 1923. Maxton rose from the delegates and in impassioned tones denounced the conciliatory attitude of head office. Maxton and Allen symbolised their differences in their contrasting appearance. Maxton, lean of face, black hair curling round from ear to chin, his dark skin seemingly dirty, his tobacco-bespattered clothes hanging loosely on him, fierce of eye, voice and gesture – rebel incarnate. Allen exquisitely groomed, hair waved, features delicate, the perfect gentleman in speech and manner, a little consciously superior.

Allen carried the conference then, but within two years Maxton had the party behind him. At the Liverpool Labour Party Conference Maxton committed the ILP to a resolution supporting confiscation when industries were nationalised, contrary to ILP decisions which had favoured taxation of the rich to pay compensation. When the Party's National Council met he explained that he had accepted the resolution to secure the inclusion of wider ILP demands, but Allen, knowing that Maxton was in favour of confiscation, was morally outraged, and denounced the whole thing as a slick trick. The crisis arose, however, over a different issue. MacDonald, despite differences, remained editor of the ILP theoretical monthly, the *Socialist Review*. The Maxton group moved that this should end. Allen stretched out his hand for the medicinal glass he kept on the table for moments of crisis, controlled himself, and in crisp sentences asserted the principles of tolerance and liberty of thought and paid a glowing tribute to MacDonald's intellectual pre-eminence. Defeated, he dramatically rose, announced his resignation as ILP chairman, and left. I followed him to his room and for the first time saw him crumpled in despair. I sought to sympathise, but he knew I was on Maxton's side and I failed to make contact. At the ILP conference at Easter Maxton was elected chairman. Allen did not even attend.

CHAPTER NINE

THE ÉLITE DEPART

Under Maxton's chairmanship the ILP was transformed overnight. The middle-class experts disappeared from Head Office, some resigning, some retaining nominal membership. Among those who resigned was Philip Snowden. MacDonald did not, holding it was better to be expelled. Almost immediately it came near to expulsion. Although MacDonald was entitled to attend the Labour Party Conference as its treasurer, the ILP had always included him in its delegation. In 1927, because of the conflict of policy our National Council decided to drop him. His friends, organised by Ernest Hunter, still secretary of the Information Department, prepared a formidable protest, signed by many MPs and leading members throughout the country, recommending that MacDonald should continue to represent the ILP. It looked as though they would win.

At the annual conference Emanuel Shinwell moved the rejection of the recommendation in a violent speech, sarcasm and fury mingled. A young girl followed him. This is how I described her at the time: 'A puckish figure, with a mop of thick dark hair thrown impatiently aside, brown eyes flashing, body and arms moving in rapid gestures, words pouring from her mouth in Scottish accent and vigorous phrases, sometimes with a sarcasm which equalled Shinwell's.' It was Jennie Lee making her national debut – the fact that we still think of her as Jennie Lee rather than as Mrs Aneurin Bevan reflects her personal eminence. She won the mind of the conference by insisting that ILP support for 'Socialism in Our Time' would be hopelessly compromised if the best-known member in its delegation was put up by the Executive to advise rejection. The argument was over, but Hunter was confident of the committed votes of the delegates. It was my duty to reply and I was equally confident. I had with me a letter from MacDonald in which he said it would be better for him not to be an ILP delegate; apparently, although he had countenanced the Hunter campaign, he had not informed his supporters. I had only to read this letter for the opposition to collapse. From the chair Maxton said: 'Our movement knows and needs no giant.'

A second effect of the Maxton revolution was more distressing. I have told of the rare distinction of Brailsford's editorship of the *New Leader*. Its influence among thinking and sensitive people was immense. It was a spiritual as well as a political inspiration. But it did not satisfy the party. They wanted a bluntly worded, hard hitting paper to sell on the factory floor. When the subject was raised in the National Council I had to report this view, but I never did anything with more reluctance. I revered the *New Leader* and I revered Brailsford. I was the more self-conscious about this because I knew that if Brailsford went I would be proposed as his successor. It was a cruel thing for me to do.

David Kirkwood made the situation worse by criticising the salary paid to Brailsford, 'luxury seized from the bread of my workers'. Brailsford replied with quiet restraint. He believed the paper had contributed both to Socialism and to its spirit. He accepted that Kirkwood had a case. If the party decided on the equalisation of the incomes of all its members he would accept. Meanwhile, why should the recognised salary of an editor be selected? In his one sentence of retort Brailsford doubted whether his income was larger than Kirkwood's, when speaking fees and expense accounts were added to the Parliamentary salary. So Brailsford went and I replaced him. I tried to explain my dilemma to Brailsford but I could see he was hurt. For hours that night I discussed it with my secretary, Marguerite Louis – more than a secretary, a political colleague – as to whether I had done the right thing. I differed with Brailsford on the salary point. I felt that high payments were not consistent with the spirit of the ILP, but the determining factor was the desire of the membership for a propagandist paper. I tried as editor to retain something of the Brailsford tradition, but the result was tawdry compared with his creation.

Soon I became editor of a daily newspaper. On May Day 1926 the miners were locked out. Two days later the Cabinet rejected TUC negotiation and a general strike was declared. Never was a government decision more irresponsible. A member of the TUC told me what happened at 10 Downing Street. An agreed formula had been found when news reached the Cabinet that the compositors on the *Daily Mail* had refused to set up an article condemning the miners. Churchill in a fury tore up the agreement and under his hysterical anger the meeting broke up. Stanley Baldwin, the Prime

Minister, went to bed and the TUC delegation was shown the door. This incident launched the general strike.

To the ILP it was a revolutionary struggle: the organised working class against a capitalist government. All at Head Office brought sleeping bags to occupy floors for the duration. We offered our services to the TUC and on the third day we had a telephoned response. Could we spare an office boy as theirs was ill! Meanwhile, we duplicated thousands of copies of the *British Worker*, the strikers' reply to Churchill's *British Gazette*, and distributed them in Greater London. Appreciating our work, Tracey, the TUC publicity secretary, asked us to work out a scheme for its wider circulation and next evening I took a detailed plan to the TUC headquarters next door to Churchill's vacated house in Eccleston Square, ironically occupied by the Labour Party. My memory is of a room so filled with pipe smoke that one could scarcely distinguish individuals. Long hours in smoke were afterwards given as a reason for the TUC surrender.

The telephone rang: the Typographical Association had agreed to allow a northern edition of the *British Worker* to be printed in Manchester. What I had come to discuss was forgotten; the one question was who should go to Manchester to plan and to edit? Quietly Tracey remarked, 'I think you have the answer here.' So before midnight I was being motored to Manchester, accompanied by Marguerite Louis, with instructions to produce the *British Worker* next day. We were driven through the night by a young playwright, Hubert Griffiths, and his sister. They talked 'county' – hunting and dances – and I wondered why they had volunteered for TUC service rather than for the Government's OMS. 'Don't know much about it,' said Griffiths, 'but I think the miners have had a raw deal.' That was the beginning of Griffiths's Socialism. We educated him a lot en route.

We had an immediate set-back in Manchester. The Cooperative Printing Society declined to print unless the TUC permitted them to fulfill their other contracts. I learned there was another Cooperative printer, the Cooperative Publishing Society, and I set off by taxi to the manager's home in Southport fifty miles away. He agreed to place his plant at our disposal but we would have to run the service ourselves. The next morning I met the Trades Council and I have never been more impressed by a combination of zeal and ability. They planned the entire production and distribution of the paper, appointing leaders for every department, engineering, printing, proof reading, accountancy, typing, telephoning, selling. The Transport Workers Union organised distribution as far west as Caernarvon, east to Hull, north to Carlisle and south to Derby. I got members of the National Union of Journalists to help on the editorial side. It all worked marvellously.

This experience has influenced my thinking ever since. Socialism cannot be public ownership only; it must include workers' participation in management, the essence of industrial democracy.

On the morning of 12 May I was warned by telephone from London to be ready to get out a 'special', and just after midday the report came through that the TUC had reached a basis of negotiation and that the strikers were to return to work immediately. I took the news to the Trades Council – to a man they refused to believe it. They were sure I had been tricked by agents pretending to speak for the TUC; even when they heard confirmation on the wireless their disbelief persisted; this was a Churchill device to break the strike. They sent out messages that their members should stay out and meanwhile sought to contact the TUC by telephone.

The 'terms' reached me first. They were wired as though they had been accepted by the Government, but we learned later that they were only proposals by Sir Herbert Samuel, a semi-official mediator. They included a reduction of miners' wages, described as temporary, and we were left to assume, though this was difficult to believe, that their leaders had agreed. Our shock can be imagined when we heard that the terms had in fact been rejected by the miners, that the TUC had deserted them, and that the lock-out at the pits was to go on. With a heavy heart I prepared the special edition of the *British Worker*. Its popularity crashed.

The next day was chaos. Churchill's *Gazette* chortled over the great surrender, but the mood of the workers was more militant than ever. In Manchester there was no thought of going back and telephone calls came to me from all over the North of England asking whether it was true that the strike was 'on' again. Feeling was bitter against employers who were everywhere victimising local leaders; even the TUC responded to the general anger, particularly against the railway companies. That day's *British Worker* was the most outspoken yet authorised; it looked as though the end of the strike might be the beginning of the revolution. But the following day there was utter humiliation. The railwaymen's representatives, led by J. H. Thomas, signed an incredible document acknowledging 'wrongful actions' and promising never to repeat them. Despair succeeded anger. With heads down workers returned to their jobs, but in Manchester I sensed that mingled with disillusionment was pride in the solidarity and self-reliance they had shown.

The General Strike failed because the TUC never believed in it; the Government forced it on them by the impulsive Downing Street action. It was said the strike was beginning to break, but in most industrial centres the problem was not to keep the workers out but to keep the exempted workers in. The betrayal of the miners was the worst consequence. Under the leadership of Yorkshire Herbert Smith, the chairman, dour and of few words, and of Welsh Arthur Cook, the secretary, extrovert and of many words, they decided to carry on alone. I came to admire Cook greatly. In contrast with many union leaders he never left the rank and file. During the nine months' struggle he refused a salary, taking the lock-out pay and nothing else. He was loved by his men, and never spared himself, travelling night after night from coalfield to coalfield. Admittedly he failed and the miners were driven back to work at cruel wage reductions. Admittedly a shrewder negotiator might have gained a better result earlier. But Arthur Cook expressed and kept alive the spirit of the men, a spirit which has since transformed the mining industry.

The ILP became the humanitarian and political voice of the miners. We collected money, food and clothing and ran a scheme for miners' children to stay with sympathisers. My family had moved from Thorpe Bay to Loudwater, near Rickmansworth, a wooded house in lovely country well north of London, and we welcomed a Welsh boy, Raymond, from Pontypridd. By now we had two more daughters, Joan and Olive, and Raymond became almost a son. Up and down the country miners' children lived in ILP homes. Politically our main contribution was to publish for the Union a weekly paper, the *Miner*. John Strachey became editor under unusual circumstances. One morning Arthur Ponsonby brought to my office a tall seemingly overgrown boy, arms and legs spreading all over table and floor. Arthur explained that his protégé was the son of St Loe Strachey, the famous editor of the Tory *Spectator*, that he had been converted to Socialism whilst a student at Oxford and that he wanted to find a niche in the movement. 1 got him to help in our research department and, finding he could write persuasively, encouraged him to do a series of articles for the *New Leader* on 'What Youth is Thinking', the first literary effort of one who was to become known for his provocative books. The articles were certainly provocative, very frank about freedom in sex relations, so frank that Labour MPs said they would lose the party the next election.

When we decided to publish the *Miner* I nominated Strachey as editor. One of his duties was to interview Arthur Cook each week and convert what he said into an article. He captured Arthur's fiery personality and the article did much to ensure a circulation of 90,000. As an editor Strachey had one drawback. Despite his Oxford degree he could not spell even simple words – 'which' became 'wich' – and his handwriting was unreadable. We had to employ a special typist to master his orthography and calligraphy, and that too had a sequel. Our manager, Leslie Plummer, fell in love with her and she became Lady Plummer. Subsequently she followed his service in the Commons with her own in the Lords, when, his widow, she was made a Life Peer. She became a farmer and spoke expertly on the problems of agriculture. It was a blow when she died in 1975.

The close association between the ILP and the miners led to a challenge to official Labour which promised a revolution but which significantly failed. John Wheatley, the brains behind it, prepared what came to be known as the Cook–Maxton Manifesto. It restated in popular terms the drastic demands of 'Socialism in Our Time'. The idea was to follow press publicity by mass demonstrations to try out the readiness of the working class to overthrow the compromising leadership of the Labour Party. The first the ILP knew of the project was when it burst into the news, and John Paton (afterwards MP for a Norwich constituency), who became General Secretary when I went to the *New Leader*, was bitter with resentment that Maxton as Party chairman should have acted without consultation. I was as much in the dark, but I welcomed the propaganda value of the campaign without being aware of Wheatley's calculated objective. The demonstrations began well, but petered out and the campaign had to be written off as a failure. This was significant, illustrating what later became evident – that the rank and file of the Labour movement, however dissatisfied with the leadership, will not countenance the destruction of unity.

The Maxton regime in the ILP meant that we lost the financial resources which Clifford Allen had furnished and we had to leave our grand head-quarters in Westminster for an unpretentious residence at Finsbury Park. One inheritance from the Allen regime was maintained: our summer schools, which continued to attract notable lecturers and distinguished visitors, many from abroad. We held successive schools at Lady Warwick's ancestral Easton Lodge in Norfolk and she began by greeting us as hostess, large and laughing, proudly announcing herself as a committed Socialist. We used to be shown the bedroom where she was said to have slept with Edward VII. H. G. Wells, chubby, high-pitched and faint in voice, was a frequent visitor from his neighbouring home. On one occasion he intervened in a discussion, insisting that we needed technicians to implement our transformation to Socialism. Oswald Mosley attacked him demagogically as a paternalist intellectual, which made me very angry. There was no recognition of the contribution which Wells had made to our generation in Socialist and liberal thinking and I went for Mosley in what was perhaps our first conflict. The future Fascist leader was a regular participant in the schools, accompanied by his wife who sang Negro spirituals. He would invite us to his home at Denham where he played brilliant tennis despite an injured leg. But in the summer school debates he was already revealing intolerance and a growing impatience with the indifference of public opinion, the first indication of a repudiation of democracy.

We had many visitors from abroad, including Willi Brandt, square-faced, reserved, always considerate, who came to a school near Letchworth. I spent an afternoon with him sitting on the grass watching a local cricket match. He could make nothing of the game, anticipating America's Andy Williams by asking why the bowlers rubbed the tops of their trousers. Brandt shared the ILP approach to Socialism in those days. Some years later he was libelled in Germany by the Communists, who alleged that he had not resisted Fascism and Nazism. I provided evidence for him, but the case did not go to court.

One of the most popular students from overseas was a young Peruvian who had been expelled from his university for refusing military service. He was adopted by an American woman pacifist who financed visits to Europe and the Soviet Union finishing with our summer school. He was Haya de la Torre who became one of the most prominent politicians in South America. I saw him off from Victoria station and he told me of his plan to form an alliance of workers and Indians, which he did in APRA, winning the Presidential election but denied office by an authoritarian junta. In the 1960s he visited me in Parliament, telling of his exciting experiences as a refugee in the forests when a price was on his head. I was disappointed by his repudiation of radicalism. He had become Peru's pro-American representative at the United Nations and a *Guardian* report now names him as a Rightwing leader. One never can tell.

Perhaps the summer schools represented the best in the ILP in those days. They were above all occasions of good fellowship. Maxton was a supreme entertainer and as he acted the most ludicrous parts we laughed until we were exhausted. He would have made a fortune on the stage. Indeed, later he told me laughingly that after the Press had enthused about his performance as the 'Pirate King' at a social at Lambeth Baths, he had been offered a leading part in Galsworthy's *Strife*. At the schools we enjoyed a comradeship which we rarely know now. Socialism was to us a personal relationship as well as an ideal for the future.

CHAPTER TEN

REBEL IN PARLIAMENT

In the general election of May 1929 I was elected to Parliament. When the MPs met it was just like the first day of a term at school. For me it was a reunion rather than an initiation because my visits all over the country meant that I knew local leaders who had now become MPs. In the Members' Lobby we slapped each other on the back, linked arms, laughed excitedly. Jack Hayes, the large, suave policeman's Member, distributed red carnations among us to serve as defiant buttonholes when we assembled on the Government benches.

I had been nominated for East Leyton as Labour candidate by the local ILP and had been accepted on a 'Socialism in our Time' and anti-war programme. By coincidence my brother-in-law Reg Sorensen, comrade of Myddelton Square days, had been nominated for West Leyton. We both won and our sister wives stood with us at the Town Hall to respond to the cheering crowds. My poll was 11,111. I could probably have made it more if I had claimed spoiled ballot papers but I wanted to leave it at that – 'won, won, won, won, won'. Four victories still to come?

My Conservative opponent was a local businessman of limited political ability. At the count the Liberal candidate, Wynne Davies, a young Welsh solicitor, told me I had converted him to Socialism during the contest and that he was prepared to join the ILP. He was as good as his word and became voluntary manager of the *New Leader*. Later, he was a Labour candidate and for quite a time gave me legal help in my constituency cases.

When the Parliamentary Party met it became clear there were divided views. John Wheatley opposed the acceptance of office because, though we were the largest party we were a minority. Some whispered that he was disappointed because he was not in the Cabinet but suspicion was forgotten after a sentence or two. Let me quote from what I wrote at the time:

There are few men who can speak so impersonally as Wheatley. His thick-set body did not move, one could not see his eyes behind the thick pebble glasses. Nevertheless he gripped; there was a quality of strength and certainty in his voice and his reasoning was remorseless. Members listened and temporarily they were convinced in spite of themselves.

Wheatley argued that at a time of depression reductions in the standard of living were inevitable within the capitalist system and a Labour Government would become their instrument. This was not, in fact, entirely ILP policy and I rose to correct it. I was very nervous, more so than when later I made my first speech in the House, but soon forgot myself in the theme. I did not oppose minority government but urged that we should introduce a Socialist programme, first popular measures dealing with the immediate grievances of the workers, then fundamental measures of public ownership and workers' participation. We would be defeated but it would make Socialism the dominant issue in politics. I could sense that the meeting was against me, and MacDonald, rapturously received, dismissed Wheatley's policy as cowardly and mine as romantic. Thus early in Labour's second Government the internal division was defined.

The conflict in the Party brought also a conflict in the ILP group. There were a hundred or so members of the ILP in the House but Maxton as chairman ruled that the group should consist only of Members who accepted ILP policy. This was vehemently opposed by Shinwell and others, but was endorsed by the National Council of the Party with the result that our group was reduced to seventeen. We acted closely together, appointing John Beckett as secretary. He had won Peckham and was an aggressive young rebel, but without basic Socialist philosophy. I had spoken at one of his election meetings in a crowded music hall. My speech was heard with indifference; then Beckett spoke with unrelieved denunciation of the rich and much abuse of his Tory opponent. The audience loved it.

Prophetically, in view of my subsequent interest, my first speech was on a Bill for Colonial Development, which immediately brought the ILP into conflict with the Government. Reading the Bill carefully I was shocked to find it permitted the use of forced labour and even child labour, and I denounced this forthrightly. Oswald Mosley, in charge of the Bill, failed to reassure, and the ILP group decided to vote against the measure unless the offending clauses were removed. Mosley then agreed to discuss our objections with me and he gave way. An early victory, but it did not prove to be a precedent.

Leaving the Chamber after my maiden speech I met Lady Astor in the corridor. She stood in front of me and placed her hands on my shoulders. 'Oh, Mr Brockway, I agreed so much with what you said,' she exclaimed. 'I am having a party tonight, do come and tell us all about those poor African children.' I had been told that it was her custom to cultivate promising newcomers and was a little flattered, but I declined the invitation. Lady Astor's features straightened. 'I didn't think you were so narrow-minded,' she commented. 'Maxton, yes, but not you.' I told Maxton of the incident. 'Och,' he said, 'keep your self-respect. You can't afford to invite them to your home, don't be obliged to them by going to their homes.' In the House itself Maxton was socially agreeable to all, probably the most popular Member irrespective of party. Tories and Liberals alike, he would take them by the arm and have them laughing at a story. It is not too much to say that he was loved by everyone, but never did he bow his head.

Lady Astor was the first woman to be elected to Parliament. In recognition the suggestion was made that her portrait should be placed in one of the corridors of the House and I supported this despite the opposition of Labour Members, including my ILP colleagues. Years later Lady Astor showed that she had not forgotten my refusal to attend her party. I was to be the guest at a dinner in her hometown in Virginia, USA, and she was asked to attend. 'As Fenner won't speak to me it wouldn't be much fun,' she declined by telegram.

On a second Empire issue, confrontation between the ILP group and the Party developed and again I was involved. Wedgwood Benn (father of the present Tony) was appointed Secretary of State for India and, acknowledging that he knew little about India, indeed mischievously suggesting that that was why he was appointed, invited Maxton and me to a discussion. I asked the Minister whether we could bring with us the young secretary of our committee on Indian affairs, Tarini Sinha. 'He is not a hot-head,' I said. 'He rebuts wild ideas in the Indian group in London.' 'I know that,' Wedgwood Benn said smiling, picking up a typescript. 'That's our report of their last meeting.' Scotland Yard Special Branch were certainly on the spot.

When we met the Minister I suggested the Government should do three things: release the political prisoners, make clear Labour's recognition of India's right to self government, and invite representative Indian organisations to a round-table conference to plan the transition. Benn promised consideration and asked for a memo about the political prisoners. With Sinha's help I prepared a detailed statement, including particulars of young men who had been in prison for twelve years for war-time offences committed when they were students. The statement was cabled to the Viceroy for his opinion. Three weeks later Benn informed me that a majority of the Provincial Governors were against releasing the prisoners. 'What can I do?' he asked despairingly. 'If I insist I shall have their resignations in my hands, and when I tell the House it will mean defeat. We can't go to the country on an Indian issue.' I was sorry for him. I had admired him greatly when, as Radical MPs, he and Josiah Wedgwood had stood courageously on issues of liberty, but I warned him that unless he acted he would have to face formidable resistance in India.

I thought this was the end of the matter for the moment, but by luck I won a ballot for a Private Member's Motion, and I put down a demand for the liberation of the prisoners. Benn persuaded me to amend the motion so that it requested the Viceroy to release only political prisoners not suspected of violence. The House accepted the motion and a considerable number of prisoners were released; but I wondered if I should have compromised. My original motion would have been defeated, but speaking to it Benn and the Opposition could have voiced the lesser request and the Viceroy couldn't have ignored them. There was a similar compromised adaptation of the two other suggestions I had made. The Government initiated a declaration of policy through the Viceroy but it merely announced dominion status as an ultimate goal. My proposal for a round-table conference was accepted, but Indian opinion was alienated when the nomination of delegates was left to the Viceroy rather than to representative organisations. My warnings were fulfilled to the letter. Gandhi initiated the Civil Disobedience Campaign by defying the salt tax and within six months sixty thousand Indians, including the Mahatma and Nehru, were imprisoned.

I took all Parliamentary opportunities to protest but was frustrated because these were limited to questions. Then I got into trouble. The session was ending and the Prime Minister announced from the front bench a string of Bills and Orders still to be considered. I rose and asked if the House would be allowed to discuss the imprisonments in India. 'No, sir,' came the reply. I rose again and asked if the Prime Minister was aware that thousands of Indians were in prison for demanding the freedom which he himself had claimed for them? (I had in mind his book, *The Awakening of India*.) The PM did not answer. I addressed the Speaker: 'I wish to protest, sir, against the adjournment of the House whilst this injustice is done.' The Speaker rose – I should have resumed my seat but I remained standing. 'I mean no disrespect to you, sir,' I said, 'but I cannot be silent whilst this injustice persists.' The House so far had been silent recognising the depth of my feeling, but now the Tories shouted, 'Order, Order.' In dignified tones the Speaker warned me: 'I must name the honourable Member if he continues to disobey the Chair.' My further words were drowned by angry cries and the Speaker warned me a second and a third time. When I continued the protest the Speaker 'named' me. The Prime Minister moved my suspension from the House, and the Members divided.

The ILP group alone supported me and Beckett was one of the tellers (responsible for counting the votes) on our side. With the Government tellers he advanced to the clerk's table, on which stood the mace, to announce the figures. Suddenly his hands plunged forward, he gripped the mace, lifted it to his shoulder, and strode towards the doors of the House. Members were scandalised, a storm of ferocious cries of 'shame' and even 'swine' breaking out; but the sacrilege was short-lived. Beckett was stopped by two ex-Guardsmen custodians, the mace was regained – and he too was suspended. I was irritated because I knew that the rape of the mace would divert attention from my political protest. As Beckett and I were escorted across Old Palace Yard by the police superintendent I asked, 'What in the world was the idea, John?' His reply had some sense. 'The House can do business only when the mace is on the Table. If I had got away with it you couldn't have been suspended.' The suspension was only for three days. My Indian friends felt it was worth while.

Let me continue with references to India, though these events happened later. In 1931 Gandhi came to London for a second Round-Table Conference. With others I met him at Dover – I can still see him smiling at his cabin entrance, white cloth half covering his body. In London at Friends' House we gave him a crowded welcome. My daughter Margaret presented him with flowers and he bent to her, touching her hair. He stayed in rooms in Kensington and I often visited him; always he was sitting cross-legged on the floor twisting his spinning wheel. On one occasion he spoke with unusual emotion. At the Round-Table Conference, Ambedkar, the representative of the Untouchables, had accepted separate representation for them in the Legislature. Gandhi was outraged. Stopping his wheel to leave his hands free to gesticulate he exclaimed, 'If I were the only person to resist I would do so with my life.' Why? 'Sikhs and Muslims may remain in perpetuity,' he explained. 'I would rather Hinduism died than Untouchables lived as a class in Indian society.' Ramsay MacDonald decided in favour of communal representation and when, on returning to India, Gandhi was arrested he began in prison a 'fast until death', ended only when Ambedkar agreed to abandon separate electorates for Untouchables.

One of my happiest memories is a dinner which I gave to Gandhi on his sixty-second birthday in October 1931. Two hundred were present from India as well as Britain. Maxton and the ILP group came and Labour MPs led by Clem Attlee. Intellectuals included Bertrand Russell and Kingsley Martin, the Church was represented by the 'Red Dean' of Canterbury, the Rev. Hewlett Johnson, and from India there were C. F. Andrews, revered Englishman; V. Patel, speaker of the Legislative Assembly; Sarojini Naidu, the poetess; and P. M. Patel. The meal was vegetarian, mostly fruit and nuts, and Gandhi made all laugh by saying he had imposed a hunger strike on us. He paid a tribute to the ILP as a 'friend in need, a friend indeed'. Many were surprised by his geniality.

It was on domestic policy, however, that the decisive clash came with the Government. Unemployment was rising seriously and J. H. Thomas, responsible for handling it, proved disastrously inadequate. He once spoke with pride of an overseas order which he had negotiated for steel rails. It was so utterly irrelevant compared with the need that the House dismissed it with laughter. I was sitting next to John Wheatley; he muttered his contempt and rose and in his quiet, strong way put a series of questions which destroyed Thomas completely – I have never seen a Minister so humiliated. How many workers had been put into jobs? How many thousand pounds had been expended for each job? Thomas dodged the questions, but remorselessly Wheatley pressed them, the House silent, allowing him to rise again and again, an unusual concession. Thomas had to give way. The work provided was shown to be insignificant and the expenditure was out of all proportion to the small results. The Minister's balloon was a deflated wreckage.

Thomas then appointed George Lansbury, Oswald Mosley and Thomas Johnston, a Clyde Leftist, to prepare proposals to reduce unemployment. The ILP had already published constructive suggestions and I was one of a deputation which took them to the three Ministers. We found them disillusioned with the Government and particularly with Thomas. They prepared a plan which embodied most of our ideas and presented it to the Cabinet over the head of Thomas. When the plan was rejected Mosley resigned from the Government.

I have told how Mosley cooperated with the ILP and its policy-making committees under Clifford Allen's chairmanship. I always had the impression, however, that he was using the ILP as a stepping stone to promotion within the Labour Party, more for that than any identification with us. He wooed the friendship of Ramsay MacDonald assiduously when it became clear that he was likely to become Prime Minister, and Cynthia Mosley fussed over him, seeing that his every little need was met on trains and in hotels. Just before the election the Mosleys invited MacDonald to be their guest on a journey over a large part of Europe. When the election took place Oswald expected to be Foreign Secretary, but accepted a junior post. On resigning his Ministerial post Mosley did not join the ILP group. He sat on a bench below us with Cynthia and faithful John Strachey, who had been his Parliamentary Secretary. He was forthright in criticism of the Government, but did not vote with us against them, playing his cards carefully, anxious not to antagonise Labour Members, already hoping that following the failure of MacDonald he might become Leader of the Party. He kept aloof from Maxton, Wheatley and me, but cultivated friendship with two members of our group, W. J. Brown, the able Secretary of a Civil Service Union, and Dr Forgan, a charming but rather naive Scot, who were attracted by Mosley's positive alternatives to the Government's inadequacies.

Mosley's hopes of gaining the leadership were immensely strengthened by what happened at the annual conference at Llandudno in 1930. The ILP had planned to make it the occasion for an all-out attack on the Government's policy and for a statement of the Socialist alternative; we arranged for James Maxton to follow MacDonald's leadership speech. On the morning of the conference the papers carried the news of the disaster to the airship R101 and the loss of many lives, including that of Lord Thompson, the greatly respected Minister for Aviation. MacDonald devoted most of his speech to a panegyric of Lord Thompson, which hushed everyone in solemn sympathy. He concluded with a personal reference which made it impossible for Maxton to follow with effective criticism. 'Ah, my friends,' he said, his voice trembling with emotion, 'at moments like this we remember the eternal verities which unite us, not the temporary differences which divide. My good comrade Maxton has known, as I have known, what it is to stand at the marble gates of death and see one who is dearest pass through.'

I was sitting next to Maxton. He had loved his wife dearly. I turned to him, tears were watering his cheeks. I offered to take his place in following MacDonald, but his answer was a startling exclamation, 'the bloody bastard!' Maxton ran his handkerchief over his face, brushed past me and strode to the platform. His speech inevitably failed in our purpose. He joined in tribute to Lord Thompson and in sympathy with the bereaved, every sentence deepening the emotion. He ended with a mere hint of criticism and with characteristic Socialist evangelism. Our better course would have been to postpone the challenge to the Government to a later point. Oswald Mosley was wiser. He waited until unemployment was discussed and then delivered one of the most effective speeches I have heard at a conference, indicating the measures which could be enacted, urging the Government to stand up to the financiers who were sabotaging action and assuring MacDonald that he would have the support of the common people if he did so. This was exactly what the delegates wanted and they gave Mosley an ovation which lasted minutes. Here was a potential leader, authoritative, courageous, passionate.

Mosley's reception at Llandudno went to his head. I do not think there is any doubt that at this point he thought that leadership was in his hands, but he became disillusioned when he tried to repeat in the Parliamentary Party his triumph at the conference. He was arrogant and contemptuous and angered the MPs by saying that if they rejected his proposals he would appeal from them to the movement outside. The ILP group voted with him, but without enthusiasm. The dangers of his personality were becoming apparent. Isolation within the Parliamentary Party then led Mosley to take his first step to separate himself from it. One evening W. J. Brown asked to see me privately. I admired Brown. He had a great reputation as a trade union negotiator; one understood why when listening to his speeches, captivating in their persuasiveness and their clarity. He had personal charm and a touch of mysticism which was intriguing. He took me to a silent corner of the House and produced a manifesto outlining a new policy under the leadership of Mosley and asked me to sign it. I declined because I held that the proposal should go to the ILP group; I was loyal to Maxton as leader and I saw in it the implication of a new party. Mosley had planned the signature-collecting cleverly. He had listed those to be approached in order of anticipated willingness. I was the sixth and was the first to refuse. The five names before mine were Cynthia Mosley, John Strachey, W. J. Brown, Robert Forgan and John McGovern. When I reported the incident to the ILP group, McGovern withdrew his signature saying that he had misunderstood. One other MP signed, W. E. D. Allen, a Unionist representing a Belfast constituency. Within a few weeks the new Party was announced and in time it gave way to the British Union of Fascists. Mosley had gone the full circle. Both Brown and Strachey broke their association with him before the Fascist stage was reached.

Meanwhile, the Labour Government was succumbing to pressure to reduce expenditure by cutting the wages of public servants, unemployment benefits and the social services. We were seeing day by day a literal fulfilment of our forecast, 'from moderation to compromise and from compromise to humiliation'. Then came the decisive test. The Liberals proposed an Economy Commission to recommend further cuts. We had no doubt that a Commission initiated by the capitalist majority in the House would demand slashing reductions at the expense of the jobless and homeless. With despair we heard Government acceptance and with still further despair the announcement of the members of the Commission. The chairman

Sir George May, was the director of a powerful insurance company and other members were equally reactionary. The ILP group challenged a division but were overwhelmingly defeated by a combination of Tory, Liberal and official Labour votes. It was this May Commission which recommended the hateful means test and the savage reductions in unemployment pay and the social services which were subsequently introduced by the succeeding National Government.

The Tories and Liberals were not content to await the recommendations of the Economy Commission and, giving way to their threats, the Government unbelievably introduced a Bill to deny unemployment benefits to seasonal workers, casual workers, weekend workers, to a large number of women workers and to workers alleged not to be genuinely seeking jobs. We were outraged and fought the Bill as strenuously as I have ever known in Parliament. Seventeen of us carried on the struggle from 3.45 pm to 10.30 the next morning, one of the longest sittings of Parliament recorded. We were particularly incensed by the patronising attitude of Margaret Bondfield, the Minister of Labour, who said that many unemployed did not want work. We had instance after instance of men wearing out their shoes tramping from factory to factory, always to be told, 'No vacancies'. A few Labour loyalists joined our criticism as did one independent-minded Liberal, Frank Owen, the youngest member in the House and one of the best, but mostly the fight was left to us. By this time the ILP was frankly in opposition to the Government, indeed the only real Opposition. Our failure was in not alerting the rank and file of the Labour movement outside to what was happening.

Let me interrupt the sequence to record an event of some historical significance as well as of individual significance, though I did not realise it at the time. Two of my daughters wished to become nurses (Joan and Olive did so) and I made some enquiries into the conditions of work in hospitals. I was shocked by the long hours and the low wages; the Florence Nightingale devotion to service to the sick was being inhumanly exploited. I introduced a Bill to establish an eight-hour working day and a minimum living wage, and letters of support poured in by their hundreds from nurses all over the country; my post was a mountain. Many of the letters begged me to take the initiative in forming a trade union and I invited a representative of the TUC to attend a meeting of nurses which I called at the House of Commons. The largest room, used for aggregate party meetings, was crowded, the girls excited and tense. The TUC representative was the secretary of a union catering for allied public-service workers and he offered to form a section for nurses. The girls were not enthusiastic, wanting a distinctive nurses' union, and appealed to me to establish one. I declined, but I have sometimes wondered if I was right. If I had agreed it would have altered the course of my life, linking me with domestic events rather than the overseas affairs to which I turned. My Bill was defeated, but perhaps it deserves to be remembered as an anticipation of what was won forty years later.

Estrangement from front bench Ministers had one exception. I was very friendly with Charles Trevelyan, Minister of Education, with whom I had had association ever since the war. We used to have dinner together once a week at his home in Great College Street and whilst he was scrupulous in not reveal-ing Cabinet secrets he was sympathetic to ILP views and gave me advice. He had a division bell in his hall and often we would have to leave our soup to dash through a maze of passages underneath the House of Lords to record our votes. It was Trevelyan who urged me to specialise. His experience taught him that it was impossible for a Member to be active about every-thing and that to get results one had to be recognised as knowledgeable in one sphere. My interests were wide, but the ILP group asked me to watch Empire affairs and I made this my particular subject as it continued to be from then on.

One evening in June 1931, Trevelyan was deeply worried. He told me that he had heard from a fellow Minister that MacDonald was engaged in discussions with Conservatives and Liberals to scuttle the Labour Govern-ment and to form a National Government. This had not been officially discussed but he had reason to believe it and he urged that the Labour move-ment should be alerted. I immediately rushed off a front-page article to the New Leader, the first public anticipation of coming events. The national press took it up and Arthur Henderson issued a denial, though MacDonald and Snowden were significantly silent. Later Henderson said that they had con-ferred without informing their Cabinet colleagues.

I had arranged to address meetings in Poland and Germany during the recess. Marguerite Louis accompanied me and we were sitting in a café in the Unter den Linden, Berlin, when newsboys came displaying their papers. I saw the heavy top line on a front page. It was in German but I could under-stand what it said: 'MacDonald Forms a National Government'. We pain-fully made our way through the German text and it became evident that the bankers at Zurich had given an ultimatum to MacDonald and Snowden and that they had surrendered. I got back to London in time for the re-assembly of Parliament under the new Government and was taken aback by the fury against MacDonald of many who a few weeks earlier had called the ILP group traitors for attacking their leader. Now we were the more philosophic because we had accustomed ourselves to the inevitable. In the General Election which followed, the Labour Party was overwhelmingly defeated and the ILP group, associated by the public with Labour, was reduced to five: Maxton, MacGovern, Buchanan, Kirkwood and Wallhead. My vote in East Leyton fell by only 678, but I was defeated.

I have told of some of my ILP colleagues in this Parliament but there were others of distinct personality. There was Geordie Buchanan, Glasgow trade unionist, working class of the working class, down to earth, practical, and when later he surprisingly became chairman of the National Assistance Board he proved himself a good administrator. There was David Kirkwood, big, black haired, blunt in speech in exaggerated Scottish accent. There was Campbell Stephen, ex-minister of religion, philosophic, and Dorothy Jewson, daughter of an influential Norwich family, whom he married. There was Jennie Lee, combining passion and reason, flashing eyes, voice like music. There was Oliver Baldwin, son of the Conservative leader, not actually a member of our group but who often voted with us. He quickly became disillusioned with Parliament and sat withdrawn on the most distant seat. He was a strange man, for long periods a mystic – he was a spiritualist – and then breaking out as a man of the world.

Whilst Parliament sat I had a room at the home of the McNultys in Bloomsbury to save travelling late at night to my Rickmansworth home. Hilda McNulty worked in the ILP research department and acted as secretary of the ILP Parliamentary group. She helped me on a book on India which I wrote at this time, and later became secretary of the Fabian Colonial Bureau, marrying Sir Selwyn Selwyn-Clarke, Governor of the Seychelles. The McNulty home became a social meeting place for the ILP MPs, and often Aneurin Bevan would join us, agreeing with our political point of view but criticising the ferocity of our opposition to the Government. 'The party is greater than MacDonald,' he urged. 'You must not cut yourselves off from it.' How right his analysis proved to be! Would that we had listened.

CHAPTER ELEVEN

WITH EUROPE'S SOCIALISTS

So far I have written mostly of domestic controversies to maintain a sequence of events. But I was an international Socialist concerned as much about peace and the freedom of peoples as about Labour's progress at home. All through the period I have described I was campaigning on these issues, selected by the ILP to move resolutions at Labour Party conferences which were often successful.

The ILP became affiliated to the Socialist International separately from the Labour Party and in 1925 I was appointed its representative on the Executive. It was only a sudden crisis between Britain and Russia which kept me from the inaugural conference when the International was reconstituted at Hamburg in 1923. Frank Wise, who was acting as an adviser to the Russian Trade Delegation, telephoned me of the danger of its imminent expulsion and of a rupture in diplomatic relations which could lead to war. I got in touch with foreign affairs correspondents in Fleet Street who confirmed the danger and I decided to remain in England to help alert the Labour movement. I phoned Jim Middleton who as Assistant Secretary was acting for Arthur Henderson already in Hamburg, and he agreed immediately to cooperate. Whilst he phoned Henderson to arouse the European parties, I drafted a letter to working-class organisations throughout Britain. The result was an avalanche of telegrams, phone calls and letters to 10 Downing Street, and the Press front paged our statements and activities. Memory of the threatened general strike in 1920 undoubtedly influenced the Government. Wise phoned that the British negotiators had become conciliatory and for the moment the crisis passed.

The ILP was disturbed by the division in the European working-class movement between Social Democrats and Communists. At the Hamburg conference the strong ILP delegation, including Allen, Brailsford, Wallhead and Roden Buxton (a notable recruit) succeeded in leaving the door open for consultation. The headquarters of the International were at first in London and I became very friendly with Friedrich Adler, the secretary. Before I met him I had expected a hard man. He had assassinated the Austrian Prime Minister, Count Stürgk, which he justified as expediting the end of the war as it certainly did. He was, I found, the exact opposite of the tough revolutionary I had pictured. He was kindly with the features of a philosopher rather than those of a pugilist. It must have cost a lot to Adler's sensitive nature to have fired that fatal shot.

Headquarters were moved in 1925 to Zurich and I went there three or four times a year, enjoyable occasions with bathing in the lake. My membership of the Executive led to invitations to address meetings in many European countries, Germany, Austria, France and Switzerland. The fact that I belonged to the Left encouraged rather than discouraged invitations; the Left wanted me because of my views, the Right to prevent Left breakaways. Henderson remained chairman until he became Foreign Secretary in the MacDonald Government of 1929. He was a successful Foreign Secretary initiating serious consideration of collective security, but he nearly ruined his opportunity even before elected to the House. Defeated at the General Election he stood at an early by-election at Burnley. Suddenly the world was startled to read that the British Foreign Secretary had made a heavy attack on the Versailles Treaty. The French were outraged and it took all MacDonald's diplomacy to restore good feeling. The explanation, as told to me, was amusing. Henderson used to read his speeches from prepared manuscripts; in fact he was a dull speaker, his ability was in administration. His texts at Burnley ran out and he telephoned Labour headquarters for more. Among those sent was an old speech on the Versailles Treaty and Henderson had the misfortune to pick it from the bundle for his next speech. Apparently he did not check its significance.

There was a congress of the International at Marseilles in 1925. We met in a vast pavilion, the fifteen hundred delegates sitting at long trestle tables, each with the name of its country above it. I remember only two contrasting speeches, one by Turati, leader of Italian Socialists, a living statue of working-class solidity, the other by the French leader, Léon Blum, professional bourgeois politician. Turati's contribution was the voice of revolt against the grinding poverty of his people. Blum's was a pragmatic presentation of current problems, each with a conclusion delivered with the rhetoric of a peroration, received rapturously. France's future Prime Minister had a genius for popular leadership. When he attended the Executive there was always a glamour about him, his smiling features and extravagant gestures suggesting that the camera was permanently directed upon him. At the same time he was fellow-well-met, joining his admiring followers at a café at night, paying for their drinks.

The ILP was disillusioned by the Marseilles congress, particularly by its unbalanced antagonism to Soviet Russia and by the self-satisfaction of the German Social Democrats. Our National Council decided to challenge this sectarian complacency and instructed me to press three issues: first, the need for an all-inclusive International; second, total disarmament and resistance to war; third, extended activity in colonial territories against imperialism. Our resolution for the unification of the Internationals aroused world-wide interest. It called for working-class solidarity against not only capitalism and imperialism, but immediately against Fascism in Europe (interesting that this phrase should have been used as early as 1926) and proposed a joint conference between the Executives of the two bodies to explore the possibility of unity. At first there were indications of considerable support; then came the *coup d'état* – the Communist International contemptuously rejected unity even before we had met to discuss it.

Nevertheless, we maintained the resolution and to my surprise it was debated seriously. The Socialist press of the world was represented, the staff left their typewriters to crowd at the door, and unusually the delegates listened to what I said in English before the translation was made. I did not hide our differences with the Communists on such issues as the inevitability of armed revolution, the destruction of Parliamentary democracy, the repression of personal liberty, the imprisonment of dissidents and the disintegrating effects of Communist policies on working-class movements in democratic countries. I urged, nevertheless, that discussion might build a bridge for united working-class action and it should be tried. Every subsequent speaker was complimentary, but, except for Joseph Kruk of the Polish ILP, a faithful friend, I had not a single supporter. I was not disappointed. The calm political atmosphere had lifted the issue to another plane.

One of the issues I had suggested for discussion between the Internationals was the imprisonment of non-Bolshevik Socialists in Russia. I was deeply distressed about this and the ILP made representations to the Soviet Embassy and to Moscow. We spent hours in studying the enormous tomes of evidence supplied by the Mensheviks and Social Revolutionaries, to which the Soviet Union replied with equally large tomes, but finally we had to give up with little achieved. I was a member of the Political Prisoners Commission of the International and we got Executive members to realise that there were prisoners in Italy, Spain, India and other colonial territories as well as in Russia. At the same time I could not ignore the stories of oppression in the Soviet Union, and when Moscow invited me on a visit I declined on the ground of the imprisonment of provenly sincere Socialists. My letter was widely published, and Social Revolutionaries told me it had some effect because the Soviet Government at that moment was anxious to cultivate better relations with the British Labour Movement.

Temporarily I had some response from the International Executive on armaments and war resistance. In the late twenties anti-war feeling was strong and I got the Labour Party conference of 1926 to accept an ILP resolution which reads incredibly today. It called on workers to refuse to bear arms, produce armaments, or render any material assistance to war and urged steps to convene a world conference of the Socialist, Trade Union and Cooperative Internationals to prepare concerted resistance. We took this resolution to the International Executive which agreed to refer it to all affiliated Parties asking them to reply within six months. Few Parties took the request seriously and the proposal was dropped. The ILP persisted however. At the triennial congress at Brussels in 1928 when we raised the issue again it was referred to a commission which went so far as to endorse resistance by direct action to any Government which refused arbitration. I put the full ILP view and we received a large minority vote including the Swiss German–Czech and American Parties, together with sections of the German, French and Polish delegations.

An ILP plan for increased assistance to the peoples in the colonies received the support of the Austrian, French and Swiss Parties and a Commission was set up to work out details. I proposed that the International should act with the International Confederation of Free Trade Unions (ICFTU), that deputations should be sent to India and other countries, that selected persons from the colonies should be given political and industrial training, and that technical and monetary assistance should be given to develop workers' organisations. The reception given to this programme was encouraging, but months passed and little was done. Meanwhile, a development occurred which complicated the whole issue.

In February 1927 the German Communists took the initiative in calling a conference at Brussels of representatives of national movements in the colonial countries and of working-class movements in Europe to establish united action against imperialism. The organiser was Willi Manzenberg, head of Communist publications in Berlin, and with great skill, making a broad appeal, he secured the cooperation of most of the recognised Nationalist movements, as well as of Left-wing Socialists who had no association with Communists, including George Lansbury. I attended as ILP representative and became involved in one of its dramatic highlights. The British Government was in conflict with China over the Treaty Ports and the ILP had been prominent in a 'Hands off China' campaign. As I stepped on the platform Munzenberg whispered to me, 'End by declaring unity with the Chinese people', and I did so. Immediately the leader of the Chinese delegation sprang to my side and embraced me whilst the whole audience, black, brown, yellow and white, stood and roared applause. The conference established the League against Imperialism and due perhaps to this incident I was elected chairman. Munzenberg broke with the Communists later, but showed great courage in opposing Hitler. He was found strangled in a wood in France in 1941, a victim of the Nazis.

When the Executive of the Socialist International met, I was in hot water. Otto Wels charged me with stabbing colleagues in the back. He said the Communists in Germany were using my chairmanship of the League to attack him and Social Democratic leaders who had forbidden Party members to join it. Wels, a heavy bull-like man, stormed with roaring anger and interrupted me frequently when in reply I urged that we should deserve to be brushed aside by the movements in the colonies if we left support to the Communists. Adler lowered the temperature by saying that the International itself should do more, but deprecated my association with a Communist organisation. In the end I was given the choice of resigning from the Executive or from the chairmanship of the League. The ILP decided that I should remain on the Executive, Maxton taking over for a short time the League chairmanship.

There was another issue, even more controversial fifty years later, in which the ILP took a leading part. In 1926 the Trade Union and Socialist Internationals jointly called a conference to discuss migration, particularly the problem of immigration from Asia and Africa. It was the most representative conference I had attended so far, delegates coming to London from the USA, South America, Canada, Australia, New Zealand and India as well as from Europe. Fred Jowett and I represented the ILP and our amendment to the official motion became the chief subject of debate. The executive of the ICFTU asked the conference to accept a statement that migration could not be treated on the liberal principle of freedom of movement and should be subject to what was described as the Socialist principle of control and direction. Our amendment accepted the right to control immigration if it threatened to lower standards of life, but insisted that there should be no exclusion on grounds of race and colour. We were opposed by the delegates from Australia and Canada, fearing Chinese and Japanese incursions, but supported by New Zealand, putting principle before expediency, by India, Latin America and most of the European delegations. I had the new experience of receiving acclamation from the great majority of the delegates, but eventually it was decided to refer the issue to the two executives for report. So far as I know no report ever came.

My membership of the International Executive was a great experience. I came to know Socialist leaders whose names are legends, Karl Kautsky, Emile Vandervelde, Léon Blum, Otto Bauer. I was one of a group of twenty or thirty who gave a party to Kautsky on his seventieth birthday in a Soho restaurant, appropriate as a haunt of Karl Marx. He was by now a shrivelled little man with a large head buried in shaggy grey hair, a broad forehead under which kindly eyes peered through thick glasses. He spoke little, but listened and smiled. I shall never forget the tribute by Vandervelde, the greatest orator I have heard, rich voice, perfect rhythm, every thought reflected in movement of body and gesture, a triumph of art. He made Kautsky's academic Marxist works come alive, relating them to the struggles of the time, extolling them as a guide amidst dying beliefs in a period of doubt and confusion. Raising his voice to a climax he spread his arms and advanced down the table, his voice trembling, fingers trembling simultaneously with his words, and embraced Kautsky. I have never seen anything done more movingly.

I had the greatest respect of all for Otto Bauer, the Austrian leader. He was a Socialist in the deepest sense, friendly in his equality with others, identified in feeling with the under-privileged everywhere, a thinker, always seeing the essentials of an issue, yet a realist, drawing a distinction between what was right and what was possible. Otto Wels called me the rebel within the Executive. Otto Bauer called me its conscience. I can see him now as I asked the Executive to call on the Labour Government in Britain to liberate Gandhi and Nehru and the 60,000 Congress prisoners. He walked the length of the room, head down, arms behind his back, worried, seeking the fair thing to do. Then he strode to the table and suggested a form of words which were a perfect compromise. They endorsed India's right to self-government, declared solidarity with the National Congress, understood the difficulties of the Labour Government, a minority inheriting an imperialist-minded administration, and expressed confidence that the Government would do everything to hasten political liberty with the release of political prisoners and with the acceptance of the right of the Indian people to independence. The Executive adopted his motion with relief.

Visits abroad were not all stern controversy. I remember how during a Brussels conference Pat Dollan, master of ceremonies at our summer school socials (he afterwards became Provost of Glasgow), took command of the Moulin Rouge, brushing aside its nightly programme and improvising a medley of song and fun which entranced the audience for an hour. Oswald Mosley was his star prop.

CHAPTER TWELVE

RETURNING TO INDIA

India interrupted my activites in Europe. I received invitations from the National and Trades Union Congresses to attend their conventions at Madras at the end of 1927 as a fraternal delegate of the ILP. I was delighted to revisit the land of my birth. The long journey by boat was a wonderful relaxation, the Mediterranean blue and calm, the sand banks of the Suez canal in moonlight white as snow, the glowing sunsets in the Indian Ocean. Only Aden was horrible, a volcanic desert, no colour except the bowling green at the Officers' Club with soil brought specially from India. I was fascinated by brown-skinned divers catching under-sea coins thrown from the ship, distressed when I saw them diving into the dust left in the coal barges. I have a memory of Clara Butt, a statuesque figure in white robes, throwing threepenny bits from the first-class deck, epitomising the parable of crumbs for the poor. It spoiled my picture of the great contralto. She had come to Silvester Horne's church and I had fallen for her. She had written out for me in large round hand the verses of her song, a sentimental ode to a baby.

At Bombay I was met by N. M. Joshi, the secretary of the Indian TUC, a picturesque figure in a loose muslin garment with a red and gold turban, and by a welcoming crowd who garlanded me with huge halters of flowers. Then they stood back whilst a representative of the National Congress presented me with a Gandhi cap 'to commemorate your honouring it in Parliament'. I had almost forgotten the incident, but grouped pressmen insisted I recount it. I had held up the cap in the Commons whilst protesting that Indians had been arrested for wearing it. 'Put it on,' shouted Tories and I did so. I found in India that this was remembered, a positive image, more than my suspension.

I was appalled by much I saw in Bombay. At night the pavements were covered by the bodies of people, homeless or so overcrowded that sleep in the heat indoors was impossible. I visited some of their homes, single rooms smaller than prison cells on either side of a dark tunnel where mill workers lived. We visited a family of seven, four adults and three children, who incredibly existed somehow in a space of seven feet by five – I measured it. I was startled by the prostitutes' row in the main street, girls soliciting behind iron bars, open to their bedrooms. Joshi was leading a campaign against their conditions. He said prostitutes were scandalously exploited by landlords and usurers, paying rents so high that they could not buy dresses or bedclothes which they had to hire at fifty per cent interest. On the other hand, I was fascinated by the light and colour and diversity of India – through the fierce sunlight women glided in saris, red, gold, green and purple, the turbans of the men were as brilliant and different, policemen in blue and yellow uniforms directed motors, horse carriages, bicycles and bullock carts. To Joshi I expressed my appreciation of this colourful variety in great contrast then (not so much now) to the monotony of London streets. 'It is our curse,' he responded, 'our disunity in race, caste and religion.'

During an exhausting programme of meetings and visits in Bombay I renewed acquaintance with M. A. Jinnah, leader of the Muslim League, whom I had met over tea at the House of Commons. He lived in a mansion on the wealthy Malabar Hills overlooking the bay. Jinnah was the most anglicised Indian leader I had met, light in complexion, English-dressed, English-spoken. A brilliant barrister, he had a keen, sharp mind. His wife was, I think, the most beautiful woman I have seen. As we talked he gave me the impression of resenting the occupation of India because he knew he was abler than British Governors and Ministers. Of the Simon Commission, which was coming to India to decide its future, he was contemptuous. 'Who are these men?' he scorned, laughing when I reminded him that Stanley Baldwin had called them 'God's Englishmen'. I was amused because I had already dubbed Jinnah the Sir John Simon of India.

I also met the Muslim leaders associated with the National Congress, including Maulana Azad, ex-President and President again in 1940. They were impressive, heads of universities and scholars. We had lunch together in the home of Dost Mohamed, founder of a college at Poona to which parentless girls from all Muslim countries came. His sitting room was an astonishing mixture of East and West. There were Greek statues, ancestral vases, two grandfather clocks, a huge mechanical musical instrument, English paintings, Indian sketches. From the ceiling a swing was suspended, two men sitting on it conversing as they rocked to and fro. On a mat our

F.B. speaking at Caxton Hall, having just lost the poll in the Westminster by-election. With him, his first wife Lilla and his daughter Margaret

F.B. editing the *New Leader* at the headquarters of the ILP

This cartoon, depicting F.B. and Jean Rous, respectively Chairman and Secretary of the Congress of Peoples against Imperialism, opposing white

host was praying, kneeling, touching the floor with his forehead. No one took any notice of him. At table the discussion showed that these Muslim leaders were acutely aware of world events. They foresaw a second world war and confrontation between the subject peoples and the richer nations. I went on to a tea party given by Sarojini Naidu, the distinguished Hindu poetess; she was a plump woman, dressed in English style, laughing, emotional, bursting into eloquent assertions of the Indian cause. I was glad to have the opportunity to attend the annual conference of the Peoples of the Indian States, ruled by Rajahs under British protection. There were a thousand delegates demanding democracy within an independent India, demonstrating a strength at that early stage which I had not appreciated.

The journey by train to Madras took thirty-six hours. I spent two days with my sister Nora who was principal of a teachers' training college on the outskirts of the city. On the way to the college we passed the Congress camp which amazed me. In Britain the annual conferences of the Labour and Conservative Parties alternate between Blackpool and Brighton because nowhere else are there halls large enough or the accommodation for delegates sufficient. In India they had done better than this. They had built a hall and accommodation for the occasion. The hall, a thatched pavilion, held seven thousand. Around it were avenues of wooden dwelling huts, gleaming white, and larger buildings for offices, ambulance stations and canteens. A special railway station had been built for the ten thousand visitors expected. My sister had planned a visit to an Ashran (community project) run by two doctors, S. Jesudason, an Indian, and Forrester Paton, a Scotsman, in a village ninety miles away. We travelled in a car lent by George Joseph, a rare Christian among Congress leaders, and his son drove us. There is something uniquely fascinating about the Indian road, a yellow strip stretching straight to the horizon, raised above the green rice fields, under the shade of the continuous banyan trees, monkeys swinging from branch to branch, lonely men and women at work in red loin cloths and saris.

On the journey back, as we passed a bullock cart, the driver asleep, the animals trudging with leisurely ease, I remarked to my sister that motor cars were a crime against the leisure of the East. She agreed – and then a dull thump on the side of the car and a sudden swerve. The driver pulled frantically at the wheel but could not prevent us from overturning down the embankment. Nora was thrown into a prickly pear bush, Joseph's face was badly cut, my thigh was broken and my shoulder and neck dislocated – much worse, an Indian pedestrian was killed. As I lay waiting for a lift to a village hospital eight miles away I heard the piercing moans of a woman, but I did not know that her man had died.

The next morning, lying on a stretcher, I was taken by train to the general hospital at Madras where I remained for three months. I was placed in the 'European Officers' Quarter' which I resented as reflecting both race and class; later I found that the whole hospital was segregated with separate wards for Europeans, Anglo-Indians and Indians. My room, containing only two beds, was so large that I felt I was in the open. Sparrows built nests in the rafters of the ceiling and grey squirrels with yellow streaked backs climbed the verandah blinds. I used to be wheeled through an Indian ward for visits to a therapist; it was so crowded that patients lay on the floor between the beds. The staff was multiracial, the two principal doctors English, the rest Indian, the sisters English, the nurses Anglo-Indian. Working conditions were disgraceful, particularly for the Indian bearers and sweepers who were paid eightpence for a twelve-hour day or night. As soon as I was well enough I protested by letters to the Press, which led to a full dress debate in the Legislative Council where the Indian Minister of Health stated that he had asked for more money but the English Finance Minister had refused. I was encouraged when I found the nurses asked for copies of the *Labour Leader*, sent to me from England, disillusioned when I discovered they were wanted for their advertisements of contraceptives.

I was bitterly disappointed to miss the National Congress and the Trades Union Congress, but had daily visits which compensated a little. Gandhi, white loin cloth and loose muslin garment hanging from shoulders, came to see me on each of the four days that he was in Madras. His personality was more vital than I had remembered, his eyes twinkling as he smiled. I was weak and his presence had a soothing effect on my feverishness. On one visit he was observing his 'silence day'; he did not speak but, a little illogically I felt, wrote questions and answers. I had been having a rather bad time and he wrote, 'how are you sleeping?' He had perceived my greatest difficulty, I had not slept naturally since the accident. When I told him he closed his eyes in concentration, pressed my hand, and an influence almost physical seemed to pass into my body bringing relief and calm. That night I slept for the first time without a drug.

Jawaharlal Nehru came to see me every day despite the pressure of a controversy in the Congress where he was leading for independence. We conversed easily as old friends. I had first met him when he was a student in England and later we had enjoyed evenings together on his frequent visits to London. He had spent his last weekend in England in our Rickmansworth home and, after the children had reluctantly been packed off to bed, we had passed a large part of the night in discussion, my tired wife making us repeated cups of tea. In London Nehru was a well-dressed Englishman; here in Madras he wore Indian robes and a Gandhi cap. He is naturally gentle and in my illness he was as tender as a woman. We discussed politics more than I did with Gandhi and I was impressed again by his knowledge of the international scene and his dedication, even when he was so much involved in the national struggle, to the freedom of all peoples and to peace.

Mrs Annie Besant came. She was dressed as a priestess in long cream-coloured robes and wore the golden insignia of the Order of the Star on a heavy chain round her neck. She was one of the pioneers of the modern movement for self-government in India through her Home Rule League, but was now more involved in theosophy. When I was well enough to make journeys by car I visited her large estate near Madras where she had churches and temples of all the religions. Dr Ansari, the retiring chairman of Congress, a wise and kindly Muslim, paid me an official visit accompanied by twelve uniformed volunteers, and Sreenivasa Iyengar conveyed the sympathy of the Congress party in the Legislative Assembly of which he was leader.

I had many English visitors, among them Clem Attlee, Labour representative on the hated Simon Commission (it was as well his visit did not clash with the Congress leaders), and Sir John Simon sent me a kindly message. The two members of a TUC deputation to India looked in, Alfred Purcell and Joseph Hallsworth – I was to enjoy their company on my return journey to England. Miss Creighton, daughter of the late Bishop of London, engaged in educational work in Madras, came and many civil servants and inevitable journalists. So many visitors, Indian and English, queued that a large notice was displayed prohibiting them without permission. Of course Nora came each day.

I had a serious operation performed by the head surgeon who fortunately had been assistant to Taylor Taylor, the famous consultant at Middlesex Hospital, during the Mesopotamian campaign in the war. When I returned to London, Taylor Taylor was proud of the way his junior had done the job. One transformation in my personal habits took place in hospital. I had been a teetotaller. I was given port to revive me and I liked it so much that I have drunk alcohol ever since. Sometimes I say laughingly that I took to drink the day I met Gandhi, the great prohibitionist. His first visit to me was on the day when the bottle of port was put beside my bed.

I was able to see a great deal of Madras by car before I left. The Congress Party invited me to a garden party and I was driven across large open spaces crowded with bare-footed hockey and football players, along the five-mile promenade on the sea front, through some residential suburbs with large houses and vast gardens and through slums with mud huts. I visited the luxurious mansion of an Indian lawyer; at the door to its drive were dung-walled hovels. I had not seen wealth and poverty in such proximity. With K. S. Venkataramani, Indian novelist, I visited a working-class ghetto. We drove down alleys so narrow that a car had never been there before. Men, women, children, bits of string round their loins, crowded round us. They knew me by newspaper reports and poured out their stories of hunger and overcrowding, low wages and long working-hours. Middle-class Nationalism seemed irrelevant.

CHAPTER THIRTEEN

CONTRASTING AMERICA

I visited the USA twice whilst still an MP and once after I was defeated. I went on lecture tours, by no means the profitable engagements generally assumed, but perhaps this was because my sponsors were propagandists: the League for Industrial Democracy, a kind of Fabian Society, and the Friends' Service Committee, Quaker radicals whose spirit reminded me of the early ILP. My visits dramatically coincided with three distinct phases of America's economy. In 1929 the USA was enjoying a trade boom; in 1931 facing deep depression; in 1932 recovering with Franklin Roosevelt's 'New Deal'.

I travelled by boat, which I enjoyed immensely, intervals of relaxation and fun which one now misses on aeroplanes. The first time Ramsay Mac-Donald's son, Alistair, allotted the top VIP suite, was on board, travelling to New York to look at cinemas which as an architect he was designing in London. I had met the MacDonald children often: Isobel who defied respectability by running a public house in Buckinghamshire; Malcolm, devoted ILP speaker, later becoming High Commissioner in Canada, Asia and Africa, quiet, able, likeable; and Alistair, Bohemian, inheriting his father's magnetism, indifferent to politics but by nature a Socialist. I was travelling tourist class but as a friend of the Prime Minister's son I was allowed the freedom of the boat. We made friends with two teenagers, a boy and a girl, and the four of us ran riot. One night we found a young couple asleep in each other's arms on deck. We surrounded them with large ornamental plants gathered from all over the ship. When they awoke they must have thought they were in the Garden of Eden. Tired of excitement I was just going to sleep in my cabin at 3 am when I was awakened by Alistair and his two companions, who solemnly presented me with an 'illuminated and

101

perforated address'. Having delivered a ceremonial speech, Alistair un-ravelled a toilet roll and festooned the cabin with it from floor to ceiling. I was too sleepy to remove the mad chaos. What the cabin boy thought next morning I cannot guess.

After a Washington luncheon speech I was fortunate to meet Dorothy Detzer, secretary of the Woman's International League for Peace and Freedom. Someone in London had given me an introduction to Dorothy and I had expected a middle-aged bourgeois do-gooder. Instead, she was young, attractive and dynamic, a practical realist, working out ideas for action and yet a revolutionary in her own pacifist sphere, I think the most stimulating person I have met. She was the star lobbyist in the Capital. Lobbyists did not all have a good name; many represented vested interests employed to bring pressure on Congressmen and Senators. Dorothy's concern was to influence decisions for peace, justice and liberty. She was described by the *New York Times* as the most famous woman lobbyist in Washington, and I found that she had a genius for persuasion.

The Women's International League was then an influential organisation, and afterwards I often met Dorothy in Europe at Peace and Disarmament conferences where we became close allies. I convinced her on evidence which I had collected for my book, *The Bloody Traffic*, that armament manufacturers supplied weapons to both sides and even incited national hostilities to secure orders. She went back to America and mobilised her influential contacts in the Congress to set up a special non-partisan committee, under the chairmanship of Senator Gerald Nye, to investigate the munitions industry. The hearings lasted for nearly a year and were publicised all over the world. The findings, particularly in relation to South America, justified all I had said. Dorothy tells in her book, *Appointment on the Hill*, of her disappointment that the far-reaching recommendations were never implemented – the armament interests were too powerful – but the report remains a classic exposure of armament makers, British as well as American. With Frederic Mullally I described these revelations in a second book on the war industry, *Death Pays a Dividend*. Dorothy married Ludwell Denny, wise and kind, a famous columnist and influential author, and they were companions in international assignations in many parts of the world.

Dorothy opened all the doors in the capital to me. She introduced me to what was known as the 'Rebel Group' in Congress and, under the sponsorship of Bob la Follette, its leader, I had the strange experience of being welcomed on the floor of the Chamber during a debate and presented to the President of the Senate who, with two members of that body, adjourned to entertain me in his private room. Dorothy also fixed interviews with

Cordell Hull, Secretary of State, and with Harold Ickes, one of Franklin Roosevelt's right-hand men in the Cabinet. I was surprised by the informality of these occasions. I had been on deputations to British Secretaries of State, the public excluded from the Department, officials stationed on each floor, and we met in a secluded office, the Minister seated at the head of a table, with civil servants at his side, all immaculately dressed.

In Washington, the Government offices were like a public place, and in the lift were clerks seeking jobs, Negro workmen, women cleaners. In the Department of the Interior, where I went for an appointment with Harold Ickes, I found him at the far end of a long room, sitting in blue shirt with a broad belt, looking like a Western sheriff in the movies, listening to the grievances of a farmer, supported by a lawyer and a Congressman. I sat with about twenty people awaiting our turns, lounging in easy chairs, smoking, chatting. They included three Indian chiefs, dolled up in feather head-dresses and beads, impatient to pour out their grievances to Big Chief Ickes himself. I was told that this meeting of applicants in semi-publicity was to show that everything was above board (no doubt true during the New Deal), but in later years I wondered how far it became a façade, hiding the private pressures of vested interests.

The Watergate scandals of the 1970s certainly gave weight to that suspicion, but in the New Deal period there was a genuine desire for democratic participation. I spent a week seeing the heads of different Departments and was impressed by their enthusiasm and by the spirit of their staffs. In one office, I met a man who on my visit two years before had been a hard-boiled cynic. Now his eyes were alight with belief. 'We are on a mighty big thing,' he exclaimed. 'We are rebuilding a continent.' It was clear to me that those working for the New Deal believed they were engaged in a revolution and were glorying in the fact.

I wrote a book, *Will Roosevelt Succeed*, where I was less optimistic, but the New Deal was certainly important in stimulating trade union organisation and action. During my visit I became involved in a strike of silk workers at Patterson in New Jersey and over tea in his home a striker told me how, whilst three months previously they had no organisation, eighty per cent now belonged to the Union. At Detroit I found an ex-ILP-er from Scotland leading a strike of engineers. He took me to a huge demonstration in a theatre but was fearful that the men's solidarity might be prejudiced if a non-American, and particularly a Socialist non-American, spoke. Eventually he asked me to say a few words of greeting and to his surprise I received a tumultuous welcome. It wasn't for what I said, but for what I was – a conveyer of solidarity from workers in Britain.

Arriving in New York on my first visit, I was astonished to see posters announcing a three-day debate on Palestine, with Jewish, Arab and British speakers, and myself billed to represent Britain. I protested to Mary Fox, the secretary of the League for Industrial Democracy (my sponsors) that I knew little about Palestine and that I certainly did not wish to voice the official British view. She retorted that the Press had carried reports of my Commons questions, which in fact were efforts to save both Jews and Arabs from execution, and she added that the League was counting on the fee from the Foreign Policy Association to meet a large part of the cost of my tour. So I spent the three intervening days in research at Columbia University and became reasonably well prepared. The Israeli advocate was a leading Jewish rabbi; the Arab spokesman an Egyptian of international repute. The chairman was J. G. MacDonald, afterwards head of the International Committee for Refugees at Geneva. Two things happened after the debate which amused me. The Foreign Policy Association published my speech in its series of 'expert' pronouncements and, following a broadcast of the debate, we received invitations from half a dozen cities to repeat it.

My speaking schedule was full, though with less remunerative engagements, and to the regret of Mary Fox we could repeat the debate only once – at Detroit. There an extraordinary incident occurred. The audience was largely Jewish and were roused to high excitement by their spokesman, emotion gurgling in his throat before words reached his lips. Following him I had some difficulty in cooling the atmosphere and when question-time came every challenge was made to me. At the end I was exhausted, but to my consternation I was surrounded on the platform by Jews and Arabs fiercely putting other points. Relief came in an astonishing way. Three young women thrust themselves through the battling crowd to my side. Two took my arms and one was at my back; my interrogators were as surprised as I and let us through. 'What's the idea?' I asked the girls. 'We weren't going to allow you to be put under third-degree interrogation by that bunch,' one explained. 'Where are you taking me?' 'For a meal at a club with a strict rule that no word of politics shall be spoken.' We had a delightful meal and I left for my train for Chicago. To this day I do not know who those three young women were.

I took part in another spectacular debate in New York on Capitalism, Socialism and Communism. It was held in the Mecca Temple, crowded after vast publicity. The defender of capitalism was Professor Seligman, a Columbia professor famous for books championing American individualism. The Communist was Scott Nearing, in the unfortunate plight of having been expelled from the Party three days before. Over the years I have come to respect Nearing greatly. He has shown courage as a kind of libertarian Communist. Debates are rarely satisfactory but this was a success. We had three rounds of speaking, the professor was knocked out in the first, and then Nearing and I went for each other, the audience cheering excitedly. The New York press carried reports as dramatic as football stories. One celebrated columnist wrote that I was wearing a suit which I must have bought from Horne Brothers three years previously and which had not been pressed since; my neck stretched from a collar three sizes too large, like a hen from a chicken coop; nevertheless I was a 'gentleman' – Jesus College, Cambridge, he guessed, and behind my English pince-nez 'shone the eyes of Savonarola'. Phew!

Norman Thomas, succeeding a hero of my youth, Eugene Debs, was Socialist candidate for the Presidency during one of my visits. I met him many times and through the years we remained friends. He was originally a minister of religion and still had the appearance of one, tall, silver-haired, clean-shaven, domed forehead, a distinguished scholarly figure. I found he was respected throughout America by members of all Parties. I remember at a football match the spectators round me discussed the election whilst waiting for the game to begin. 'Thomas is the best of the three, but he's got no chance. I'm voting Roosevelt,' said a man, and I was impressed by the many who agreed. Thomas had a continuously developing mind. On my first visit he was a typical Social Democrat of the Centre, except that he was a pacifist. On my third visit he had moved far to the Left. He was a pioneer in denouncing America's part in the Vietnam War.

I was intrigued by Jay Lovestone, who journeyed from leadership of the Communist Party to apologist for Americanism. At the time of my visits he was head of the Communist Opposition associated with the ILP, and I went to his headquarters, a long, low room at the top of a narrow staircase in Fourteenth Street, New York, and had the good fortune to meet Diego Rivera, the remarkable mural painter of Mexico. The whole of one wall was covered by his work and he was engaged on final touches to a painting of the First World War. He had still to paint one head and paused to ask me whether it should be of Montagu Norman or Lloyd George. I said Lloyd George, and at once he began to sketch the familiar figure. But Diego was doubtful. He held that high finance was behind all wars.

I saw more of America than most Americans, travelling from Niagara Falls in the north to Texas in the south, and west to San Francisco. I visited Canada twice, first to speak at Toronto University, second to get a glass of beer. Prohibition was the order of the day in the USA, so at Niagara with my guide, I crossed the frontier bridge only to find that under Canada's restricted hours, no drink was available. When we returned to the States my companion took me to a café where in the back room we drank to our throats' content. San Francisco was the most beautiful city I visited, but I was most moved when crossing the Rockies by the beauty of the eternal blue of the sky above, the eternal white of the clouds below, pierced by coned peaks of snow. Never had I felt so much a part of infinity. On the return journey we came through a violent storm, the wings of the plane almost perpendicular, first one side and then the other. Strangely I was not frightened – I became madly drunk with excitement, defying the wind to do its worst. Our hostess, tending to a sick passenger was knocked out. Chicago seemed to be rocking when we landed.

America both depressed and inspired me. I was shocked by the almost universal habit of measuring personal achievement in terms of income and wealth; to make money was the object of life and success the sole reason for pride. On the other hand, I had never met such friendship and generosity towards others as I found among those who rejected these values. Judged by Socialist ethics I had met the worst and the best. I came back to England pessimistic, yet in no country had I experienced a feeling of so many men and women dedicated both in ideals and in their lives to human fellowship and cooperation.

CHAPTER FOURTEEN

BREAKING WITH LABOUR

The ILP left the Labour Party after the General Election of 1931, a stupid and disastrous error, and, appointed chairman at Easter, I was largely responsible. It was stupid because we departed just when the party was turning Left in reaction to the MacDonald failure and betrayal. It was disastrous because, outside the Labour movement, the ILP dwindled to relative insignificance and because the Labour Party lost the inspiration of the Socialist evangelism and dynamism which the ILP at its best contributed. My support of disaffiliation was the greatest political mistake of my life. All I can say is that I did my damnedest to reach a settlement.

The specific cause of the break lay in the Standing Orders of the Parliamentary Party which prohibited an MP from voting against its decisions. The nineteen ILP candidates at the 1931 election had been refused endorsement by the Labour Party Executive because they declined to give an undertaking that they would always obey this rule. We felt there were occasions, for example on armaments and a threat to living standards, when we should follow our conscience. Immediately after the election there were meetings between Arthur Henderson, the secretary of the Labour Party, and James Maxton, then our chairman, who mutually agreed that the dispute could be amicably discussed; but for some reason the negotiations were held up. I had the impression that Maxton, who was against continued affiliation, permitted things to take their course, but when I followed him as chairman I received consent to renew contacts.

I saw both George Lansbury, who had been appointed Leader of the Party in succession to MacDonald, and Arthur Henderson, the secretary. I had expected Lansbury to discuss policy and Henderson organisation – Lansbury was a recognised Leftist and Henderson had a reputation for party management rather than political theory. Exactly the reverse happened. When I met Lansbury in his modest Bow home he was concerned only with organisation; he was kind as always, but insisted that there was no place for a Party within a Party – the ILP must either be wholly in the Labour Party and subordinate its own views to the Parliamentary decisions or get outside. When I raised with him his own pacifist convictions against armaments and his past breach with the Party on women's suffrage, he said that on issues of conscience he would abstain, a negative view of conscience which I could not accept.

This interview was disappointing but I did not feel it was final and I travelled to Geneva to see Arthur Henderson, who was putting in much time there as chairman of the Disarmament Conference. I had a fleeting glimpse of Philip Noel Baker, his Parliamentary Private Secretary, handsome in white flannels, tennis racket in hand, waving to me through the window. I had admired Philip ever since meeting him on his return from the war when he told me he would devote the rest of his life to ending war and armaments, which he surely has done.

Over tea Henderson brushed aside Lansbury's constitutional doubts and the controversy about Standing Orders. 'Get policy right and these are details,' he said; the fundamental issue was: 'Did the ILP believe in Parliamentary democracy?' In fact the issue of the Parliamentary approach to Socialism was at that moment controversial in the ILP. We were alarmed by the threat to democracy by Nazism in Germany and by the Fascist emergence in Britain and there were those who held that Parliament would be thrust aside and that the final struggle would be outside. I told Henderson that the ILP would use Parliament so long and as fully as it could be used, but this did not satisfy him. He insisted we should not think of other methods than Parliamentary democracy.

I reported these discussions to the ILP National Council and found it acutely divided. Maxton, Fred Jowett and Campbell Stephen were for disaffiliation. Frank Wise, Pat Dollan and David Kirkwood were against. That meeting was difficult to chair, Wise lecturing us, Kirkwood emotional, Dollan tricky. There was no alternative to leaving the decision to the annual conference without a recommendation. The conference was interesting for the part played by Jack Gaster, bright young solicitor, son of the famous rabbi, and Dr C. K. Cullen, an East End Medical Officer of Health. They wanted not only disaffiliation, but association with the Communist International. The majority of delegates, however, were uneasy about a break with the Labour Party and voted in favour of continued negotiation.

As chairman I was mainly responsible for the discussions which followed. I leaned backwards to find agreement. The issue turned on the Standing Orders of the Parliamentary Party. The ILP put forward two proposals: first that the policy of the Labour Government should be decided by the Party, and secondly that an MP should not be absolutely prohibited from voting against a decision by the majority of the Parliamentary Party, but if he did so he should be reported to his constituency Party and his nominating body. We made it clear we were not tied to this formula and would consider alternative suggestions. When our deputation, which included pro-affiliationists, met the Labour Executive we found them unresponsive; they insisted that we should accept the present Standing Orders before consideration was given to the ILP amendments. I then proposed a procedure which would not infringe this right: a preliminary discussion between four members on each side, and, if agreement were reached, a recommendation from the Labour Executive to the Parliamentary Party, which would retain unimpaired its right to decide. The Labour representatives, however, were adamant. There was complete deadlock, and the majority of the ILP National Council concluded there was no alternative but to recommend disaffiliation to a special conference. I supported that recommendation, but writing now from hindsight I know it was wrong. Later the Parliamentary Party itself modified its Standing Orders and much greater liberty was permitted. Within a Leftish Labour Party the ILP MPs could have accelerated that realisation.

The Special Conference met in July 1932 in the Jowett Hall, splendid headquarters of the Bradford ILP, named affectionately after its veteran leader. The debate was tense but serious. Only once, when David Kirkwood stormed from the back of the hall roaring defiance, was order threatened. The vote for disaffiliation was 241 to 141, an influential minority including Frank Wise and P. J. Dollan, and among the majority were disquieted figures like R. C. Wallhead and Jennie Lee, both of whom subsequently rejoined the Labour Party. The debate demonstrated that opposition to the Labour Party was based more on policy than on the Standing Orders. The majority were convinced that Fascism would have to be met outside Parliament more than from within.

The months, indeed the years, which followed were an appalling experience of sectarian controversy about revolutionary theory. The first response of the ILP National Council was a statement which dismissed the view that Socialism could be achieved simply through Parliament, 'the instrument of the capitalist State'. Nevertheless, the Legislature should be used for propaganda and occasional concessions. Ironically, this statement was recommended to the conference by one of the most skilled Parliamentarians, James Maxton.

I sent a copy to Bernard Shaw who said it left him without the faintest notion of what ILP policy was. 'All I know is that you feel bound to use the old Marxist catchword "revolutionary" as often as possible. When you have frightened off enough people with it you will have to explain that it means just nothing.' Shaw even went to the trouble of submitting in one thousand words an alternative statement, remarking that if he were a young man he would not join the ILP on our own presentation of policy. 'My object has been to produce a statement that would attract young Fenners and Shaws.' He explained that his alternative did not express his own views but was an endeavour to help us express ours, but it was, nevertheless, typically Shavian. We rejected Shaw's text, but reading it now I am impressed by much of its good sense. It was an essay on current events rather than a permanent thesis, giving much attention, for example, to the Distributist League of G. K. Chesterton and Hilaire Belloc, forgotten today.

The casualties and dangers of Fascism led the ILP into its first united front with the Communist Party. Our National Council approached the Labour, Cooperative and Communist Parties for a joint campaign to assist the victims in Germany and to resist the advance of Fascism at home. Only the Communists agreed. Maxton, Harry Pollitt, J. R. Campbell and I had frequent consultations. Pollitt was as skilful a negotiator as he was a speaker, not afraid to think twice. A short time before I had debated with him and he had declared war to the knife on the ILP, but here we were cooperating on common issues as I had proposed. Soon the cooperation extended to anti-war demonstrations, hunger marches, rent disputes, protest against cuts in unemployment benefits and practically all day-to-day activities. These united campaigns ended partly because of Communist complaints of the criticism I was beginning to make of Soviet foreign policy and partly because of a revolt by ILP membership.

The Head Office took a census of Branch opinion which revealed that two thirds of the party were cooperating uneasily with the Communists. They objected because they preferred united action with the Labour Party and trade unions to whom the Communists were anathema and because in the localities the Communists were using united action for sectarian purposes. The Lancashire leadership and a large section of its following broke away from the ILP and formed an independent party. One of our few recent recruits of distinction, Middleton Murry, went with them. I was greatly attracted by him; he was a gentle, lofty soul who set out to convert us to a spiritual interpretation of Marxism; he appealed to something strong in my nature. Still more serious was the resignation of John Paton, the Party secretary. John had had a magnificent record as a Socialist pioneer in Scotland and had ably served as secretary in circumstances of dwindling support. The National Council were at a loss to replace him. We were meeting at Digswell Park and it was Jack Gaster, the rebel, who suggested a solution. He took Maxton and me by the arm and led us across the lawn. 'Jimmy,' he said, 'you must return to the chair and, Fenner, you must return to Head Office.' And that was what happened.

Meanwhile, despite our break with the Communist Party here in Britain, at the 1933 conference a resolution was carried, in face of the opposition of the National Council, instructing it 'to ascertain in what way the ILP may assist in the work of the Communist International'. An exchange of letters followed, the replies from Moscow signed on behalf of the Secretariat by O. W. Kuusinen, later notorious as head of the ill-fated government set up by the Soviet Union in Finland. The correspondence was of some historical importance to those interested in the principles and practices of the Communist International, but it extended to thousands of words and cannot even be summarised here. Soon it became apparent that Moscow was concerned not to win the ILP to association but to divide the Party by winning a section of its members. The leaders were attacked as 'reformists' and I was described as 'a slanderer of the Soviet Union', no doubt because, as I shall tell later, I criticised Russia's collaboration with Fascist Germany and denounced the Stalin trials. By ninety-eight votes to fifty-one the annual conference rejected a motion for 'sympathetic affiliation' to the Communist international. It was still a disquietingly large minority. The ILP was now isolated. It had left the Labour Party. It had turned down the Communist Party.

Abroad, however, our contacts remained with independent parties and with the Left within the Social Democratic parties. In 1932 I did a tour of meetings in Germany – the last British Socialist to do so before Hitler triumphed. The Nazis were already gaining ascendency. I was held up at Weimar where the Führer was reviewing a massed army. Brown Shirts attacked our meetings, Red Guards accompanied me whenever I was in the streets. I delivered the funeral oration at a moving gathering in Breslau at the graveside of Ferdinand Lassalle, pioneer libertarian Socialist, on the sixty-seventh anniversary of his death, the only time a non-German had done so. The leader of Breslau Socialists was Eckstein, loved and courageous. He was one of the first victims of the Nazi terror, exhibited on a lorry as a Jew, imprisoned and dead within a week. The ILP named its fund to assist the underground movement against Hitler the Eckstein Fund. I spoke in

Thuringia, Leipzig and Berlin, the audiences ringed by the paramilitary force which the Democratic Front was already raising. Often they had to beat back assaults. I was inspired by the spirit of the Socialist Youth with their bright blue shirts and spreading red ties, bravely defying the Nazis; but the Swastika was everywhere, and I feared. A year later Hitler came to power.

CHAPTER FIFTEEN

BREAKING WITH STALIN

The ILP had reservations about the Soviet Revolution, but supported its basic change. We had the friendliest relations with the Soviet Embassy and I became closely associated with its ambassadors. Maisky had been a colleague during the First World War and comradeship remained when he returned to London. I got to know Krassin, Rakovsky and Sokolnikov well. An indication of the mutual trust was the practice of the Embassy to approach me for nominations when appointing English members of their staff.

An unusual proof of confidence occurred during the crisis over the trade delegation to which I have referred. The Embassy anticipated that the directors of their undertakings would be asked to leave the country and through Frank Wise, their adviser, they asked the ILP to nominate substitutes. We agreed, but in ILP tradition insisted that this should be regarded as a political gesture and that any duties should be fulfilled without fees or salaries. Looking back, I am surprised that we went as far as this and perhaps it was as well that the need did not arise. The most personal instance of trust was a request to me to speak at the funeral service of Krassin at the Golders Green Crematorium. I was reluctant because of the nature of the occasion and I felt acutely embarrassed as I stood almost within reach of the bereaved family. Krassin's death was natural. It is a sadder memory that Rakovsky and Sokolnikov were both victims of Stalin's purge. Rakovsky was shot, Sokolnikov imprisoned.

Our first crucial severance from the Soviet Union and the British Communist Party arose from the agreement which Moscow reached with Nazi Germany. When Hitler triumphed in the Reichstag Fire Election, the ILP urged international action to bring him down. We proposed that the Trades Union, Cooperative and Political Internationals, in association with the

Russians, should organise world-wide refusal to make or handle goods destined for Germany. The proposal was not impractical. Within the Trades Union Movement there were strong elements advocating a boycott and the International Transport Workers Federation planned to give a lead. The idea was killed by the announcement that the Soviet Government had extended a Trade Agreement with Germany in operation before Hitler came to power. This made Russian support impossible and inevitably Communist Parties outside Russia were inhibited. Indeed, in Holland, when transport workers refused to handle goods on boats carrying the Swastika flag, the Dutch Communist Party restrained them.

After I wrote an article criticising the Stalin–Hitler Agreement, the *Daily Worker* revealed how committed British Communists were to the Soviet Union, right or wrong. It carried a page streamer, 'Brockway Goes Over to the Counter-Revolution' and another Communist journal described me as 'a Hound of War and Fascism'. I was attacked for sabotaging common action but, appalled by what was happening in Nazi Germany, I could not remain silent. Thousands of Socialists and Communists were thrust into concentration camps, their Parties outlawed, their premises occupied, their papers suppressed. An agreement with Hitler seemed to me under these conditions a betrayal. My article created a controversy within the Communist membership and Pollitt called a discussion meeting, announcing that I had been invited. In fact I did not receive the invitation until three days later when I immediately offered to debate the issue. This time I was on top. Pollitt declared that boycott was not a working-class weapon, whereupon I quoted an earlier Communist International call for the very policy against Fascist Italy which I was urging against Fascist Germany.

Our second serious divergence from the Soviet Union erupted from the Moscow trials of dissentients. The early arrests included Rakovsky and I could not believe he was guilty. My doubts were strengthened when in Paris I met revolutionaries who had escaped from Russian prisons and ex-members of the Soviet Administration like M. Barmene, the First Counsellor in Athens, who refused to return to Moscow. I denounced the trials in a second article in the *New Leader*, dismissed this time by the *Daily Worker* as a 'Social-Fascist'. The opportunity arose to check the allegations when Trotsky escaped to Norway. He wrote to me asking for an impartial enquiry and I began getting together a commission of French, Scandinavian and American jurists. The Norwegian Government, however, found Trotsky an inconvenient guest and he took refuge in Mexico, which made a European enquiry impossible. A Trotsky Defence Committee in America then appointed a Commission with Professor Dewey, whom I had learned to respect on visits to the States, as chairman, but the other members were known supporters of Trotsky and I did not feel that their conclusions would be accepted as impartial. When I expressed this doubt in a letter, Trotsky denounced me as 'Mr Pritt Number Two', a reference to D. N. Pritt, distinguished barrister and Labour MP, who had attended the first Moscow trial and declared it fair. Pritt was a devotee of Soviet Russia, never able to see wrong in Moscow but I admired his forthrightness and courage. And he could be generous. When I stood as an ILP candidate for Norwich in the thirties and he was invited by the Labour Party to oppose me, he declined. Later he was expelled from the Labour Party for his association with the Communists.

Meanwhile, Communist policy was justifying my forebodings by their advocacy of Popular Front alliances with the capitalist governments of France and Britain. The first effect was upon the anti-imperialist struggle. The League against Imperialism was allowed to wither away and I was moved by what George Padmore reported of the consequences in Africa. George, about whom I will have much to write, represented Blacks on the Executive of the Communist International and with Lenin had been the author of its Charter for Colonial Peoples. He had been allotted the task of strengthening the liberation movements in North Africa and particularly of stimulating conscripts to be ready to fight for their own freedoms rather than for France or Britain. When Moscow decided in favour of alliances with the French and British Governments, he was told to stop his activities. I should be fair to the Communists – they maintained activity in India and British Communists were sentenced at the notorious trial at Meerut. Perhaps this was because India was further from the European scene.

Much of my involvement in happenings in the Soviet Union arose from my chairmanship, after the ILP left the Second International, of an international bureau of independent parties and groups. It included the Norwegian Labour Party, fairly strong parties from France, Holland, Italy, Spain and Israel, the Communist Opposition from Germany, a breakaway from the Communists in America and twelve parties and groups from colonial territories, including India, Indo-China and Northern Africa. I was captivated by the personalities of their representatives, of a stuff quite different from the professional politicians I had met in the Second International. They were Socialists in their lives, aliens in a capitalist world, dedicated to a new society.

There was a remarkable woman, Angelica Balabanoff, of the Italian Party, white-haired, in her sixties, but exciting in features, gestures and speech, as enthusiastic as a teenager. She was born in Tsarist Russia, was exiled and went to Italy. Ironically, she was responsible for starting Mussolini on his political career. She was addressing a group of Italian exiles in Switzerland, and noticing an ill-clad, distraught lad listening eagerly, she spoke to him. Finding that he was hungry, she gave him a meal, bought him clothes, smuggled him into Italy and trained him to speak and write. Proudly she saw him progress, first as popular orator, then as editor of the Party paper and finally secretary of the Party. The young man was Benito Mussolini. Swollen by his own power, he led Italy to Fascism and among those he exiled was Angelica. She found her way to wherever the struggle against Fascism was most critical, Vienna, Berlin, Barcelona, travelling hard, living hard. She knew six languages and acted as interpreter at our meetings, translating until the early hours of the morning, never seeming to be tired. Another Italian, Enrico Nenni, large physically and mentally, later so influential in his country, came to our meetings in Paris. We have remained friends ever since, talking of these difficult times whenever I have visited him in Rome.

Three of the most impressive representatives were ex-Communist leaders from Germany, Brandler, Thalheimer and Froelich, famous for their part in the struggles at the end of the First World War. Lenin selected Brandler as leader in Germany after his masterly handling of the Chemnitz revolution in 1920 when, having won power, he had the wisdom to retreat rather than invite suppression. He was not so wise a year later when, with Thalheimer and Froelich, he led the ill-fated rising in 1921 which was followed by the imprisonment of all three. Released, Brandler and Thalheimer became chiefs in the Communist Party Executive, Froelich, editor of its paper, but all three were thrown out of the Party when they opposed its ultra-Left line. On their expulsion, Brandler and Thalheimer formed the Communist Opposition, whilst Froelich joined the Socialist Workers' Party (SAP), a Left breakaway from the Social Democrats. I was present at the inaugural conference of the SAP and was struck by its similarity to the ILP.

In appearance, Brandler reminded me of Lon Chaney's impersonation of the hunchback of Notre Dame. An accident when an infant left him hunchbacked and hugely broad of shoulder, but from his stunted body rose a head of remarkable strength in shape and features, whilst the muscles of his arms and hands were like cords of steel. He was volcanic in speech and gesture. Thalheimer, on the other hand, looked like an academic, tall, silver-haired, quiet spoken. He was the theoretician, whilst Brandler the man of action. Froelich was more human than either of them, open and genial.

I would like to dwell on the personalities of other members of our Committee. I select two for whom I had special affection and admiration. The first was Marceau Pivert, leader of the French Party of Socialist Workers and Peasants. He had been an influential leader of the Left in the French Socialist Party, but his conscience made him leave when the Popular Front Government of Léon Blum declined to help the democrats of Spain resist the Fascist rebellion of General Franco. He was gentle in character and reluctantly became a revolutionary by the inescapable force of events. The second was Joaquim Maurin, head of the Spanish Party of Marxist Unity (POUM). Maurin was MP for Barcelona, and was known as 'the Lenin of Catalonia'. He had been a leader of the CNT, the dominant trade union in the province, unique because its ideology was philosophic anarchism aiming at Syndicalism rather than State Socialism. He had gone to Russia in Lenin's day and had been converted to Marxism, but he broke with Stalin and joined with Andres Nin, Trotskyist, popular author as well as politician, to establish POUM, which soon became a considerable force in Catalonia, cooperating with the CNT in industrial struggles, despite ideological differences.

When the Franco rebellion broke out, Maurin was in another part of Spain and was caught by Fascist forces on his way back. In September *The Times* reported that he had been shot. It was in Spain that my disillusionment with Soviet Communism under Stalin became decisive.

CHAPTER SIXTEEN

IN WARTIME SPAIN

The Franco rebellion in Spain erupted on 19 July 1936. The ILP immediately planned help to the democratic forces. POUM asked us to send a representative to Barcelona and fortunately we had just the right man. I had heard of John McNair before the 1914 war as a Socialist propagandist in the North East. In 1923 he walked into our Head Office and offered his services in any capacity. He had been a merchant in Paris since the war, was fed up with capitalist trade and had made enough money to offer free service. We gave John a trial and he proved so efficient that we made him organising secretary, but a breakdown in health necessitated his return to France after a few years. In June 1936, my telephone rang and I heard John's voice. His health was better, he wanted to come back and we jumped at the opportunity. Early in August we sent him to Barcelona, taking the first financial aid from Britain to the anti-Fascist forces, and he remained there, with short consultations in London, until the end of the war, not only assisting POUM, but serving as contact for the ILP contingent at the front. Let me turn from immediate events to complete the McNair story. His first dedication was to Socialist service, but he had a second ambition. He came from a poor family and although he longed to go to a university had to leave school at fourteen. The desire to further his education remained all through his life and when he retired from the ILP secretaryship (he succeeded me) at sixty-five years of age, he enrolled as a student at Newcastle University and took his degree. He wrote a thesis on George Orwell for his doctorate but died before his last hope was realised. He wrote the biography of James Maxton, *The Beloved Rebel*. He was a Socialist of the same quality as his hero. But I was writing about Spain.

In the province of Catalonia the Franco rebellion was met not only by military resistance, driving the Fascist forces a hundred miles from Barcelona, but by a social revolution. The CNT and the POUM led the workers and troops in taking over everything. The soldiers arrested their Fascist officers and transformed the army into a workers' militia. Factories, farms, railways, buses, every place of employment, came under workers' control. Even the brothels were run by the prostitutes, the pimps and matrons sacked. A united Workers' Council, representing POUM, the Social Democrats, the Communists (then weak), both sections of the Trades Union Movement (reformist UGT as well as revolutionary CNT) coordinated the administration of the economy. The Provincial Government, much of it bourgeois, formally remained but with very restricted functions. Andres Nin was appointed Minister of Justice, establishing People's Courts with an amended criminal code making human injustice a greater crime than damage to property. The Catalonian revolution became a divisive issue among the anti-Fascist forces, but the ILP rejoiced in it.

Although by now much diminished in numbers, the ILP turned all its energies to campaigning for democratic Spain. Despite the aid given to Franco by Hitler and Mussolini, the British Government declined to send arms to help the elected Government and unhappily the Labour leadership supported this policy of non-intervention, with the French Popular Front Government, under Léon Blum, and other European governments taking the same line. Through our International Bureau in Paris we convened a large conference in Brussels which planned to send medicines, arms and men by all means available. The ILP sent an ambulance to Barcelona, packed with medical equipment and medicines, naming it Joaquim Maurin. On the initiative of Bob Edwards we mobilised a group of volunteer fighters of which Bob took command. I was proud of the way the Party rallied.

An amusing incident happened as I was organising the despatch of the ILP contingent. They left before the Government prohibited volunteers, but a young man in a shop on the other side of the road from Head Office (then in St Bride Street) reported that detectives had taken an office on the floor above to watch us. I rang up the firm and asked to speak to the police inspector. 'Our staff is flattered by the attention you are paying us,' I said, 'and we invite you and your men to join us for tea this afternoon.' The inspector was embarrassed, falling back on regulations. 'We couldn't do that without the permission of the superintendent,' he said. I rang up Scotland Yard and asked for the Head of the Special Department. He was even more taken aback than the inspector, remarking at first that he saw no reason why his men should not accept the invitation, but then remembered that they would be off duty. In a mischievous mood I told the story to the Press Association and the next morning the whole country, except the Home Office, was laughing. We never saw the Scotland Yard men again.

It was just after this that I met Eric Blair, already known as George Orwell for his *Road to Wigan Pier*. He came to see me at Head Office, tall, fair, reserved, to talk about going to Spain. He was attracted by the ethical, libertarian Socialism of the ILP but had been disillusioned by visits to London branches where Communists and Trotskyists had wrangled. We had lunch together and he unbent, lively and laughing, saying he was in- different as to whether he joined the International Brigade or the ILP contingent in Spain – all he wanted to do was to have a 'whack' at Franco. I gave him an introduction to John McNair but left him to decide which force he should join when he reached Barcelona. I am not sure whether it was at this luncheon or later that he told me he was in some difficulty about a publisher. I gave him an introduction to Fredric Warburg (of Secker and Warburg) who was sympathetic to the ILP and had asked me to write for him. In his autobiography Warburg afterwards thanked me for putting him in touch with Orwell, grateful when *Animal Farm* became such a success. Orwell joined the ILP contingent.

In August 1937, Joaquim Maurin's wife, Jeanne, was one of the lecturers at the ILP summer school. After her husband's arrest and reported execu- tion, she had taken refuge in Paris, replacing him in our International Bureau, and I used to stay with her. I presided at her lecture and paid a tribute to Joaquim, saying what a loss his death had been. Jeanne was not normally emotional and I was surprised when she clasped my hand. 'Come to my room,' she said, and there she asked me to read a letter. It was from Joaquim! Jeanne told me that he was a prisoner in Franco's hands but had disguised himself, giving another name and was unrecognised. To Jeanne he sent his monthly letter addressed to her maiden name, but she had not dared to tell a soul because if it were known that he was living Franco would search the prisons until he was found. I hugged the secret to myself until the unknown Joaquim was released at the end of the war. Jeanne and he went to America, where he wrote his *Revolution and Counter Revolution in Spain*.

I was chairman of a broad-manned committee which organised a Spanish Exhibition in Ludgate Hill under the shadow of St Paul's. Two colleagues in this were Emma Goldman, the veteran anarchist, and Roland Penrose, the Surrealist artist. Emma was in appearance the anarchist of Establishment misrepresentation with the stocky figure of a peasant, a face like a pugilist, a harsh voice and a ruthless personality. Yet to her friends she was kind; she would make tea for me in her little bare room with housewifely care and she was sincere to the point of sacrifice, caring nothing for herself. Roland Penrose was a gentle friendly person, working on the problem of the relationship of art to revolution. I went to his house in Hampstead and was startled by the pictures, a woman holding her severed head at her breast and other eccentricities which I could not understand. He had a wonderful collection of records of primitive music, playing an African piece which was strange and exciting. Roland went to Spain to gather material for our exhibition and designed its lay-out beautifully.

I cooperated with Emma also in distributing Spanish CNT films. Ethel Mannin, the novelist, was active in this. Ethel, worshipper of James Maxton, had been a member of the ILP for several years. Her personality surprised me when I met her. I had read her *Confessions and Impressions* and seen her photographs, but she was neither the adolescent Bohemian suggested by the former nor the mystical Madonna suggested by the latter. She came from a working-class home, a Socialist by nature, welcoming everyone as an equal, unassuming and simple in her taste. She married a Jewish businessman, had a daughter, quarrelled with her husband from whom she was later divorced, became anti-Zionist and pro-Arab, and spent her days typing novels. Later she married Reg Reynolds, Left-wing pacifist, a disciple of Gandhi, and also an author. Despite their different temperaments a warm friendship grew up between Ethel and Emma.

Our allies in Catalonia, the POUM and the CNT, came under increasing denunciation from the Communist, Labour and Liberal supporters of the International Brigade who were defending Madrid. At the time I did not appreciate their case, but it had some strength. They were at the core of the military conflict, defending the capital, the headquarters of the Coalition Government with its Social Democrat Prime Minister, Largo Caballero. They had no time for a social revolution; all effort was needed in the battle against great odds to defend democracy. Looking back it was tragic that cooperation was not reached. For the ILP, however, it was enough that a workers' society existed in Catalonia, and we invited Julian Gorkin and two colleagues to come to England to tell us about it. The phone rang and they were at Croydon airport – but they were prisoners in the police station, refused admission, to be sent back on the next plane. With my voluntary secretary, Edith King, I rushed to Croydon and spent an hour with them. One of Gorkin's companions was a younger brother of Joaquim Maurin, so like Joaquim that I thought at first it was he. He returned to Spain to fight for months at the front; then he was arrested by the Communists and died in prison.

Madrid was in danger and part of the besieged Government took refuge in Valencia. Retreating towards the coast, the Communists and their Liberal allies were confronted by the hold which the CNT and POUM had in Catalonia. To influence their own ranks, including the International Brigade and democratic supporters abroad, the Communists let loose a campaign of incredible slander against POUM (they refrained from directly attacking the CNT because of its industrial strength), describing the party as Franco's 'fifth column', as Fascist agents and spies, as guilty of betrayal at the front by retreating at critical moments of the battle, and finally as conspiring to assassinate Caballero, the Prime Minister; Azana, the President; and La Passionaria, the heroine of the Republic. Every newspaper carried these stories and even in Barcelona, where the Communist Party had grown in appreciation of Russian aid, the daily repetition of the calumnies made an impression.

I saw that the scales were weighted heavily against POUM and advised John McNair and Gorkin, whom I met in Paris, that an accommodation must be sought to prevent civil war within the Republican ranks. With some misgiving, the POUM gave permission to McNair to approach Communist representatives. On five occasions he met them and was told his proposals would be taken to the leadership in Madrid, but there was no response. In May 1937, the crisis came. The Catalan Government, restored to authority by the Communists (the Workers' Council shorn of power), decided to occupy the telephone exchange where workers' control persisted. The CNT staff resisted and within an hour the workers of Barcelona, from one end of the city to the other, were on strike and throwing up barricades in the streets. For four days all work stopped, but the CNT leadership called off the strike because they did not wish Republican strength destroyed in physical conflict. The Communists, who now entirely dominated their Popular Front colleagues, ascribed the Barcelona 'rising' to POUM and so the Liberal and Social Democratic journalists told the world. The Madrid Government outlawed POUM and authorised the imprisonment of its leaders. When there were objections in the Cabinet, the Communists forced the resignation of Largo Caballero and other Social Democratic colleagues. Nin and his POUM colleagues were arrested.

I heard this news with dismay, concerned for Spain, for POUM, for John McNair and for our ILP contingent. I heard that our boys were in Barcelona, enjoying the normal fortnight's leave after three months' service at the front. The Press reported that foreign sympathisers with POUM were being arrested and this seemed to be confirmed by the news of the death in prison of the nineteen-year-old Robert Smillie, one of our volunteers, son of Alex Smillie, Scottish ILP leader, grandson of the miners' pioneer president, the great Robert Smillie. Young Bob was our most promising youngster, chairman of the ILP Guild of Youth, of which my daughter, Audrey, was secretary. His death affected me deeply. Should I have acquiesced in his joining our contingent at his young age?

I decided to leave for Spain. In Paris two members of our International Bureau were assigned to go with me, but after forty-eight hours I was tired of waiting and took a train alone to Perpignan, a border town. There I had the great relief of finding John McNair, accompanied by George Orwell and a youthful ILP volunteer, Staff Cottman. Hunted in Barcelona, they had slept in a cemetery and fortunately reached the frontier before the guard had news that they were wanted. They told me that others had taken refuge in the CNT headquarters, but that Bob Edwards, commander of the ILP contingent, had set off to climb across the border over the Pyrenees. Orwell had missed death at the front by a fraction of an inch, a bullet scraping his windpipe, and his voice was thin and husky. He told me he had resolved by accident the problem of which brigade to join; the ILP contingent was just leaving for the front and he had gone with them. He was still uncommitted, but was deeply impressed by the workers' revolution and later wrote his *Homage to Catalonia*. I think it was experience of Communist behaviour in Spain which aroused his loathing of dictatorship expressed in his *Animal Farm* and *1984*. George Orwell was joined at Perpignan by his wife, Eileen, and together they went to a village on the coast for a short holiday. McNair and Staff Cottman made haste for Paris and London.

I left Perpignan at 4 am arriving at Cerbère, the last French village, an hour later. A crowded little train took us under the frontier mountain and we came into the light at Port Bou, the first village in Spain. One of John McNair's proudest possessions was a worker's passport, bearing the stamps of all the Catalonian working-class organisations, given him on entering Spain. Now Communist officials were in charge, everything was searched, my documents (the minimum) examined in detail. I successfully surmounted the interrogations.

The train for Barcelona did not leave for three hours and I made my way down to the village through which a river tumbled to the sea. I became excited. On the walls, on cottage fronts, on the concrete banks of the river, *everywhere*, were POUM posters. The Party was outlawed, but here already was evidence of its strength. The train journey to Barcelona revealed the life of the people as vividly as any street scene. We stopped at every station and peasants got in and out with every conceivable article from home and field. A woman climbed in, her back buried under a huge bundle of newly-cut grass, another clasping in her arms a gobbling turkey. A man struggled through the crowded carriage trying to control two dogs pulling in opposite directions, one eager to get at a rabbit on a girl's lap, the other a goat clutched round the neck by a boy. The journey took seven hours, but it never ceased to be lively. The carriage buzzed with excited talk and I often heard CNT and POUM uttered, straining to understand. I soon had evidence. At Gerona, the only large town, a jumble of small houses dominated by a fortress and a church, every family bought papers, four out of five the *Solidaridad Obrera*, the CNT daily. When my neighbour stopped reading and joined the fierce verbal storm which had broken out I borrowed his paper and puzzled out the news. The front page carried a CNT manifesto in black type condemning the suppression of POUM, demanding to know where the imprisoned leaders (particularly Nin) were, and declaring that the workers and peasants of Catalonia had not fought to set up a Stalinist dictatorship in place of a Franco dictatorship. I became as excited as the others and grasped the hands of the peasant beside me and shook them. When I got him to understand that I came from the British POUM he exclaimed 'Camarado,' took my face in his hands and kissed both cheeks. Food and fruit were showered on me.

In Barcelona, broad streets, large buildings and avenues of trees, I took a taxi to the Continental Hotel, the driver refusing a tip. The hotel, clean and comfortable, had been collectivised, and the staff also refused tips. Later, whenever I visited a country which had gone through revolution (Yugoslavia, Egypt, Poland) I sensed that the refusal of tips was the test of its depth, the assertion of equal status.

The next morning I went to the CNT headquarters, a massive seven-storey monument which, before the revolution, had accommodated the capitalist Federation of Industries. I was welcomed by Antoine Souchy, the International Secretary of the Anarcho-Syndicalists, a fair-haired German, a good friend whom I had known in Paris. He took me to see half a dozen ILP refugees on the premises; my first job would be to get them across the frontier. With them were a group of foreign sympathisers, men and women, German, French, American, among them Willi Brandt representing a Vienna Socialist paper, whom I had last met at an ILP summer school. Brandt was depressed, broken-hearted that workers should be fighting each other rather than the common enemy, fearful for the future of Austria and indeed Europe, with the rising arrogance of Hitler and Mussolini. I was impressed with the depth of his analysis.

A meeting of the Regional Committee of the CNT followed. They insisted that I should travel to Valencia immediately to see Ministers. During the afternoon I saw the head of the Catalan Passport Ministry, and was relieved to find that he wanted to get the ILP boys out of the country as soon as possible. They left that evening. I also visited a convent which had been converted into a printing press, delighted with its enthusiastic and smooth running workers' control. I was concerned about what had happened to the nuns. Were they raped and shot as the Fascists charged? The chairman of the workers' committee brought me a letter from the mother superior posted from Paris, praying that God would show them the errors of their ways but expressing gratitude for safe conduct to the frontier.

I left for Valencia the following morning. Souchy, who accompanied me, thought he was honouring me by assigning Spain's ace racing driver as our chauffeur. I have never had a more frightening journey. We went along the curving coast road, one side mountain, the other sheer drop to the sea. The driver never braked, skidding round the corners, the car within inches of the edge turning to grin at us with his white teeth, enjoying the narrow escape. On the day we were to return from Valencia he came to me, his face bandaged. 'Car no esta,' he remarked, smiling as ever. He had shattered it and must remain. I was never more thankful.

Valencia was very different from Barcelona, a town rather than a city, and the psychology was different, little thought of social revolution, concentration on the military struggle against Franco. Yet when scared employers fled, the social revolution had automatically spread. Our hotel and the cinemas and factories had been taken over by the trade unions, but here the Social Democratic UGT was dominant. The junior CNT, nevertheless, occupied the magnificent mansion of a marquis where I saw the secretary, Vasquez, who looked like a bear, thick black hair and beard, massive shoulders and long hanging arms. He had a conquering personality; tragically he was drowned in 1939 in Paris to which he had escaped on Franco's toes. He told me details of Bob Smillie's arrest and death, calling in a Spanish friend who had been with Bob. They had gone to the frontier together, Bob intending to return to London; he was arrested and charged with having anti-Republican documents on his person and carrying a bomb. In fact, he had only his diary, no doubt containing some criticism of the Communists, and a 'dud' bomb which he had kept as a souvenir. He was taken to Valencia and died after a few days in prison. Later I made an appointment with the Communist Home Secretary, but he had hurried away to Madrid, leaving a statement about Bob's death which was read to me. It said he had developed appendicitis, received medical treatment, but had died. I put questions to the official, but they were unanswered. I left with the conviction that there had been negligence at least. A strong boy should not have died from appendicitis.

Vasquez surprisingly advised me to see first the British Chargé d'Affaires. 'You want two things,' he said, 'access to Ministers, and protection from the Communist terrorists, so adopt the cloak of respectability of the British Government. What you wear does not determine the beat of your heart.' The British quarters astonished me. In contrast to the workers' headquarters I had seen, at the top of ramshackle stairs there was a scruffy little room, two partitioned boxes, one for the Chargé d'Affaires, the other for his secretary. Mr Leche was typical of the old school of aristocratic diplomats. When I spoke of Robert Smillie and the POUM prisoners he was nervous about intervention in Spain's internal affairs, but he was sympathetic and he was concerned about two blue-blooded Spanish ladies confined by the Republicans to their mansion, 'so charming they could not harm a fly'. He agreed for me to see Ministers and offered to interpret – a little embarrassing because he would hesitate to voice my interest in internal imprisonment.

Whilst interviews with Ministers were fixed I went to see the deposed Prime Minister, Largo Caballero, who had resumed his secretaryship of the UGT. He continued to act with the pomp of a Head of State, waiting for Souchy and I to be seated before he entered, preceded by four officials, acknowledging our standing to him with a ceremonial bow. He was bitter about the Communist conspiracy which dismissed him, but excused himself from action on behalf of POUM prisoners because of the growing influence of 'Reds' in the UGT. I was saddened by this visit. Caballero had done great things for Spain but he was now weak and indecisive. The Communists had exploited his unfitness for their *coup*.

The next day was Sunday with no opportunity to meet anyone influential. I was taken to a Peasants' Collective at Segorbe and I think I was more thrilled by this than by anything I had seen. Eighty peasants had taken over the estate of the local marquis, pooling land and stocks and sharing the proceeds equally. In the stable there were six horses – three expropriated thoroughbreds and three small ponies contributed by the peasants, who were far prouder of their own gifts than of the marquis's magnificent conscripts. The chairman of the collective was the Mayor of Segorbe, a young man of thirty-five, efficient and enthusiastic. He had an excitable assistant who told me he was learning French to examine the Fascist documents left by the marquis. I asked him to show them to me – they were cheap French novels. I was interested to learn that the collective was an economic success. Half a dozen Kulaks with large holdings had declined to join, but they had asked to market their goods through the collective which had the advantage of selling directly to the shop-keepers.

The following day the Chargé d'Affaires took me to the Foreign Secretary, Señor Giral. He received me in his home. the atmosphere informal, and it was evident at once by his gracious manner that our grey-haired host was a member of the cultured élite; he was one of the Liberals whom the Communists had allowed to stay in the Government. Conscious of Mr Leche's doubts I approached the subject of Smillie and the POUM prisoners discreetly, establishing first the anti-Fascist record of the ILP. To do him justice Mr Leche, whilst disassociating himself from my questions, interpreted them fully, and Señor Giral replied as though I had not committed any impropriety. He knew the record of the ILP, he regretted deeply Bob Smillie's death, the POUM leaders would not be charged with Fascism, and as a Cabinet Minister he would press for a public trial. So far so good, but I was not really reassured.

The appointment with the Communist Home Secretary, as I have indicated, fell through, and over lunch we heard why from Señor Pabon, the POUM lawyer. 'Your arrival scared him into action,' he said. 'He flew to Madrid to get some information about the POUM prisoners.' Before leaving the Minister had assured the lawyer that Nin was alive, and that Gorkin and their three colleagues, Bonet, Andrade and Esquador, were with him in Madrid. We decided to telegraph the Minister for assurances about their prospects, and the following day received a reply that the prisoners would be brought to Valencia within three days, that the trial would be held in public and that the normal Popular Tribunals would judge them, not a Military Court. I took this encouraging news to Mrs Bonet and Mrs Nin who were hiding in a workmen's hut. I do not think Mrs Nin believed her husband was alive: she listened without a flicker of an eyelid or movement of her mouth, her only expression of emotion was the grip on my hand as she said 'thank you'. Instinctively she knew the truth, her husband was dead.

I had overstayed my leave and had to return to London. Before going, I met the Valencia executive of POUM with their lawyer to plan arrangements for the trial. They were in good spirits because that morning the Valencia Council, composed of Social Democrats, Liberals and Communists, had declined to expel the POUM member; only the Communists had voted in favour. The Paris delegation had at last caught up with me and we agreed to leave them to liaise in Valencia, Souchy to accompany me to Barcelona to report to the CNT headquarters. We left that night but had not got far when our car was stopped by an armed officer who demanded that we carry him to Barcelona to join the anti-POUM forces. How we hid our identities I do not know. We even had breakfast with him at a roadside café and drank his red wine, the only time I have taken wine at breakfast. We dropped him at the City Hall and climbed the steps of the CNT quarters.

My adventures were not over. A POUM activist was wanted by the Communists; he must be got out of the country; the only possibility was that he should go as my companion. When he was refused exit by the immigration control officers at the frontier because he had no papers, I asked that they should phone their Barcelona chiefs. As they lifted the phone, we dashed out, leapt into the waiting car and passed the frontier barrier, raised under the impression that we had been endorsed. We were in France.

Back in London news came fast. Madrid fell. The Franco forces captured Valencia and then Barcelona. In the confusion the POUM prisoners escaped and got to Paris. They confirmed that Andres Nin had been assassinated.

I think it must have been my anger with Stalinism in Spain which led Arthur Koestler to invite me to a meal in a restaurant off Sloane Square. He could see nothing except the barbarity of Communism, even deprecating my opposition to imperialism because it weakened the Western Powers. He was certain a nuclear war would come and was retiring to Snowdonia where he would hide his books in mountain caverns in the hope that possible survivors a few generations hence might find them. He was tremendously dynamic, but I could not accept that one should acquiesce in one form of oppression from fear of another.

My Spanish journey did, however, revolutionise my thinking. I could no longer be a pacifist in all circumstances. I was utterly disillusioned with Communism under Stalin. Libertarian Socialism became my faith.

4, Whitehall Court (130) London, S.W. 1.
Telegrams: Socialist, Parl - London.
Telephone: Whitehall 3160.

Ayot Saint Lawrence, Welwyn, Herts.
L & N.E.R., Welwyn Garden City, 5 miles, Wheathampstead, 2½.
Telegrams and Phone: Codicote 218. 1ˢᵗ Dec. 1945

From
Bernard Shaw.

I will not touch this now.
Imperialism is a form of Inter-
nationalism, and Nationalism of
Isolationism. Starting an Anti-Imperialist
movement now will only add to the
confusion, and be taken as Anti-Russian.

When does a Commonwealth become
an Empire? And vice versa?

Are we to back the tribes who kill
every stranger against ourselves in north
west India? against Russia in north Persia?
as we backed the Danakil savages of
Abyssinia against Italy?

Every case is different. Slogans are
useless. My advice is Drop it.

G. Bernard Shaw

A postcard from George Bernard Shaw, replying to a request to sponsor a movement against imperialism and colonialism

Barbara Castle, Anthony Greenwood, F.B. and Anthony Wedgwood Benn presenting
a petition at South Africa House, 1950

With Anne Kerr and Sydney Silverman at a CND demonstration

CHAPTER SEVENTEEN

DIFFERING WITH MAXTON

Whilst the Spanish war moved to its tragic conclusion Mussolini and Hitler began their territorial aggression, Italy invading Abyssinia and defying League of Nations sanctions. What should be the attitude of Socialists? We did not trust our own governments, but we opposed Fascist Italy's action. It was on this issue that I had my first serious difference with James Maxton whom I admired unreservedly and with whom I had worked in close cooperation for more than a decade.

Our International Bureau in Paris decided to press for action independently of governments by working-class refusal to handle arms or goods for Italy. This was the course, near to success, proposed against Nazism when it came to power in Germany and I had no doubt of ILP support. The National Council of the Party gave endorsement, the membership responded enthusiastically, and Maxton did not dissent. Three weeks later, however, he summoned a meeting of the Inner Executive (composed of three MPs, London's John Aplin and myself) and informed us that he could not support workers' sanctions because he believed they would encourage war with Italy. He carried his Parliamentary colleagues with him and Aplin and I had to agree to refer the issue to annual conference.

At the conference C. L. R. James, pioneer Black leader, immensely popular in the ILP as Socialist orator, moved the rejection of the Inner Executive view. George Buchanan and John McGovern spoke for the MPs and I had the distasteful task of publicly disagreeing with Maxton and them. The vote was taken in a tense atmosphere. When it was announced that the resolution had been carried by seventy votes to fifty-seven, Maxton said calmly that the Parliamentary Group would have to consider their position, but I knew from his demeanour that crisis was upon us. And so it proved.

At an emergency meeting of the National Council that evening Maxton tendered his resignation as chairman and told us that the MPs could not conscientiously apply the policy of conference; they would act independently on Abyssinia whilst hoping to reflect ILP policy in other respects. I realised at once that if we came into such conflict with Maxton and his colleagues it would mean the destruction of the Party and with relief accepted a proposal by James Carmichael, Scottish representative, that the difference should be submitted to a ballot of the Party membership. I had no illusions about the result. Maxton was not only revered but loved to a degree I have known of in no other leader. At the resumed conference next day I moved a compromise resolution, booed by some of my supporters for having 'ratted'. The vote showed a hard-core minority of thirty-nine; the plebiscite gave Maxton a majority of three to two. He remained chairman.

I did not take this set-back gravely. I was convinced of the policy of workers' action and was sure it would win support. Two years later the ILP conference endorsed it unanimously as a means of opposition to Japan, the MPs not opposing, perhaps because they felt they had already made clear their position. Japan had attacked China and our appeal to trade unions for action received promising response. The International Transport Workers Federation (its secretary, Edo Fimmen, a great Socialist, often cooperated with us) announced its readiness to operate a world boycott of goods to Japan, and at home the National Union of Railwaymen called on the TUC General Council to consider measures to the same end. It was the mounting crisis in Europe, submerging all other concerns, which diverted attention from China.

The parties attached to the Paris Bureau had established an International Front against War. Its representatives met in Europe (at the time I wrote for secrecy 'somewhere in Europe' and forty years later I do not remember where it was) and planned action across the frontiers should war occur. Our aim would be to end the war by Socialist revolution, political or insurgent according to national circumstances. We were depressed by the imminence of war but confident it would end in a workers' revolt. We parted sadly, knowing that some of us would not meet again. When war came many of our members were executed in Germany and Italy and even beyond. One of the most courageous was Heinricht Sneeveliet, chairman of the Revolutionary Socialist Workers Party of Holland. He was shot by the Nazis in July 1942.

When Neville Chamberlain returned from Berchtesgaden without a settlement, it seemed that we were faced by either extending Nazi oppression or a war in which neither side would be free from imperialism. The ILP

National Council adopted a statement drafted by Fred Jowett concentrating on the immediate need to stop hostilities but also giving endorsement to a fuller manifesto from the London ILP which sounded a warning both against war and a Hitler–Chamberlain patched up peace. John Aplin and I were authorised to edit and publish the manifesto and we did so to the evident satisfaction of the Party. At this point there was no hint of the renewal of any difference with Maxton and the MPs.

Then Chamberlain brought back from his Munich meeting with Hitler a peace which handed over thousands of people to Nazi oppression. As I read the agreement I was depressed almost to tears. I was relieved that war had not come, but I could think only with bitterness of the fate of Socialist comrades in Czechoslovakian Sudetenland, many of whom I had met. I saw them hounded to concentration camps and death, and was filled with anger against a situation which offered as alternatives the massacre of war or a peace of cruel injustice.

Before the debate in the Commons John Aplin and I saw Maxton at the House and urged him to refrain from endorsing the Munich Agreement. I have never seen him more distressed; his one aim was to stop the war and he would not commit himself on Munich. When I listened to the BBC report of the debate only one sentence of Maxton's speech was quoted, his congratulation to Neville Chamberlain. I was dismayed, but a little reassured when John McNair, who had been at the House, reported a strong indictment of imperialism, German and British. Next morning, however, the Press headlines blazoned that Maxton had congratulated the Prime Minister, and this was the public effect of the speech. I felt it imperative, therefore, that we should make clear that we did not endorse the Munich terms and at my request the Inner Executive met. When I asked permission to dissociate myself publicly from Maxton's acceptance of the Hitler–Chamberlain Agreement, with his usual tolerance he raised no objection, asking only that I should think it over for twenty-four hours. John Aplin alone supported me and together next morning we issued a statement to the Press. I learned later that Maxton was more hurt by my failure to wait twenty-four hours than by the statement, and I regretted that I was precipitate.

A word about John Aplin who cooperated so closely with me. He had been a skilled engineer, posted, though young, to large projects abroad; but he gave up his industrial career for Socialist activity. He was not magnetic as a speaker, but objective, clear-minded and logical. He married my earlier secretary, Marguerite Louis, and we were good friends.

When the Munich Agreement was discussed at the succeeding annual conference the delegates refused in successive resolutions either to condemn or congratulate the MPs. 'Well,' said Maxton to me as he rose from the chair, 'that means the Party did not like what we did but was not prepared to chastise us for it.' I think that was a correct estimate.

As chairman of the International Front against War I became involved in exciting adventures to assist our comrades in Italy and Germany. For the Italian Socialist Party we printed their paper, *Avanti*, smuggling it to Milan, and, because the normal size would be difficult to distribute, we produced a miniature *Das Banner* for the German Socialist Workers' Party, for whom we also prepared pamphlets camouflaged as cheap novels. I hesitated about doing this because I knew that anyone in Italy and Germany found with our productions would be sent to concentration camps, but those who faced the danger insisted. In fact, many were arrested, and in our Paris office they were listed on a roll of honour. The courage of the resisters was wonderful. There was a Viennese girl who crossed the frontiers three times in 1938 and 1939 to strengthen contacts and to make arrangements for comrades in danger to escape. On one occasion she told us of a heroic girl who was being hunted by the SS. Could we find a British boy to marry her so that she would obtain our nationality? I sent her photograph – she appeared to be very beautiful – to a leading young ILP-er in the North. I believe he would have agreed, but his mother would not hear of it. I do not give his name because he is now a colleague of mine in the House of Lords. A young man in Stockholm offered to marry the threatened girl and she gained Swedish nationality and they were both happy.

I could tell many stories. Perhaps one can safely be recorded now. The London representative of the Austrian Socialists wished to go to Vienna on an urgent mission to plan common action with German Socialists against Hitler. Had we anyone like him in appearance whose passport he could use? My mind leaped to Viscount Churchill who had fought against Franco in Spain; they were extraordinarily similar. The Viscount loaned his passport and when it was presented at the frontier the immigration officers were so impressed by the name that they waved on the Austrian Socialist without further questioning. Because he would still be proud of it, I can mention the name of another member of the Upper House who loaned his passport for a similar mission. Although modestly in the background, Lord Faringdon has never hidden his deep pacifist and Socialist convictions. Passports soon proved of first importance. We became experts in London and Paris in forging them for anti-Nazi purposes. I was alarmed when one of ours with evidence of its source was discovered by the police in the East End of London, but no interrogation followed. Were the authorities unwilling to prosecute illegal anti-Nazi activities? In Paris the production of false passports was extensive, saving many lives. My colleague in the House of Lords still recalls with a chuckle how he helped in the process.

We had the duty of caring for refugees when they reached this country. During the period between Hitler's occupation of Sudetenland and Prague an urgent appeal came to get forty-eight Socialists to England; their lives would not be safe for a day if they fell into Nazi hands. They had an inspiring record. They were of German origin but had devoted themselves to securing unity with Czech workers and had achieved considerable success, gaining control of several local councils. When we received the rescue call John McNair put everything aside. Through our Paris contacts he arranged false passports and a hazardous journey across Poland, and great was our relief when they arrived.

On the morning of Christmas Eve I was preparing to leave London to join my children at Rickmansworth when the Kensington police phoned. There had been a fire at the small hotel where three of the refugees had been placed; one of them had been burned to death and the two others were under treatment at Paddington Hospital. With Edith King I went to the hospital and brought the two injured men to our rooms, Edith tending to them. One was slightly burned, the other with smoke-filled lungs. The dead comrade was Bruno Reichart, deputy mayor of his home town. I could not throw off a feeling of responsibility for his death. It was not a happy Christmas.

Edith and I were now living together. I had a deep love for my wife Lilla. She had been wonderful in the way she had supported me in difficult times, particularly during the war when she had brought up two babies in a caravan whilst I was in prison. She was a marvellous mother. For some years we had been separated maritally. I had been a bad husband. I had had several affairs, some serious but not enduring. With Edith it was different. We were co-operating closely in Socialist activities and this developed into complete identity. I did not hide our association from Lilla and at weekends I would go to Rickmansworth to see the girls and she was always kind. To anticipate, in 1945 Lilla agreed to divorce and Edith and I married. My close friendship with Lilla remained.

Edith and I lived in Keir Hardie's rooms in Neville's Court, not the rooms where thirty years ago I had first interviewed him, but in the squire's house of the old Elizabethan village to which he moved when the crumbling buildings on the other side of the court were demolished. Our mansion was strong, with a marvellous timbered staircase. The rooms were let mostly to journalists. Above us was Ian Mackay whom I admired greatly for his forthright contributions to the *News Chronicle*. Opposite us was a well-known woman journalist on the *Daily Express* who shocked us all by committing suicide.

During the summer of 1939 the clouds of war became blacker and blacker. I campaigned all over the country, two occasions still in my mind. I was to debate at Aberdeen University with Oswald Mosley's first lieutenant, William Joyce, later the infamous 'Lord Haw Haw'. I had been doing a series of meetings for the Scottish ILP and was wearing grey trousers and a sports jacket. An instruction came that for the debate I must be suitably attired. Fortunately the ILP comrade with whom I was staying was a tailor and he adorned me appropriately. Great was my disgust at the dinner table before the debate to find Joyce in his Fascist black shirt. Worse was to follow. Joyce delivered a clever speech, winning sympathy by pointing to a scar on his cheek where he said a 'Communist thug' had slashed him and then indicting capitalism with a thoroughness no Socialist could have surpassed. The Fascist Corporate State was the answer. After this my democratic Socialism was too tame for the Aberdeen students and when the vote came Joyce won. This was less than six months before the outbreak of war. I have never been so humiliated.

The second occasion was a debate on conscription at the Gray's Inn Union in London. My opponents were St J. Hutchinson and Randolph Churchill. Randolph outdid his father in denunciation of Neville Chamberlain's appeasement of Hitler. Of course in such company I was defeated, the KC chairman expressing surprise that 'Good King Charles' and 'Good Queen Bess' had not descended from their portraits on the wall in protest against my views. I once met Randolph Churchill afterwards. With both hands he was angrily banging a table in a self-service restaurant at the Kensington terminal of the British BEA. I asked him what was the matter. 'Scandalous!' he exploded. 'They won't serve me. Expect me, the son of the Prime Minister, to help myself at the counter!' I regret to say that the staff gave in to him.

At the Gray's Inn debate Randolph Churchill prophesied that war would come within three months. He was right.

CHAPTER EIGHTEEN

DILEMMA OF THE SECOND WAR

Edith and I were in Keir Hardie's living room on Sunday, 2 September, awaiting eleven o'clock when Britain's ultimatum to Germany would expire. I thought of Hardie's hope that workers' action across the frontiers would prevent war. The clock struck and Neville Chamberlain's voice came across the radio announcing war. Immediately the siren sounded a warning of approaching German planes. We went down to the cellar, but it was only a try-out.

Hardie's hope was far away, but that afternoon's post brought a message, posted through Sweden, from our group of German Socialists. I read it with a sense of almost spiritual identity. It ran:

In the moment before the cannons speak, before the world faces horror and manslaughter, we send our message to you. The German workers do not want this war; the German peasants do not want war. Hitler begins the war with Poland against the will of large masses of the population. This war is not our war, this fight is not our fight, and we ask you, in the midst of death and destruction, do not forget the ideas for which we have died under torture, do not forget the ideals for which we have suffered in the concentration camps. Comrades, you love your country and we love our country, but our common fatherland is humanity.

Alas, the German masses soon supported the war, but I wondered how many of those who sent these moving words would in the months ahead face imprisonment and the firing squad.

The war forced on me a dilemma. I was in all my nature opposed to war. I could never see myself killing anyone and had never held a weapon in my hands. But I saw that Hitler and Nazism had been mainly responsible for bringing the war and I could not contemplate their victory. In a sense, the

Spanish civil war had settled this dilemma for me; I could no longer justify pacifism when there was a Fascist threat. It had not quite settled it. I was prepared to defend the workers' revolution in Barcelona, but I had no wish to defend Britain's capitalist regime or its imperialist government. I had to compromise. I could not oppose the war unreservedly as I had in 1914, but I would cooperate in civilian activities, and I would work for the ending of the war by Socialist revolution – democratic one hoped. This was not wholly the attitude of the ILP. During the war I twice stood as its Parliamentary candidate, at Lancaster and Cardiff, and it was evident when Maxton read my election addresses that he was disappointed I had not come out forthrightly against the war. Characteristically he said no word of disapproval and in his speeches went no further than to say we must stop the war by Socialism.

Lancaster was old ground – I had fought it in 1922 – but now conditions were very different. The Labour Party had joined the Coalition and my opponent, Fitzroy Maclean, was endorsed by the three Party leaders. He was an officer in a Highland regiment and excused himself from speech-making on the ground that his uniform prohibited him from political utterance. I am sure his uniform won him more votes than speeches would have done; he had a fine figure, and his short kilt revealed splendid legs; he would wander round my open-air meetings, and women would pay more attention to him than to my speeches. He even turned up for nomination in uniform, dumbfounded when the Returning Officer told him that his papers could not be accepted whilst he was in army dress. Eventually he was permitted nomination on condition that he removed his belt. Maclean did a brave and broadminded job as British intelligence officer with Marshal Tito's rebel army in Yugoslavia in the war and wrote of his experience in *Eastern Approaches*. Later I was with him in the Commons, and the contrast between the fine writing in this book and his pedestrian speaking surprised me. He won the election at Lancaster by 15,783 votes to my 5,418.

My second election was at Cardiff against Sir Edward Grigg on his appointment as Minister of War. The campaign against me was ferocious. On the morning of polling day the local daily had a heading across its front page: 'Hitler the First to Vote for Brockway', justifying the streamer by a German broadcast, camouflaged as 'Workers' Voice', which urged support for me, and during the day a loudspeaker van toured every street denouncing me as a coward who would not fight for his country. Sir Edward Grigg himself was friendly, telling me at the count that to a considerable extent he agreed with my Socialist aims. I polled a third of his vote, 3,311 to his 10,030, regarded by us as quite good against a Minister of War in the middle of a war. Significant were three by-elections won by the Commonwealth Party started by Sir Richard Acland, organised spectacularly by Kim MacKay with his much-photographed 'glamour girl canvassers'. Whilst supporting the war, the Party was challengingly anti-Establishment, which reflected the growing mood of the people.

The idea of a Socialist revolution after the war was not fanciful. Had not the First World War ended with the Soviet Revolution? At war-time Christmas, less than four months on, British and German troops fraternised across no-man's-land despite the orders of the High Commands. What did that promise? Perhaps romantically the ILP took the prospect of revolt too seriously. We gathered the equipment for a mobile broadcasting station to send out its revolutionary call to Europe when the time came. The plan was nearly revealed. The essential crystal could be obtained without licence only in Paris, and Bob Edwards, Edith and I took advantage of a meeting with associates there and bought one. At the customs at Dover I had the crystal in a back trouser pocket. We got through, but I showed my relief too blatantly and was called back to be searched. By good luck there were two back pockets. The officer emptied one of my diary, thumbed through it, and waved me on. The smiles on the faces of Bob and Edith should have told him he had not been thorough.

The announcement of the Hitler–Stalin Pact, under which Germany and Russia would divide Poland, had a devastating effect on the Left in Britain. Overnight it changed the attitude of the Communist Party from pro-war to anti-war and it stunned Socialists. The news came over the radio whilst the ILP National Council was in session. Again it caused a difference with Maxton. Our chairman was Dr C. A. Smith (about whom more later), and he supported me in urging a strong denunciation of Russia. Maxton advised caution and only mild criticism was expressed.

I admit that my reaction was partly subjective. I thought of many comrades I knew in Poland, among them Joseph and Eirene Kruk. Joseph was secretary of the Polish ILP and we had been colleagues on the Executive of the Second International, often a minority of two against the great battalions. Eirene was a doctor in charge of a clinic for tubercular children; Joseph had named a workers' education centre at Czenstochowo after me. What would be their fate if the German and Russian armies advanced from two sides on their Jewish ghetto? The fate of many thousands when heroic Warsaw was destroyed we now know. As the tanks arrived Joseph and Eirene escaped to Estonia, then to Stockholm, and finally to Israel, where later I visited their vine-covered cottage. Joseph became an acclaimed historian of international Socialism.

Another sequel to the Stalin–Hitler pact was more tragic: one of the crimes for which I have never been able to forgive Stalinist Russia was the arrest and execution of the two leaders of the Polish Social Democratic Party, Ehrlich and Adler. They also had served on the Executive of the Socialist International and on many issues, though not invariably, supported my Leftist challenges. I admired them greatly. They were captured by the Russians, taken as prisoners to Moscow and shot. An infamous crime.

C. A. Smith, the ILP chairman, was an extraordinary man. A brilliant scholar, he rejected academic appointments to devote himself to lecturing for the Workers' Educational Association. I was at one of his classes and marvelled at the way he involved the students. But he had a mind so incessantly active that it responded to events with startling changes – he was like Richard Crossman in that respect. At the beginning of the war he urged Maxton and me to issue a call to all young members of the ILP to become conscientious objectors and regarded us as faint-hearts when we declined. When the Soviet Union revoked its pact with Hitler and joined the Allies against the Nazis, he became pro-war; when Soviet troops attacked Finland he became anti-war again. He was engagingly sincere, but his inconsistencies made it impossible for the ILP to retain him as chairman.

For many months Britain experienced the 'Phoney War'. The Nazi armies massacred Poland, but in the west there was little action. Then the German forces drove back the French and the isolated British were rescued heroically from Dunkirk. Chamberlain's feebleness was replaced by Churchill and a Coalition Government which the Labour Party joined. The war became vicious with the bombing of London, Coventry, Plymouth. A German invasion of Britain was possible, saved by the epic courage of Air Force pilots in the Battle of Britain. I could not be indifferent to these events. My eldest daughter Audrey lived at Westerham, a few miles from Biggin Hill, the air base from which the pilots flew. I visited her sometimes and heard the roar of the aircraft, German bombers aiming at London, British fighters intercepting them, the explosion of guns and once the crash as a plane fell. However sceptical about war aims, one was inescapably involved.

My uneasy conscience and frustration were relieved by action when I returned to Neville's Court. It arose from a frightening night. We were in the cellar when the swish of incendiaries through the air was followed by a loud thud above. I raced upstairs – two floors, three, four. There was sizzling behind a bedroom door, it was locked, I crashed it. In the middle of the bed was a fountain of flame. I bent the mattress, but could not reach the opposite end. I looked round and there was one of our journalist residents. Together we carried the burning mass to the window and threw it out. We saw that Neville's Court was covered by flaming incendiaries, ran down and emptied buckets of sand on the nearest fires and dug up earth to cover them. I became aware of a young lad digging at our side; he lived next door and was awaiting call-up to the navy. Together we worked our way down the Court, putting out fires, and met others doing the same. This gave me the idea. Six of us formed ourselves into a Voluntary Fire Guard for the Court. Two watched each night, the four others on call. It was this which lifted the burden of doubt and guilt from my mind; I was doing a positive service. I sent the idea to my old colleague, Herbert Morrison, who was Home Secretary. He replied cordially that he was thinking of setting up a national Fire Guard Service. Later he did.

There was a terrible night when a bomb roared deafeningly and earth hit the house like a giant wave, the walls rocking. I ran out and there was the lad from next door. He was shattered. The bomb had fallen fifty yards away on waste land where the demolished Elizabethan houses had been, and he had been flung heavily to the ground many yards away. There was no time to linger. We heard muffled shrieks – and remembered there was an underground shelter. We hurried with our spades. The Home Guard was already there and soon the Fire Brigade. We dug hysterically, still hearing the cries below. Fifty bodies were brought up.

Two old ladies lived in our basement, one eighty years of age looking after a mentally deficient sixty-year-old; we found her one night hunting for her pet cat whilst incendiaries fell around her. During the bombing they slept under the open chimney in the cellar, blankets covering their heads, but when the bomb hit the Court shelter we decided this was not protection enough. One of our journalists invited us to bring them when things were hot to the *Daily Express* offices where, three floors down, they would be 'as safe as in the Sahara'. Safe when they got there, perhaps, but the next night, when Edith and I shepherded them to Fleet Street, we were all near to death. Incendiaries fell all about us as we shuffled the old dears through Gough Square. The *Express* was only a stone's throw away, but it was the longest walk of our lives. The incendiaries hit the pavement a few yards ahead, a few yards behind, dropping straight, ricocheting off Samuel Johnson's house. Somehow we escaped. From then on we took the old ladies across to Fleet Street before the bombers were due to arrive.

There came the Great Fire when every building within a mile of St Paul's Cathedral seemed to be alight. We looked at the approaching flames; the building behind us was already burning; our walls were hot; and, in-formed on the phone by the Fire Brigade that they were too busy to help, we decided to leave. We gathered together the few essentials we could carry and said farewell to many things dear to us and to our revered Hardie rooms. A lighter incident brought relief. 'The cat – the old ladies' cat!' exclaimed Edith. They were at the *Daily Express*; the journalists were with their papers; we were alone in the building except for the pet in the basement. Edith gave me a cushion cover, but it proved impossible to catch the cat. Frightened by the flames and noise, it leaped madly from floor to table, from table to sideboard. All I could do was to stun it with a blow to the head. 'There's your cat,' I said to Edith as the cushion cover collapsed on the inert body. But we carried it to safety.

Our retreat was the ILP office in near-by St Bride's Street, but everything between was alight. We had to make a long detour of Holborn, stumbling over a confusion of hoses, through clanging fire engines, beneath ladders straight in the air with little men at the top directing streams of water on burning buildings; drenched to the skin, brushed aside by impatient officials, two lonely refugees struggling under heavy loads and surrounded by a destroyed world. Somehow we reached the ILP headquarters – miraculously standing with flames all around – lighted a gas fire (ironically operating), threw off our clothes and collapsed on uncomfortable office chairs. The cat came to life and was strangely amiable.

In the early morning, still dark, we made our way along Fleet Street – almost unscathed except for St Bride's Church whose wedding-cake steeple, silver-lit by fire within, looked incredibly beautiful – and found a haven in the Strand Corner House, open all night. We did not expect to see 10 Neville's Court again, but the Fire Brigade were better than their word. When we returned at dawn, Number 10, though scorched, was uniquely standing.

The minister of the Moravian church, of which the old ladies were members, persuaded them to evacuate with their cat to Somerset. That was a relief – but they were back in three weeks. I thought the story of returning Londoners was a fable but they said fantastically, 'We found it too quiet.' When, however, the bombing continued they were fortunately persuaded to go to a small town in Hertfordshire, apparently noisy enough.

We also decided to leave, taking refuge in a block of flats on Holly Lodge estate at Highgate, one of several previously restricted to women. Ours was pleasantly named Makepeace Mansions. I became sector captain of the Fire Brigade, standing on the roof at night watching the approaching bombers, able to tell their direction by the point at which they crossed the horizon. I was the only man in our voluntary Brigade, which gained a reputation for its enthusiasm and efficiency, so much so that the North London commandant came to observe us. Alas, the first couple were so nervous that they failed to attach the hose to the engine, and our model display was a flop. News came that Number 10 Neville's Court had gone, and also the ILP Head Office, which caused me special distress because my papers and books were there, including autographed first editions of Shaw.

I continued to edit the *New Leader*, taking copy late at night to St Pancras station to despatch to the ILP printers at Leicester. The journeys to the station were bomb-molested: one night our bus was lifted into the air by an explosion. My most vivid memory is of a wet night when I found a boy huddled on St Pancras steps. He sold papers and had not earned enough that day to pay for a bed. He was hungry and I took him to a swell restaurant which was opposite King's Cross. The manager placed brown paper over the velvet seat to protect it from his muddy clothes, and both staff and customers were shocked when he took the tureen of soup in both hands and put it to his lips. I got him into a home to train for a job.

In addition to my editing, I was writing a biography of Fred Jowett, part-time worker in a mill at the age of ten, rising to become Cabinet Minister. Jowett, feeble at eighty-four, clung to life to see the book, but, alas, died before it was published. I chose the title *Socialism Over Sixty Years* because I knew no one whose story more reflected the struggle at the grass roots than Jowett's from the 1880s to the 1940s. I was also doing a lot of speaking about the country, often travelling by lorry with an ILP driver rather than by uncertain trains. Lorries did not come into London during the bombing, stopping at London Colney in Hertfordshire from where we would start at dawn.

My divided view of the war prevented me from endorsing the attitude of conscientious objectors, but I believed so profoundly in personal liberty that I became chairman of the Central Board for Conscientious Objectors which represented a remarkable grouping of pacifist, religious and liberal bodies. I negotiated with Ernest Bevin, then Minister of Labour, and was impressed by his breadth of view. He offered to exempt from military service all associated with our organisations if they would limit their personal incomes to soldiers' pay, diverting the surplus to a charitable purpose, 'even to a peace society'. I thought this just, but the Board turned it down, regarding such an agreement as condoning conscription. I represented many COs at tribunals and courts martial. Two occasions I particularly remember. The first was the case of an Indian who was not prepared to fight for Britain whilst self-government was denied to his country. After a short term in prison, he came before the Appellate Tribunal where I succeeded in getting him exemption. This was an important case because the supreme tribunal accepted the view that a political conviction could be regarded as conscientious under the Act. The second occasion was at a court martial where I represented a young Jehovah's Witness who had been imprisoned five times for refusal to obey military orders. An officer expressed surprise that I should be defending a man with whose beliefs I had no sympathy. I told him that the boy's courage and willingness to undergo repeated punishments proved sincerity, and I got him off. My motivation was a belief that conscience cannot be ruled by the State – a principle which became important later when the dissidents were penalised in the Soviet Union and, alas, in many countries.

I came into conflict with Communists again over the case of a refugee from Nazism. Wolf Nelki and his blonde girlfriend Erna, both members of the Leftist Communist Opposition in Germany, had escaped with our help just before the war broke out. At the beginning of hostilities they had been interned with all of German origin in the Isle of Man, but as an anti-Nazi Wolf was soon freed. Erna, however, was kept in custody, and Maxton learned from the Minister that she was under suspicion and was to appear before the Aliens Tribunal. I investigated her record in detail. She had been arrested with four Communist leaders for underground activity against the Hitler regime, but evidence of her complicity was insufficient and she was discharged whilst her colleagues were sentenced to imprisonment. With the aid of our associates she had escaped to Paris and had joined Wolf in London. I found that she had the complete confidence of her German comrades and was puzzled why doubts had arisen, particularly since the Refugee Committee, investigating cases in the first instance, had given her a letter for the Aliens Tribunal certifying her *bona fide*. I went to see Sir Norman Birkett, chairman of the Tribunal, who revealed to me that an official of the Refugee Committee had simultaneously sent him a confidential letter saying that she was a suspected spy, suggesting that she had been discharged from her trial in Germany because she was an informer. Sir Norman went to infinite pains to get at the truth and had no doubt about finally releasing Erna. I was shocked to learn that the conflicting communication from the Refugee Committee had been sent by a prominent member of the German Communist Party who was bitterly opposed to the breakaway Communist Opposition of which Erna was a member. I have remained a friend of Wolf and Erna ever since. Two more dedicated Socialists could not be found.

The British Communists followed the Soviet Union slavishly. They had advocated a Popular Front coalition with Churchill before the war and were expectedly pro-war at the start of hostilities. With the Stalin–Hitler pact they became anti-war, changing again when the Soviet Union and Germany broke. The leadership was not united in these turns. I remember meeting Palme Dutt, consistent Marxist theorist, on a train the morning the Party became anti-war and he was overjoyed that it had returned to the classical line. The rank and file obediently supported their leaders, sometimes with confusion. The day I travelled with Dutt I met a Manchester Communist who had not heard of the change, and I provoked him to defend the Party's support of the war, which he did fervently. Then I handed him the *Daily Worker* with the announcement of the reversal of policy. He was dumbfounded.

The ILP, concentrating on advocacy of post-war Socialism, did not become involved in military controversies such as the campaign for a European Second Front, but we challenged the massive destruction of civilian populations in German towns to which the military resorted after the Nazi bombing of London and other cities. Air Chief Marshal Sir Arthur Harris had the support of Anthony Eden, the Foreign Secretary, who termed it 'psychological warfare', but the Air Minister, Sir Archibald Sinclair, was on the defensive when anxious church leaders made enquiries, saying that the civilian losses were incidental to the bombing of military targets. After the war I saw the devastation in Hamburg and Dresden where thousands of men, women and children were slaughtered – approaching the number destroyed by the atom bomb on Hiroshima.

As always in war, there were the extreme patriots who identified all the people of enemy territories with their rulers. Lord Vansittart was their spokesman, hating the German people as much as he hated Hitler. The ILP prepared a manifesto signed by an extraordinary list of liberal-minded leaders reminding the British people that thousands of Germans were in concentration camps for opposing Hitler: it gained valuable publicity and we organised vast distribution. The author of the manifesto was Will Cove, past chairman of the National Union of Teachers and later a Labour MP. It was one of the finest examples of political writing I have known, and when I joined Will in the Commons I was disappointed he had not made a mark. He became disillusioned with Parliamentary procedure and his talents were wasted. During the war our small group of ILP MPs was courageous but isolated. In addition to the Commonwealth Party, there was Nye Bevan, never afraid of challenging Churchill, always proving that he was a Socialist in Britain as well as an enemy of Nazism in Germany. He did much to keep the soul of Socialism alive.

I have written a personal story of the war years, sometimes irrelevant and always trivial amidst the gigantic issues fought with suffering and sacrifice of millions. I have criticised Soviet Russia, but the war would have ended in a

Hitler triumph had it not been for the epic resistance of her people to the Nazi invasion. Stalingrad was immortal. Churchill's greatness one had to recognise. I did so profoundly as I listened to his broadcast welcoming Russia as an ally despite his hatred of invasions. My thoughts were continually with my associates in France, Belgium, Holland, Norway, typifying many others in their courageous resistance. We were never invaded, never occupied, but our men and women, British and Commonwealth, held fast when all seemed lost. America's intervention was decisive. At rare moments one could escape from tension to be philosophic and recognise that a similar courage, however bad the cause, was shown on the other side. One could also contemplate on the tragedy that all this heroism, all this acceptance of suffering, was directed to war.

Towards the end of the war the mood of the people began to change. They had demonstrated national unity against Nazism, but they became increasingly alive to Britain's social inequalities and injustices. The wives of soldiers began to tell of letters expressing a growing resentment among servicemen of the class division between officers and the ranks and of a rising anger against injustice in a society which they had been fighting to defend. Our dream of Socialism after the war was becoming real; we glimpsed the gathering clouds but we did not foresee the storm which would sweep the Churchill Government away when peace came. That was to surprise us all.

I had an unexpected honour at the end of the war. Among Hitler's undestroyed papers was his list of those to be executed when his forces won. It included my name.

CHAPTER NINETEEN

AN ACTIVE VACUUM

I sat in the gallery at the Labour Party Conference at Blackpool when the decision was taken to break the Coalition Government and to fight the coming election independently. I was inspired. If dynamism for change was revolutionary, then the Socialist revolution for which the ILP had striven was imminent. I knew I had to rejoin Labour.

The General Election of 1945 came before I left the ILP. Labour swept the country. I wanted the ILP to nominate me at Woodford against Winston Churchill, whom the Labour Party was not opposing. Maxton would not hear of it, Churchill was too popular. In the event, a freak candidate ran against him and came sensationally near. We underestimated public opinion and particularly opinion in the forces. Many soldiers, sailors and airmen abroad wrote to their wives asking them to vote as Left as they could. The ILP put forward a mere six candidates; their four previous MPs returned. This pathetic showing proved completely how we had lost contact with the masses of people.

Our relationship to the Labour Party was discussed by the National Council of the ILP. Maxton was absent, stricken by the illness which brought his death before the end of the year, but his influence was dominant. We all knew his view, as tolerant as ever. If we thought it desirable to rejoin the Labour Party he would not complain, but personally he could not do so, feeling he had greater opportunity to serve Socialism by retaining independence. We took part in the discussion one by one, with myself, sitting to the left of the chairman, leading off. I urged that the ILP should become an educational organisation, continuing its fundamental Socialist teaching which had always been its strength, but permitting its members to join the Labour Party for electoral purposes. For the first time Maxton's Parliamentary colleagues, Campbell Stephen and George Buchanan, supported me, but few others did. The Council was captured by the optimism of Bob Edwards, the chairman, who prophesied that the future confrontation would be between, not Toryism and Labour, but reformism and revolution – the latter winning. The vote went overwhelmingly for romanticism rather than realism. I gathered my papers and went silently to my room. I had no doubt that I must resign from the ILP but it was a wrench. For thirty-eight years I had lived for it.

I went to see Maxton in his cottage home at Largs in Ayrshire. He lay on his bed in the front room reading Tawney, still smoking cigarettes, still that winning smile lighting his blue eyes, still flicking back his long black hair; but he knew he was to die. His clasp of my hand was tight and long, and I was a coward – I could not tell him I had resigned from the Party. I told Madeleine, his disciple wife – she was his voluntary secretary, they had married in 1935 – as we took tea on the grass in front of the bedroom. 'I hoped you would not do it until Jimmy had gone,' she said quietly. The end came a few weeks later. I delayed joining the Labour Party until he had passed.

Maxton was Keir Hardie's natural successor. Hardie created the Labour Party. Maxton sought to make it a Socialist Party. He did not succeed – few would say that it is yet Socialist in practice – but he converted more people to real Socialism, its spirit and purpose, than any man in Britain. In his sixty-one years he addressed more meetings and spoke to more people than anyone, and he rarely spoke without making converts, changing their conception of life fundamentally. He did this not only by convincing argument and inspiring eloquence, but because Socialism to him was a religion and his hearers sensed intuitively that his words were himself. When he entered prison he registered Socialism as his religion and when told that this was politics replied that it was his one guide to life. Walter Elliott in his obituary tribute on the BBC said that Maxton was a Socialist before Socialism. Everyone who knew Maxton knows how true that was. He treated all human beings as equals, the Labourer and the Lord, at the same time subservient to none. When sympathy was voiced that he had had to mix with criminals in prison he retorted that he had only twice seen criminal features – in a senior official of the High Court and in his mirror. He had an extraordinarily high sense of morality, returning any present given for service as a Member of Parliament. There was one exception. A woman whom he helped made him a pair of socks with his name knitted in white wool. He was amused as well as grateful and used to pull up his trouser legs to show them to his friends. His sincerity gained him the respect and even affection of his political opponents. Ill in hospital he received messages from Tory and Liberal leaders, and Churchill sent him a parcel of books. He used to tell with some glee how the matron excitedly informed him that the most famous man in Britain had enquired about him. 'And who was that?' asked Maxton. 'Lloyd George – I told him you were getting on well.' Maxton's sense of humour broke through. 'And did he not say that's a pity?' he commented smiling. In fact Maxton was pleased to get these messages. 'To win respect for Socialism is half the battle,' he remarked. Lloyd George had sent Maxton to prison, but no bitterness remained. He hated the politics of his opponents, but he hated no one. He used to say that if he had had their background he might have been the same. He loved the human race and was tolerant to all. That was Maxton.

I did not join the Labour Party until a year after leaving the ILP. I had to adjust myself. I spent the time in the congenial task of writing the biography of Dr Alfred Salter of Bermondsey. He was extraordinary. The most brilliant medical student of his time, he deliberately turned his back on a successful career to become a slum doctor. His identity with the people became a tragedy, his only child, a daughter, dying from an epidemic in the slum school. Salter was a Quaker Socialist, winning the local council for the ILP, beautifying Bermondsey by planting trees in every street, winning the Parliamentary seat. He died broken-hearted during the war. *Bermondsey Story* was my best book. Dick Crossman in the *New Statesman* even described it as a perfect biography. If there was merit it was due to the unique subject.

During this political interval I also participated in an ambitious project to launch a revolutionary 'Readers Digest', revolutionary in the sense that it would seek to reflect all that was progressive and creative in politics, economics, science and art. The idea of *World Affairs* came from the son of the publisher who, before Hitler, dominated newspaper production in Germany, and for a year Julius Braunthal, a cultured Austrian who had been attached to the Socialist International (and wrote its history), and I worked as prospective editors. We even reached the stage of preparing a dummy copy, but, alas, the German family got into legal conflict and there was no money to proceed.

I expected this period to be a vacuum in my life, but, instead, I had a series of surprising events. In 1946 came an invitation from the Hamburg Trades Council to address their first May Day demonstration in fourteen years. I did not think there was a chance; no British politician had been permitted to address a public meeting in Germany since the war. Nevertheless, I wrote to Ernest Bevin for permission – and incredibly it was given.

I had been the last British Socialist to speak in Germany before Hitler came to power; now I was to be the first to do so after his fall. I had not foreseen all the consequences. I was requested to report to a military command in Whitehall and when I did so began to feel like Alice in Wonderland. I entered a lift on an open space where Admiralty House now stands. We shot underground, I think three floors. There I found long passages with offices on either side, air-conditioned, fully equipped. I was told Whitehall was honeycombed like this, the passages continuing to Downing Street. This was the dug-out for the Cabinet and War Office in the event of bombing.

I learned that I could go to Germany only if I joined the army temporarily. I was given the rank of captain and handed a uniform. As I donned it I laughed inwardly at the irony of what I was doing. In the First World War I had been court martialled for refusing to put on a uniform! Yet I had no doubts. This time the uniform was the symbol not of military service, but of a Socialist mission to an enemy country.

I had a second surprise. My successor as editor of the *New Leader* asked that Wolf Nelki should accompany me as its representative. Although as a German he had been interned at the beginning of the war, amazingly permission was given. Wolf's knowledge of German was an inestimable help to me.

The Hamburg demonstration was the largest I have ever addressed, estimated at 100,000, stretching across a vast space in the city's equivalent of Hyde Park (*Planten und Blumen*) to its distant lake: people were massed on either side and even on the further bank, their red banners mirrored in the water. It was breathtaking. I spoke from a hill through a microphone which I was told had last been used by Hitler. My message was the contribution which trade unions could make to democracy, and it was received rapturously. I was hurried away to a smaller demonstration some miles distant, and then to the first post-war conference of the Social Democratic Party. I found myself sitting next to Ashley Bramall, a young Intelligence Officer for the British, later Labour MP and chairman of the Inner London Education Authority. I was deeply impressed by Kurt Schumacher, the Social Democratic leader, a heroic figure burning with fervour in great contrast to the comfortable German bureaucrats I had met in the Second International. I saw in him the tragedy of Germany. He had lost an arm in the First World War, and he bore the physical marks of nine years in a concentration camp, teeth knocked out by Gestapo thugs, glazed eyes, a starved body. Yet, when he spoke, this sickly man became transformed, his features alight, his voice strong, his personality so vivid that one forgot his deformities. It was what he said which impressed me most. He denounced German

Reaction and Stalinist Communism, but he also had the courage to attack the Western military administration, calling on German workers to be self-reliant and independent in the struggle for Socialism. Alas, Schumacher died soon after. Had he lived the subsequent history of Germany would have been different.

I went to the Ruhr and saw its devastation, and to Berlin where I met the giant Austin Albu, later a colleague in the House of Commons, then Political Adviser to the Military Governor, and General Sir Brian Robertson, the Deputy Governor, who conducted a press conference with greater ability than any Cabinet Minister I have sat under. I was shocked by the intimidation the Russians exerted to compel the Social Democratic Party to become junior partners with the Communist Party. My overall disappointment was the enforced political vacuum which the West, including Britain, imposed on their sectors. It seemed to me that after the defeat of Hitler mass opinion was ready for a basic revolution. I was dismayed by Ernest Bevin's endorsement of the American pressure to hand back the mines and steel works of the Ruhr to private ownership (ultimately to Krupps). The British need not have imposed Socialism as the Russians imposed Communism, but we destroyed even the opportunity for Socialism.

Before I left England, Victor Gollancz's campaign had made me aware of the hunger from which the German people were suffering, but it was worse than I had expected. One could never get away from it. I used to save a roll after each meal and offer it shyly to a boy or girl in the street; but soon I realised that no one was ashamed to take food. I was shown a day's ration on a small tray; as one meal it would have left an average Englishman hungry. I was appalled when I went to a mental hospital to find that the patients were still on the diet which Hitler devised deliberately to starve them to death, on the principle that lunatics were not worth preserving. When I got back to London I hurried to John Hynd, the Minister for German Affairs. He could not believe me, but sent immediate instructions for the diet to be lifted. His enquiries elicited the explanation that an order sent when the British took over to increase hospital diets had not been applied to mental institutions because they were not classified as hospitals.

All was not well in hospitals. When I went to Hamburg's General Hospital I found that malnutrition cases had proved fatal because the doctors could not get the amino-acids required in the diet. I was amazed by the ingenuity with which they collected a supply. They obtained the necessary cystines from human hair rounded up from the barbers' shops in the town. I was shown tin boxes packed with hair of all colours, cleaned and disinfected, and I tasted a sandwich of the human hair product. It might have been Marmite. Back in London, I wrote an almost minute-by-minute description of my visit, *German Diary*, which Gollancz rushed out with characteristic sympathy. Official permission to speak and tour in Germany was followed by another surprise. A letter from my publisher informed me that the Control Commission had acceded to a German request that my *Inside the Left* should be printed there. I was astonished because the book expressed my Socialist views and was severely critical of British policy. I concluded that I must have a friend in the Foreign Office.

Then came a greater surprise. An Indonesian sailor serving as a wireless operator in the Netherlands navy knocked at our Highgate door and excitedly exclaimed that he had a communication for me. He told me how he had picked up a long message from Sukarno, President of Indonesia, addressed to me. Edith and I could not believe him. We knew that the Indonesians, after the defeat of the Japanese, had resisted the restoration of the Dutch colonial administration and set up their own government. We knew that the Netherlands navy, regrettably with British help, was blockading Indonesia; contact with the outside world was possible only by wireless. Was it really true that Sukarno had attempted to reach me and that by chance this young Indonesian had intercepted his message? Over coffee we were convinced. The message, which our Indonesian visitor had roughly typed, set out broad terms for a settlement. In it Sukarno, perhaps remembering my chairmanship of the defunct League against Imperialism (although only a student, he had been present at the Brussels conference), asked me to set negotiations going.

Luck was with us. A long-time Socialist friend, a member of the Netherlands delegation to the first assembly of the United Nations, was in London en route for San Francisco. Peter Schmidt had been London correspondent of *Het Volk* during the Second World War, had joined the ILP and had married an ILP girl. Returning to Holland he had established the Independent Socialist Party, and during the Second World War was a recognised leader of the resistance to the Nazi occupation. His wife had been captured by the Nazis and was reported to have been shot. After the war he joined the Social Democrats and rose to high office.

Peter was my obvious contact with the Netherlands Government and over the phone I arranged that Edith and I should have lunch the next day with him and his new young wife. At our lunch Peter agreed that the Sukarno terms were negotiable – they offered the release of all Netherlands prisoners and compensation for property taken over – and, after annotating the document with suggested modifications (retyped by Edith), promised to submit it to his chief, the Foreign Secretary. At the same time, I agreed

150

to ask Ernest Bevin to allow me to report this development by wireless to Indonesia. Bevin declined to intervene in this way, but I was led to understand that he welcomed any prospect of negotiations and would contact the Netherlands Government. Peter saw his Foreign Secretary – and the exchanges began which brought peace.

One surprise brought another. Some months later I was lecturing in America and had reached Chicago. A handsome woman approached me at a cocktail party. 'Don't you remember me?' she asked. Her features were faintly reminiscent, but I could not place her.

'I am Mrs Peter Schmidt,' she said. I was bewildered. She was dark and buxom, and I remembered Peter's wife at that London lunch as fair and slim. I began to stammer.

'I am the *first* Mrs Schmidt.'

I have never been so speechless. *The Times* had reported her execution and I had written her obituary. I looked at her face more keenly and saw dimly on her cheek a birthmark which I recollected. She told me her story over coffee after my lecture. She had been in a concentration camp, but she had never faced a firing squad. When released she did not tell Peter, not wanting to break up his new marriage, but came to America and herself remarried. I can reveal this now because Peter has died.

Sukarno invited me to Indonesia when its independence was recognised, but I could not make the journey. Then, when on a State visit to Dublin, he insisted that I should meet him there. He hugged me at the airport; but I did not admire him unreservedly. He lived an ostentatiously luxurious and immoderate life far removed from his people, and I was not surprised when he was subsequently overthrown in a *coup*.

Again unexpectedly, an event occurred which channelled my future activities for most of my life. I had joined the Movement for a United Socialist Europe, initiated by the ILP and French and other continental Socialists. I attended a conference, held at Puteaux, a suburb of Paris, in 1948, which had the object of uniting the nationalist movements of Africa and Asia with European Socialists in a coordinated economic policy. Léon Blum and Guy Mollet, among other prominent leaders, were present and spoke. There were representative delegations from the colonial territories, but I warned my European comrades that they would not succeed in their purpose because: (1) Africans and Asians would not breach their non-alignment by coalescing with West Europeans, (2) they were dissatisfied with lukewarm European Social Democratic support for their rights, and (3) they would not commit themselves to an economic plan before they gained independence. These doubts made me unpopular, but they proved correct, and there was an unforeseen development. The Africans and Asians called a separate meeting inviting a few of us to attend, and decided to establish the Congress of Peoples against Imperialism. They agreed a little reluctantly that, for purposes of communication with territories in the French and British Empires, Paris and London should be the headquarters; and Jean Rous, columnist in the radical *Combat*, was appointed secretary and myself chairman. In the next two or three years the Congress became almost a legend for its activity in the struggle for colonial freedom in French North Africa, Sudan, Kenya, Tanganyika, the Gold Coast and Indo-China. Congress continued until the intensified Algerian war cut off Paris, and the Movement for Colonial Freedom replaced it in London. It was the Puteaux Conference which finally committed me to the Third World as my political speciality.

Indian independence, won in 1947, stimulated Africa and the rest of Asia to agitate aggressively for self-government. Despite my earlier involvement, I took little part in the last stages of the Indian settlement, though my brother-in-law, Reg Sorensen, was a determining influence in the negotiations led by Stafford Cripps in Delhi. The assassination of Gandhi robbed the world of a shining light, though there was something both tragically ironic and appropriate that he should have met his death as a result of his generosity in seeking conciliation between Hindus and Muslims. I deplored the partition of India and Pakistan, particularly the division of Bengal, but rejoiced that Ceylon and Burma had gained independence too. These historic steps strengthened my attachment to the Labour Party.

I was delighted, too, by the domestic policies of the Attlee Government, its success in transforming the war economy, its nationalisation of the mines and railways, its historic inauguration of the Welfare State; above all, Nye Bevan's creation of the free Health Service – the greatest Socialist achievement since free education. I deplored deeply the reversion to increased arms expenditure and the beginning of the Cold War, but I was very ready to accept nomination as Labour candidate for Eton and Slough when the Government had completed its work in 1950.

CHAPTER TWENTY

RETURNING TO PARLIAMENT

There were four of us nominated to the selection conference for the candidature at Eton and Slough – a prominent trade unionist, a woman Cooperator, Roy Jenkins, then Parliamentary Secretary to Clem Attlee, and myself. We sat in a small office, a little embarrassed, forcing geniality, until summoned one by one to face fifty delegates from local trade unions and ward parties, speaking for ten minutes, answering questions for ten. It was the first time I had met Roy Jenkins, though I had known and liked his father, a miners' MP from South Wales. Roy was the quietest among us, distant, reflecting his Oxford college rather than his Welsh valley. He was commended by Attlee and the favourite for selection, but on a second ballot I got the vote. We travelled back to Paddington together, and he was still distant, signing Attlee's letters which bulged a briefcase. I was surprised by the excited congratulations which I received from Left MPs who regarded Roy as a snob. Later I became associated with him when he was Home Secretary and I found him human and warm. I suspect his reserve at Slough was due to shyness rather than superiority. He had no reason to regret his non-selection. He got a much safer seat in Birmingham.

Eton and Slough had been won by Benn Levy, the playwright, in the 1945 election. He had served in the navy and like many other ex-servicemen was passionately for overthrowing the Establishment and building a new world. In the Commons he became fascinated by political controversy but was impatient with the slow procedure and frustrated because his involvement prevented him from writing. He decided to resign, but when he did so half his mind remained in politics and it was some time before he wrote well again. Sometime later he invited my wife and me to the first night of his *The Rape of the Belt* and from the glint in his eye I knew he had recovered his art. He was the most lovable of persons and the affection which Party members in Slough had for him was moving. They adored too, his actress wife, Constance Cummings, who was no less a Socialist and continued to speak for me after Benn had retired.

We won the election comfortably, getting 19,987 votes against 15,594 for the Conservative, 5,026 for the Liberal, and 614 for the Communist. Eton and Slough is a constituency of contrasts, Eton untouched by the industrial revolution, Slough its embodiment. I got on well with the College despite my Socialist views, taking tea with the progressive head-master, Sir Robert Birley, finding one or two supporters among the masters and having good-natured opposition from the boys. Three hundred seniors would attend my election meetings, crowding the gallery. When question-time came the adults would remain silent to enjoy the heckling by the boys, but it was not all opposition. In a debate at the College political society I was surprised to get a third of the votes for Socialism, and when fifteen years later I joined the House of Lords I was delighted to meet two young heredi-tary peers who said I had influenced them when they were at Eton. At one of the Eton meetings my speech was interrupted by the most dignified protest I have ever known. I was criticising Duncan Sandys when a tall boy in the front row of the gallery rose, bowed to me, bowed to the audience, and without a word turned and with head up walked out of the hall. I knew at once it was Duncan Sandys junior; he was the slim, red-headed image of his father. It was done beautifully and I could hardly forbear from joining the boys as they cheered.

Although I openly expressed my opposition to fee-paying education, the nursery of a class society, I only got into trouble with the College when I attacked a Rating Bill which exempted it from paying £7,000 in rates be-cause it was classed as a charity. The school was started philanthropically by King Henry VI in 1440, but the only charitable features which remained were subsidies to sixty scholars and to a parish school and its vicar. I felt the exemption monstrously wrong in view of the high fees charged and the extensive property owned by the College, mostly in Hampstead. I was escorted round the College by the Provost to impress on me the high cost of repairing historic buildings, but I argued that it should be met from the fund to maintain ancient monuments rather than from exempted rates.

When controversy arose about an arterial road which would have des-troyed Eton High Street, with its willow-pattern bridge, I became friendly with a house master, B. J. W. Hill, who rescued me and Clement Attlee from an amusing predicament. I was dictating letters to my secretary on the Commons terrace when a succession of custodians, policemen and staff from both the Commons and the Lords came to say that Earl Attlee wanted to see me urgently in the Upper Chamber. There was clearly something important afoot and I wondered what proposal Labour's ex-leader was to make. I found Clem in the Peers' Guest Room with Arthur Moyle, MP, who had been his Parliamentary Secretary in the Commons. Certainly, an exceptional interview. It was Moyle who spoke. Attlee was to be presented with the Order of the Garter at Windsor Castle; his daughter wished to witness the ceremony; the difficulty was that she was feeding a baby at the breast and would have to do so en route; she could not take the baby to the Castle; did I know anyone at near-by Eton with whom the baby could be left during the Garter ceremony? Mr and Mrs Hill were glad to oblige.

The problems of Slough were very different from those of Eton and much bigger. It was a perked-up town, leaping in population after Sir Noel Mobbs bought up junk deposited there by the Government after the First World War and transformed it into Britain's first trading estate. Workers poured in from the depressed areas, Wales, the North, Scotland and Ireland – as immigrants did later from India and the West Indies. The Welsh did not arrive in large numbers until the hungry 1930s and were regarded as foreigners, with some landladies putting notices 'No Welsh' in their windows. During my period as MP, feeling was bitter against West Indians, and much of my activity was to reduce tension. The varied origins of the people of Slough inhibited the feeling of belonging to one community. It was not until the 1960s that identification really developed.

The speed of Slough's emergence meant that the town lacked any overall plan, all too evident when one looked at the trading estate, the housing estates, the rows of improvised shops. It was not a pretty place and Betjeman had good reasons to write in his *Collected Poems*:

> Come, friendly bombs, and fall on Slough!
> It isn't fit for humans now,
> There isn't grass to graze a cow
> Swarm over, Death!

But during my fourteen years' association with Slough, the Borough Council, Labour-controlled, and the County Council struggled heroically to mend things. They built attractive houses within the limits allowed; their open spaces became famous for their flowers; their schools were models of design; they planned a modern new hospital and prepared an ambitious development plan. The centre of Slough today is not recognisable by those who knew it twenty years ago, though financial stringency delayed the process of improvement. I was still MP for the constituency when the London

County Council established their colourful housing estates at Langley and Britwell. Slough is on the way to becoming a balanced city instead of an unplanned town.

I had to participate in much of this progress. The explosive population growth brought the problem of sewage disposal. During wet days in the early 1950s it seeped in the streets and down garden paths. We were in danger of polluting the Thames and one of my first Parliamentary jobs was to get materials to construct a huge sewage farm. I think I was happiest in securing for the town the restoration of Black Park, an Eden of acres of beeches and pines and a tree-bordered lake, lost between Pinewood film studios and spreading housing estates. During the war the Ministry of Defence had taken over the park to hide ammunition stores, and dumps were still there five years later. It is never an easy job to get the War Office to surrender land and I took pride in my achievement. Slough is lucky in its surroundings, the Thames valley, Burnham Beeches, the lanes and villages of Buckinghamshire – and Black Park.

My period as MP resulted in a personal involvement with social wrongs such as I had not had since my Settlement days before the First World War. I had denounced poverty at hundreds of meetings; I had seen conditions everywhere which outraged me, but this was largely from the outside – I had worked from a clean office and lived in a comfortable house. But at Slough I was brought into personal contact with those who were denied a human life and I became emotionally identified with them. Like many MPs I had a political surgery on Saturday mornings, clients pouring out their sufferings. I soon learned there were many gaps in the Social Welfare State. Housing was the worst. Couples came who could get no more than one room, impossibly high rents were charged for allegedly furnished rooms, families were crowded so that parents and grown children had to sleep together; others had no home at all and slept in the open. A man came who had notice to quit. I visited his 'home'. It was a room twelve feet square with a mattress on the floor for his wife, two children and himself. With the help of the Council I got them temporary accommodation, but often the Housing Department could do nothing. I came to realise that the lack of homes was responsible for every kind of social evil. It was not only a denial of the elementary right to have a roof over one's head, but it destroyed health, brought nervous collapses, broke up families, drove young people on to the streets, stimulated juvenile crime and made miserable the declining years of the old. I devoted a large part of my Parliamentary time to this issue and Nye Bevan, who had become Minister of Housing, acknowledged that Slough was one of his greatest headaches. Old age pensioners who were half starved came to me, widowed women, disabled men existing on inadequate pensions from the First World War, ex-miners suffering from pneumoconiosis, a woman who wanted a free weekly bath, a man too poor to buy underclothes. Sometimes one could help, sometimes not. I dreaded my Saturday surgeries.

One surgery involved the Queen. A middle-aged working-class couple came to me with an unusual request. Their son had been selected as the British contestant for the world accordion championship; the contest was to take place at Amsterdam; he was serving with the RAF at the Suez Canal; could I get him to Holland? I wrote to the Minister for Aviation who replied that he would arrange for him to have a fortnight's leave, but it would be unfair to the other boys to fly him to Europe. I knew the parents could not possibly afford the fare, and was not surprised when the mother put her handkerchief to her eyes.

'To think that the dear Queen heard him play,' she sobbed.

'What?' I asked with new hope.

'Yes, at Nairobi. Just before she became Queen.'

'That's done it,' I said. 'I'll get your boy to Holland.' I wrote to the Queen asking her if she remembered and, if so and if she admired the performance, would she send me a token contribution towards meeting the cost of the air flight? She replied that she recollected the occasion, had been impressed by the boy's skill and sent me a cheque. I had only to publish the fact of the Queen's donation for money to pour in. We met not only the cost of the journey, but were able to buy the boy the best accordion on the market. A few weeks later the Queen was coming to Slough and I was asked to meet her. I was interested in the procedure. From Buckingham Palace I was sent a questionnaire about my life and record, with an enquiry if there were anything special I wished to mention. I replied that I would like to thank her for her help with the accordion player. When I was introduced, the Queen immediately asked how the boy had fared. I told her that he had come eleventh, defeated by the supreme Latin Americans, but that the previous British best was eighteenth. 'Congratulate him from me,' the Queen said with a smile. I was impressed by her homework. The innumerable question-naires she must study!

Most MPs are bored by the duty of conducting constituents round the House. I rather enjoyed it, telling irreverent stories not in the schedule of the official guides. I liked doing it particularly for the children. I arranged with the Education Officer to take the schools in turn, once every three weeks, and years later I found on many mantelpieces in Slough homes photographs of the grouped children taken on the terrace. One day five

Eton College boys arrived without notice, asking for tickets for the Commons gallery. An important debate was in progress and no seats were available. I fell back on the Upper House, saying I could get them in easily as no one was interested in the Lords. 'I am,' said one of the boys. 'I shall belong to it when I'm twenty-one.'

I had been warned that the Eton and Slough Labour Party was one of the most cantankerous in the country, and I quickly learned that it contained some assertive personalities who did not always harmonise. They had a splendid sense of rank-and-file democracy. For example, determined to be free from monetary influence, they would not allow their MP to contribute towards election expenses or to the continuing organisation. When I was proposed as candidate one of the nominees would have brought considerable trade union subsidies, another Cooperative backing; the delegates did not consider such sponsorship for a moment. It was not that the Party had money; for long periods it had not enough to engage an agent, relying on voluntary service. I learned in Slough that this rank-and-file devotion is what constitutes the strength of the Labour movement.

CHAPTER TWENTY-ONE

JOINING THE BEVANITES

My re-election to Parliament was not a happy experience. In contrast to the success of the 1945 Labour Government the Government of 1950 failed. Its majority was only eight, but the reason for its weakness was the fact that the Party had run out of policy. At the first meeting of the Parliamentary group I urged an extension of measures for public ownership and social service, but Herbert Morrison replied that our object should be consolidation of what had already been achieved. We were to mark time, fatal negation for any government. In addition, circumstances conquered convictions. Ministers did not mark time, they ran backwards, repudiating Socialist principles, both of peace and human equality. Support for the Korean war led to massive rearmament, which in turn led to a reduction of the social services, followed by economic crisis and electoral defeat.

I was in difficulty. I had rejoined the Labour Party with my eyes open. I had been out of the Party and Parliament for eighteen years because I would not accept discipline. I had decided to conform, realising that the Party was the instrument for the achievement of Socialism. Was I to go back on that decision? I did not, but my conscience was troubled.

The Korean war was the first challenge. The issue was not black and white. I was in favour of a United Nations force to resist aggression. Was not UN action in Korea that? I was disturbed by President Truman's order to American troops to act before any UN decision was made and by the American veto in the Security Council of the proposal, despite support from the other six members, that a representative of the Chinese Government should be heard. I was also influenced by the fact that the Soviet Union was not represented at the Security Council meeting which authorised military action and thus could not exert its power of veto.

In the Commons I heard Attlee's staccato announcement of British support for the war with apprehension and put to him two questions which caused a Parliamentary row. In view of Soviet absence, should not the Security Council seek means of discussion with Russia? And would hostilities be limited to Korea? On the second point the Prime Minister was definite. 'Yes, certainly,' he said. On the first he was evasive, saying that it was a matter for the Security Council, ignoring the fact that the British representative on the Council could take the initiative.

My questions seemed reasonable, but the reaction of the Tory members was hysterical. They literally howled at me, causing a Parliamentary scene. It did not end there. In *Reynolds News* Tom Driberg (later Lord Bradwell) denounced the outburst under the heading 'Tories Bay for War', which led Winston Churchill to rebuke him in the House in his most imperious manner. Tom courageously held his ground. I have regretted ever since that I did not vote against the Korean war. Two MPs with appropriate heritage from Keir Hardie, did so – Emrys Hughes, his son-in-law, and S. O. Davies, representing Merthyr Tydfil, Hardie's old seat.

An unrecognised historic event arose from the war. The Asian governments for the first time demonstrated their non-alignment from the American–Soviet confrontation. They rejected Communist dictatorship but equally condemned American support for Chiang Kai-shek in China and Bao Dai in Vietnam. They proposed a ceasefire in Korea. The result was disappointing. A ceasefire was rejected by Russia, and China insisted on impossible conditions. I supported the Asian Governments, the beginning of my identity with an independent Third World.

The Korean war had two disastrous results. First, it started the steep rise in world rearmament, not least in Britain. The Minister of Defence, Emanuel Shinwell, one-time Clydeside rebel, raised arms expenditure over three years by £3,400 million. I spoke frequently against this vast rearmament – once a Tory dubbed me 'Member for Moscow and Eton' (a strange combination) – but I did not vote; every night I asked myself if I was right in not doing so. Secondly, the Korean war finalised the tendencies towards the Cold War and consummated the Power bloc alliance between America and Western Europe. Ernest Bevin, daringly appointed Foreign Secretary by Attlee, was the co-parent of NATO as well as the Marshall Plan. As a neutralist I thought Bevin's policy wrong, but he certainly justified his appointment by ability. He was a big man with a broad sweep of ideas. I have not known any other Foreign Secretary who would address the House without a note and who allowed his thoughts to expand on an unchartered course without restraint; the civil servants on the bench reserved for them

F.B. and his wife Edith meet Joshua
Nkomo during the Kenya
Independence celebrations

F.B. greets Jawaharlal Nehru on his
visit to Tilak House, 1952

F.B. at a feeding centre at Nguru, Biafra, 9 December 1968, during his peace mission to Nigeria

In the ceremonial fur cloak of a chief of the Kikuyu

must have had an uneasy time whenever he rose. I admired Bevin, but I was fearful of his initiation of Britain's Cold War participation.

Already I was beginning to specialise on the colonies. Jomo Kenyatta organised a petition on land hunger in Kenya and over 600,000 signed it. (The illiterate made thumb marks, often in blood.) When I presented the petition to the House two officials had to help me carry it to the table. Petitions have become of little account. There was a time when they were considered before all other business. Now they are stuffed into a green bag behind the Speaker's chair and are never heard of again except for a formal report on their authenticity. My contact with Third World movements through the Congress of Peoples against Imperialism meant that I had letters from all over Africa and Asia reporting injustices, and I continually raised them in the House. The Hansard index showed that in one week I put questions about Uganda, Nigeria, Trinidad, Sierra Leone and Gambia. I had been dubbed 'Member for Moscow'. With more justice I was now called 'Member for Africa'.

On one issue I came into headlong conflict with the Government. Seretse Khama, the chief of the leading tribe in Bechuanaland – the Bamangwato – had married an English girl, Ruth Williams, whilst studying here. At first his own people objected, but Ruth won their hearts by going to Serowe to have her baby. The South African Government, which held mixed marriages to be crimes, was outraged, whereupon the Minister for Commonwealth Relations, Gordon Walker, summoned Seretse to London ostensibly for discussion. I have rarely been more angry than when I heard the Minister announce that he had deposed Seretse from his chieftainship and exiled him from his country for five years. It was beyond my belief that such a thing could happen under a Labour Government and I caused a scene by my hot words. From the Tory benches Quintin Hogg, now Lord Hailsham, supported me and Churchill denounced the devious method employed. I led a deputation to Gordon Walker and was bewildered by the weakness of his case. He got away with it, but only just. The Liberals tabled a motion of censure. I was ill at the time and the Labour Whips, anxious how the vote would go, telephoned my home and urged me to get in a car and come.

'What's the vote about?' I asked.

'Seretse Khama.'

'Good thing my doctor won't allow me to leave my room,' I replied. It was touch and go, but Labour won with the support of Tories who did not want to offend South Africa.

I got to know Seretse and Ruth well. At first Seretse was alone and when I visited him I was fearful that he would overdrink his disillusionment, but when the family joined him they settled happily in a South London home. They were heartened by an entire absence of colour feeling among their neighbours. Three of them had cars and would take it in turns to give the children a lift to school; Ruth's dark-skinned, curly-headed toddler was a favourite. All the time Seretse longed for his own land and people. He visited our beauty spots – Devon and Cornwall, North Wales, the Lake District, the Scottish Highlands – but when I asked which part of Britain he liked most, he said, 'East Anglia, its flat distances to the horizon took me home.'

When Seretse was at long last allowed to return to Bechuanaland and became head of its independent government he proved skilful in balancing economic dependence on South Africa with the maintenance of African rights. We did not meet for twenty-four years; when we did we embraced.

In 1950 I introduced a Bill to apply the UN Declaration of Human Rights to colonial territories. It was one of the longest Private Members' Bills ever presented, including clauses to cover every infringement. Clement Davies, leading the Liberals, told me I should have drafted a one-clause Bill, but my object was propaganda and in my speech I was able to give instances of how each provision was ignored. The Bill did not reach a second reading, but it helped to ventilate wrongs in British territories.

My association with De Valera, who had become President of the Irish Republic, added a personal stimulus to my political desire to help solve the problem of divided Ireland. I had discussed with De Valera a proposal that Ulster should accept federation and that Eire should accept membership of the Commonwealth for this reunited Ireland. The Republican leader doubted whether the South would accept the Queen as head of the Commonwealth, but he was not averse to the idea being discussed. I got into touch with the Catholic hierarchy and found some of them sympathetic, one of the Bishops publicly endorsing the suggestion. Encouraged, I went to see Herbert Morrison and suffered a rebuff. He would not listen to any Government initiative; it would be political dynamite, dividing the Labour movement, Protestants and Catholics, without uniting Ireland. I still believe this may be the path to a solution, perhaps through membership of the European Community rather than the Commonwealth.

I had retained friendship with De Valera ever since I had been in Lincoln gaol with him, later to be received by the Governor as 'distinguished old boys'. I enjoyed chairing a meeting at Slough when he addressed the large Irish community and twice I visited him at Phoenix Park in Dublin. He was one of the men with whom I felt almost spiritual identity, captivated by his philosophic depth and gentle charm. In his later years he became nearly blind, though he moved about his large working room with certainty. He told me he had gone back to his old love, mathematics. So often mathematics and philosophy go together.

Government policy on overseas issues caused anxiety among the more internationally-minded Socialists, but domestic issues understandably brought the most serious opposition. They led to the coming together of a number of pressure groups, culminating in the controversial Keep Left and Bevan Groups. I was associated with Ellis Smith, MP from the Potteries, in the first of these. We initiated the Socialist Fellowship to carry on the traditions and inspiration of the ILP within the Labour Party. It was open to Socialists outside Parliament as well as MPs and was soon made in-operative by Trotskyists. Ellis and I cooperated in tabling a motion which expressed the ILP plan to establish a Living Wage as a basic statutory human right. The debate split the Labour Party, some trade union leaders opposing any statutory control of wages (an indication of things to come), and Herbert Morrison summoned us to his room, where he reprimanded us in dictatorial tones for raising the issue without consulting with the responsible Minister. I admit I found satisfaction in telling him that Ellis and I had gone to Sir Stafford Cripps, the Chancellor of the Exchequer, and that, without en-dorsing our proposal, he had encouraged us to proceed. A first indication of differences at Cabinet level.

There was a second attempt by ex-ILP-ers to establish association within the Labour Party, a group known as Victory for Socialism. Its chairman was Frederick Messer a dedicated pacifist, and his son Eric, faithful to this day, was secretary. The group was too idealistic to be politically effective, but it became significant as it broadened to admit Sydney Silverman, Stephen Swingler and Ian Mikardo. Soon, however, we concentrated our activities in a still broader association, the Keep Left group. Keep Left had in fact been formed in the previous Parliament. Its origin is known only to a few. The group and the subsequent Bevan Group became known mainly for their criticism of the domestic policies of the Labour leadership, but they emerged from an unpublished letter sent confidentially as far back as October 1946 by twenty-one MPs to Clem Attlee urging a basic change in foreign policy.

This document was historic because for the first time an influential group within the Labour Party called for Britain to become non-aligned in foreign affairs by withdrawing from the American alliance. It was fundamental, comprehensive and constructive, much of it relevant today. It argued in favour of a democratic socialist middle way between American Capitalism and Russian Totalitarianism. It criticised the Government for neglecting to express concern about the extension of American military bases throughout the world whilst denouncing the Russian expansion of spheres of influence in Europe, and submitted that collaboration with the USA had deprived Britain of the moral leadership of the smaller nations. Participation in power politics, the MPs prophesied, would involve us in a burden of arms expenditure which would cripple Labour's plans for Socialist reconstruction. By the vigorous example of our policies we could bridge the antagonism between the USA and the USSR and encourage (rather than discourage) the democratic Socialist forces in Europe and the world.

Surprise will be occasioned not only by the early date of this pronouncement but by the names of some who signed it. The distinction of initiating and drafting the letter rests with Donald Bruce who, first as Parliamentary Secretary to Aneurin Bevan and later as Lord Bruce of Donnington, has maintained his Left views. But the signatories have not all done so. They included James Callaghan, now Prime Minister, who when Foreign Secretary strengthened the American alliance, the changeable Richard Crossman and the completely changed Woodrow Wyatt. There were others who are not now associated with the Left. The complete list, worth giving for history, was: Barbara Ayrton Gould, Ashley Bramall, Donald Bruce, W. G. Cove, R. H. S. Crossman, Harold Davies, James Callaghan, Jennie Lee, Mark Hewitson, W. Griffiths, Benn Levy, R. W. G. Mackay, H. G. McGhee, J. P. W. Mallalieu, Michael Foot, Christopher Shawcross, Fred Messer, Sydney Silverman, Joe Reeves, Lyall Wilkes, Woodrow Wyatt. When the next division on the Government's foreign policy took place in the Commons, seventy Labour Members abstained, and it was a core of these who decided to form the Keep Left group. It began as an innocuous study group, specialists reading papers, but in 1947 it published its famous pamphlet, *Keep Left*, advocating Socialist solutions to economic difficulties. The MPs who sponsored the pamphlet included some new names, among them Ian Mikardo, Geoffrey Bing, Leslie Hale (now Lord Hale), Stephen Swingler and George Wigg (now Lord Wigg).

By the time I was invited to join Keep Left it had been reduced by election losses to twelve. New members included Richard Acland, and we had as secretary Jo Richardson, whom I had known as a fervent Young Socialist in my local Party at Hornsey, now among the ablest woman MPs. It was a somewhat exclusive group, admitting members after a consideration of their personalities as well as their politics. I was against this closed shop, and events burst it open. Nye Bevan, Harold Wilson and John Freeman resigned from the Government and Keep Left mobilised every known supporter of the rebels. We could no longer meet in a small interview room. Fifty of us crowded a committee room and we became known as the Bevan Group.

The immediate occasion for Nye's resignation was the Cabinet's decision to introduce charges in the National Health Service. He was the father of Free Health and cherished it with parental devotion, proud that a community service for personal well-being should be available to all on the basis of need rather than money. When Hugh Gaitskell, who had become Chancellor of the Exchequer on Stafford Cripps's breakdown in health, imposed prescription charges, Nye was as hurt as though he had been physically assaulted. I sat with him and some of his admirers in the corner of the Members' smoking room where we used to forgather. For once Nye was silent, too hurt to speak.

The Bevan Group quickly extended the attack to the mounting cost of rearmament which was the immediate reason for cutting social expenditure. It published a complementary pamphlet to *Keep Left* entitled *The Only Way*. The Cold War was becoming a Hot War in prospect. 'This fear can either drive us to a despairing acceptance of the rearmament race – and the inevitability of war itself,' wrote the Bevan Group, 'or it can inspire us to hammer out a constructive peace policy.' The Group differed radically from Keep Left by positive stimulation of action within the Parliamentary Party and in the movement outside: it went all out to compel a change of policy. Inevitably the leadership acted against it. We were ordered to dissolve by a majority in the Parliamentary Party.

The evening after this decision we met in Dick Crossman's house in Vincent Square. There were one or two voices raised in defiance, but the overwhelming view was for acceptance of the Parliamentary command because of our belief, despite all disappointments, that the Party would become in time the means of realising Socialism. One decision was reached which influenced my future activities. Different members of the group were asked to specialise in exerting pressure on different aspects of policy. I was allocated the colonies and it was then that I decided to initiate the Movement for Colonial Freedom.

Meanwhile, despite the cuts in the Budget, the economy deteriorated to crisis point. Clem Attlee believed that his small majority government could not tackle the problems and decided to go to the country. The electorate returned an overall majority of seventeen for the Tories. In Eton and Slough my majority fell in a straight fight by only 309, but that could not console my distress. The leadership blamed the split in the Party for the defeat. Perhaps the confrontations of the Bevan Group contributed to it, but the Left dissension was the consequence not the cause of Labour's failure. Little remained of the Party's constructive social programme and what did could not have been carried through because of the appalling increase in rearmament expenditure which accompanied the Korean war. Defence costs have bedevilled us ever since.

CHAPTER TWENTY-TWO

RUSSELL, WELLS AND SHAW

My generation was fortunate in having so many creative writers: Thoreau, Walt Whitman, Edward Carpenter, Upton Sinclair, Sinclair Lewis, John Galsworthy, H. G. Wells, Bernard Shaw, Bertrand Russell, George Orwell. Richard Crossman has written that early British Socialism was presented by Providence with three men of genius – Russell, Wells and Shaw. I had the great privilege of knowing all three.

As I have told, Bertie, as we came to call Russell, walked unannounced into a room in Adam Street, Adelphi, where the half-dozen youngsters who organised conscientious objectors in the First World War were meeting. He offered his services, but at first we were a little in awe of the distinguished Cambridge professor. He soon won our hearts by his comradeship and mischievous fun and our minds by his brilliance in writing and speaking. He contributed every week for our underground paper, *The Tribunal*, and when the editor was arrested for an unsigned article, wrote at once to *The Times* acknowledging that he was the author. He was arrested and charged under the Defence of the Realm Act, leading to a famous exchange with Sir Archibald Bodkin, the Director of Public Prosecutions.

'If all men followed your advice,' said the outraged Prosecutor, 'there would be no war.'

'Precisely,' remarked Russell. Sir Archibald's comment became famous. We displayed it throughout the country on posters.

Bertrand Russell was a man of simple compassion, easily moved by suffering. He arrived late at a committee meeting explaining that he had emptied his pockets for a hardship suppliant; he had not kept a copper for a bus.

When I took over the chairmanship of the No-Conscription Fellowship I found among many devoted volunteers at its head office a beautiful, auburn-haired girl in her late teens and was surprised to learn that she was

167

Lady Constance Malleson, married to my friend Miles. Miles and Constance both believed in free love but married because she was under age for physical association otherwise. Miles volunteered for non-combative service in the army (it was temporary, as I have told) and Constance, who had already joined the ILP, gave her days to the NCF – she was at the theatre in the evening, already winning recognition as the actress Collette O'Neill. The NCF brought Bertrand Russell and her together. They met first at Lavender Hill police station when Clifford Allen surrendered to the police and it was at an NCF conference at which Bertie spoke that they fell for each other. I have always thought that she was the most intense of Bertrand Russell's many loves, despite his somewhat cursory dismissal of their affair in his autobiography. Constance was the daughter of Lord and Lady Annesley and when she joined the ILP her mother wrote to me deploring not so much that she had become a Socialist as her avowal of agnosticism. Bertie and Constance became inseparable in their work for the NCF and were one in ideas as well as emotionally.

It was after the war that Russell influenced me most. We came out of prison into the new world of the Russian revolution and the challenge of Communism attracted us. It was the writing of Russell which brought back me and many others to the value of personal liberty. He was decisive at a time of much mental conflict.

Three years after coming out of prison I spent a weekend with Russell in his Cornish home. Perhaps he chose the spot because it was near Mousehole whose Parish Council, Plymouth Brethren, solemnly declared the village neutral when war was declared. Following Ottoline Morrell and Constance Malleson, Bertie had fallen in love with Dora Black, a Fellow of Girton College. Dora became his wife for twelve years, but at the time of my visit she was refusing to marry on libertarian grounds. I saw more of Dora than Bertie because he was absorbed in writing a book. She was the most assertive of Russell's women, claiming equality in ideas and behaviour, a challenging personality dedicated to the rights of her sex, but with the wider perspective of Socialism and peace. She told me laughingly how she insisted on following Bertie to pre-revolution China, registered as his 'favourite concubine'. They criticised the Chinese custom of parentally-arranged marriages and, a little ironically in view of their unwedded status, the subsequent love unions there became known as 'Russell marriages'. Dora finally married Bertie because he wanted an heir to his earldom, though she teased him about this. The son is now my colleague in the House of Lords; in the Russell tradition he devoted his maiden speech to an appeal for the transference of expenditure on arms to the provision of food for the hungry millions. Dora was a little bitter when Bertie divorced her for mothering a child by an American journalist, reminding him they had agreed to allow each other freedom in sexual conduct. I kept in touch with Dora and, despite her age, I found her when in in 1975 she visited me at the House of Lords as aggressive as ever, her voice reverberating round the guest room. She remained an incorrigible rebel with a mischievous sense of fun.

I took the initiative on Russell's ninetieth birthday to arrange a celebration dinner at the House of Commons. Everyone was present – Parliamentarians and distinguished persons outside Parliament – and Barbara Wootton paid a wonderful tribute to Bertie, his service to philosophy and mathematics linked with his contribution to personal liberty, Socialism and peace. Bertie sat next to me, and I was intrigued by his diet – liquid Complan, wine and coffee. He told me he hardly took any solids. He was lively and in replying to the tribute was witty as well as moving.

H. G. Wells and Bernard Shaw had liberated my mind before the war. I came to know them both, Wells through occasional meetings, Shaw more closely. HG came from his near-by home at Dunmow to our ILP summer schools at Easton Lodge, the home of the aristocratic but sincere Socialist, Lady Warwick. He joined in the fun at our socials. I still laugh when I think of him in 'The Grand Old Duke of York', bouncing up and down excitedly, clapping his plump little hands, and squealing in his thin treble voice, 'pretty, pretty, pretty', in appreciation of the girls as they danced between the two lines. He was the youngest among us. I have a vivid memory of an evening meal in his home when Edith and I were his guests. We watched through the window a group of small birds driving away a hawk by screeching and beating their wings round it. 'A lesson for man,' said HG.

Wells and I differed during the war, as I have told, but with peace we thought on the same lines. He invited the ILP National Council to dinner at his Regency house facing Regent's Park. Dinner began rather embarrassingly for us but not for HG. Maxton enquired politely about his children. 'Which children?' asked Wells. 'Legitimate or illegitimate?' A remarkable coincidence lingers in my mind. It was told to us appropriately by HG when we were discussing the possibility of world government. In his *World History* he included a picture of a spear used by primitive man in Africa. He now turned and showed us the original adorning the wall and described how, when he planned the room, he had placed old and rare Chinese plates under the spear. They were still along the wall. He pointed to the plate in the centre – its design was an exact illustration of the spear. He assured us he had placed the plate there by sheer accident, but it indicated that in centuries unknown the Chinese had reached Africa. Since then discoveries in Africa have, one knows, strengthened this theory.

For over forty years my association with Bernard Shaw was continuous. I have told how he gave me my philosophy of life. I owe more to him in my thinking than to any man. The full story of our relationship is best told perhaps by the letters which he sent me and which happily I had saved, treasured in my flat, when the bombing of the ILP headquarters destroyed nearly all my personal papers, including priceless letters from Churchill, Trotsky, Gandhi, Nehru and others. Shaw's letters were something apart. My worst loss was a set of his first editions, all autographed. When I interviewed the Inspector for Compensation for war losses he would give me only the published price of the books, and my letters from world leaders were regarded as valueless.

Shaw's letters, which I reproduced in *Outside the Right*, covered every phase of my adult life from resistance to the First World War to my candidatures at Lancaster, Westminster and Slough. Revolted by a draft constitution for the ILP because of its repeated use of 'the meaningless catchword revolutionary', he wrote a thousand-word alternative, far too personal to be accepted but typically provocative and stimulating. He made mincemeat of the wish of G. K. Chesterton and Hilaire Belloc to make us all little property owners, but, forty years later, rereading this GBS analysis of ideologies and parties, I am most interested in his estimate of Fascism which in his later years brought him some disrepute. He endorsed the Corporate State with its trusts in command of industry and culture, but insisted that until the Corporations owned land and industries they would be as bad as city companies.

I am not sure whether Shaw's intervention in my 1950 election did not do me more harm than good. 'Slough and Eton,' he wrote, 'are inhabited largely by political nitwits who read nothing but betting pools, and simple-souled stick-in-the-muds who dread reformers more than serpents and dragons. The wiser few must do their utmost to outnumber them on the forthcoming Day of Destiny.' My opponent thought the message had won the election for him. 'Brockway's mentor says you are nitwits!' screamed the loudspeakers. I responded by a telegraph retort to Shaw: 'You are wrong. We'll show you on The Day.' GBS did not reply until the result was known. Then came a postcard: 'Ingrate. My coupon and my advice has secured you the one Independent triumph of the election in an impossible constituency. I was right – and you tell me I was wrong. Yah!'

My last meeting with Shaw was two years before he died in November 1950. My friends, the Winstens, who lived near him at Ayot St Lawrence became his closest intimates. Inca Winsten had been in prison with me in the First World War. A Russian by origin, he was still in Walton gaol when the October Revolution of 1917 made his brother Deputy Commissar for Education in the Soviet Union. His wife, Claire, was a painter and sculptor. I got Gandhi to allow her to do his portrait whilst, sitting cross-legged on the floor before his spinning wheel, he received British Ministers and deputations during the Round Table Conference in 1930. She gave Shaw a beautiful statue of Joan of Arc which he treasured in his garden.

GBS visited the Winsten's cottage for tea every afternoon. He found in it the domestic atmosphere and the intellectual companionship which he had missed since the death of his wife. Claire said her passing was a great blow to him. He could not sleep and he used to say he would not last long. For a time he could not walk because of some paralysis of the legs; Claire massaged them and got them straight and strong. Shaw's household consisted of a Scottish housekeeper (whom he described as 'an efficient tyrant'), a maid and a man secretary. They did their job, but the atmosphere of home had gone and Shaw escaped daily to the Winstens. He had no other local friends. Ayot St Lawrence consisted of two large houses and half a dozen cottages, and probably not an occupant had read a Shaw book and, if they had, they would have been profoundly shocked.

Shaw's day was: morning – the daily paper and work in his hut in the garden; he read his letters over lunch; he slept until 4 pm, then a short walk and tea with the Winstens; 5.30 pm he started work again, answering letters; supper at eight and early to bed. The continued success of his books helped to get Shaw over the depression of his wife's death. He was pleased with the filming of his plays, and with the money they brought him. In contrast to his egalitarian views, he was intensely interested in money-making.

On the afternoon of this last meeting with GBS Inca had gone to meet him whilst Claire and I went to look at the village and its demolished church. The local lord of the manor had complained that the old-time structure blocked his view, and began its destruction but, reprimanded by the Bishop, he was compelled to build a new church, erected, however, out of sight from his mansion. We were within the crumbling walls when we heard Inca calling. He and GBS were approaching.

I had not seen Shaw for some years and was a little shocked by his frail figure. He was dressed in a mustard-coloured tweed with plus-fours; his legs looked painfully thin, his face was shrunken, his beard was pure white and he walked with the help of a stock. His eyebrows were still thick and his eyes piercing, a touch of his old strength, and his back was still straight.

He smiled with a friendliness warmer than his traditional pose of superman. I took his arm and said he had not aged as much as I had. He laughed and declared that he had expected to see me with a white beard. He suggested that we should take a walk across the fields to see the new church.

Claire began to tell how the church had got £700 for war damage – a bomb had fallen a mile away and had shaken the walls. GBS acknowledged that he had given £100 towards the repairs. 'I am a rationalist,' he said, 'but church buildings are the one consolation for Christianity. The architect here was second only to Christopher Wren.' Shaw's voice had lost nothing of its vigour, with the same rich Irish brogue I remembered so well. He began to talk about the bombing.

'Two German airmen were under the impression that Ayot St Lawrence was the site of the Bank of England,' he declared. 'They swooped over here night after night, dropping bombs in a circle of three miles. Then their plane was hit and they parachuted down. The nuisance ceased.' He went on talking of his reminiscences, friendly, interesting talk, but not the GBS I had known. Then he stopped and, waving his stick, burst into a speech. We had the old typical Shaw. 'I am tired of telling my villainous scientist friends that they don't know their own business,' he exploded. 'Instead of making atom bombs they should be making volatile life-killing gas. What happens when they drop their atom bombs? They not only destroy human beings, who historically speaking do not matter – they can be procreated fast enough, perhaps too fast – but they also destroy the riches of civilisation, Gothic architecture and works of art which can never be replaced; they commit a crime against the whole history of man and against all future generations. How much more sensible a volatile gas would be! It would destroy every living thing and, having done its work, would go into the air and disperse. Simple! And the victors would march in to find everything in apple-pie order for them – factories, homes, transport, electrical power, water, food, stocked shops. All they would have to do would be to remove the corpses.'

Shaw looked defiantly at me. He knew I had been a conscientious objector dedicated to the sanctity of life. I was too much in awe of him to respond or even to think. (The answer is that human beings are the creators of evolving civilisation and by destroying them you finally leave a tomb.) 'It must be a volatile gas,' he insisted. 'Bacteriological warfare won't do; life can conquer it. There are always people immune. I am. I was once in a household which developed a serious disease. The doctor commanded that we all be inoculated. I refused, telling him I would be the test. He could prove by his safe immunisation of the others and by my death that his serum worked. What an opportunity – GBS dead!' Silence, and then he laughed. 'I didn't get the disease.'

We reached the church. Shaw pointed to 'the famous gravestone which led me to end my days in Ayot St Lawrence'. I read the inscription and found nothing unusual. He was impatient. 'Don't you see? She died when she was eighty-four and "her time was short". That encouraged me to believe I might live to be a hundred here.' Inside the church Shaw told how he gave the Winsten's daughter, Ruth, elocution lessons there, making her orate from the pulpit whilst he sat by the door, pulling her up whenever a syllable was not clear. She aimed to be an actress; instead, as Ruth Harrison, she became the leader of the campaign against battery farms, a cause which I feel sure vegetarian GBS would have espoused. As we made our way back to the Winsten cottage Shaw talked about the clergy who had been at the church. It was a good living with little to do, the congregations numbering only from six to ten. 'One parson was an atheist without a conscience, who caused a scandal by living in sin with a Russian woman.' He asked Claire what the present parson was like. 'A muscular Christian,' she replied. 'Likes his beer in the local and regards his work as a job.' 'Sensible fellow,' said GBS. 'That's the only possible excuse for being a parson.'

Talking about conscience led Shaw to relate the amusing story of how he gave evidence on behalf of objector C. H. Norman at a court martial. Norman was an atheist and had protested when GBS had lectured at the City Temple. Shaw told this to the court terming his lecture a sermon, 'and I am certain that the friendly major, who obviously didn't know me from Adam, thought I was a minister of religion who in Christian charity had come to speak to the sincerity of a dissenter'. Despite Shaw's help, disaster nearly came to Norman. His counsel insisted on speaking when everyone wanted to go to lunch, referring, said Shaw, to conscientious objectors in every war since the Israelites crossed the Red Sea. 'As this dreadful harangue continued I don't know whether the major or I became more angry. I tossed a note across the room to him; he picked it up and smiled. I'm confident it was that note which restored his good temper, resulting in a favourable verdict for Norman. I had scribbled: "If you will take this man out and shoot him, we won't hold it in evidence against you." Perhaps not the most appropriate remark for a witness on behalf of a conscientious objector, but it did the trick.'

We had tea in the Winsten's long, low room. A corner of a settee was GBS's reservation. Claire placed an electric fire at his side and Inca added another log to the blaze in the chimney. 'Walking, Shaw never wears a coat; indoors he bakes,' whispered Inca to me. 'In his little workroom hut in the garden he sits on his electric fire.' Claire knew his vegetarian tastes and pleased him with a bowl of milky food and brown-bread sandwiches of honey and nuts. GBS told us he was writing a play about a mathematician, and the Winstens were specially interested because their son was a lecturer in mathematics at Cambridge. Shaw startled them by declaring that mathematics could not content a man beyond thirty. It was not an enduring interest, only a gateway to other sciences or thinking. That was why so many mathematicians became scientists in another sphere, or philosophers and economists.

GBS challenged me politically. Why was the Labour Party making such a fuss about Soviet intervention in Czechoslovakia? When I replied that democracy and liberty were important he banged the floor with his stick and once more came a flood of emphatic words. 'Get your priorities right,' he demanded. 'Liberty begins with the stomach, not with the brain. To a man who is hungry democracy means nothing. Freedom of thought is a luxury for leisure. It is irrelevant for working hours which dominate most people's lives. Economic liberty comes first – and in Czechoslovakia they seem to be doing well in its achievement.'

I asked Shaw how long it would be before man had the sense to accept the need for world government. 'Who can say?' he replied. 'What could Adam have said about the future? For us the future is as remote as it was to him.' He paused and shook his head. 'Men will go on quarrelling and killing each other. They haven't grown up yet. World government won't come until the people of Ayot St Lawrence have learned to govern themselves. We must learn to be civilised.' I remarked that Socialists made the mistake of thinking that man is a political animal. 'Of course,' agreed Shaw. 'The average man hates government. He thinks it is for the other fellow, not for himself, for the thief and the rogue. The police and the law courts and prisons – that is government to most people.'

He pulled out his watch. It was twenty-five minutes to six. 'You've robbed the world of my genius,' he said. 'I should have been working an hour ago.' He did not want us to see him home but we insisted. On the way Claire told him that the mayor of near-by St Albans wanted him to open a ceremony on the thousandth anniversary of its Charter. 'No,' said Shaw. 'I'm an institution, not an exhibition.' I suggested he should tell the mayor so on one of his famous postcards. 'No,' he replied again. 'My postcards are for people who need to make money out of them. St Albans isn't bankrupt.' We reached the gate. He gripped my hand and without a word started off down the drive. His mind seemed to be driving his body along, straight and certain as ever. I watched him for a moment or two. I was thinking not so much of that afternoon, memorable though it had been, as of what Shaw had meant to me in my youth, and of thousands of others to whom he must have meant the same.

The last word shall go to GBS himself. Just after the First World War I asked him to comment on a statement on Palestine I had written for the ILP. 'All historical nonsense,' he replied. 'I can only put you right adequately in a three-act play.' This is the playlet he sent:

ACT I

1917. Scene: The Foreign Secretary's room at the Foreign Office. Arthur is contemplating with dismay a document which has been handed to him by an attaché.

ARTHUR: Boy, this is awful. Are you sure your figures are correct?

ATTACHÉ: They have been checked three times over, sir.

ARTHUR: This is really what the war is costing us?

ATTACHÉ: Under the mark, if anything, sir.

ARTHUR: Young man, do you realise – but no. Only a Scot can feel as I feel about it. Look at this one item alone. £5,038 15s 9⅞d for cordite enough to kill a single German. How can any country stand such a strain?

ATTACHÉ: It's not the cordite, sir. It's the acetone that is so expensive. Cordite cannot be made without acetone.

ARTHUR: I don't know what acetone is; and I don't care. All I know is that if we go on like this we shall have to give an order to cease killing Germans. Dead Germans cost too much . . . Are our chemists trying how to find something cheaper?

ATTACHÉ: They are doing their best; but nothing has come of it so far. There's a chemist in Manchester who has a microbe that makes acetone for next to nothing.

ARTHUR: Send him here instantly. Why hasn't he been sent here before?

ATTACHÉ: Impossible, sir, unfortunately.

ARTHUR: Nothing is impossible when we are at war. Why is it impossible?

ATTACHÉ: He is a Jew, sir.

ARTHUR: Is his microbe a Jew?

ATTACHÉ: I suppose not, sir.

ARTHUR: Is Sir Herbert Samuel a Jew or is he not? Is he in the Cabinet or is he not?

ATTACHÉ: But it is a coalition Government, sir. All sorts of people are let in.

ARTHUR: Any other objection?

ATTACHÉ: Well, Manchester, you know, sir. Provincial. And Owens College! If it were Cambridge now, we might stretch a point.

ARTHUR: If this Jewish gentleman is not in this room in three hours, you go to the trenches.

ATTACHÉ: Oh, if you make a point of it, of course. But we shall lose tone.

ARTHUR (*roaring*): Get out!

(*The attaché shrugs his shoulders and goes out.*)

ARTHUR (*clutching his temples as he again pores over the sheet of figures*): Five thousand and thirty-eight golden pounds to put one Boche out of action! And we have to exterminate the lot of them!

ACT II

As before, three hours later, but with Dr Chaim Weizmann instead of the attaché.

ARTHUR: Doctor Weizmann, we must have that microbe at your own price. Name it. We shall not hesitate at six figures.

DR WEIZMANN: I do not ask for money.

ARTHUR: There must be some misunderstanding. I was informed that you are a Jew.

WEIZMANN: You were informed correctly. I am a Jew.

ARTHUR: But – pardon me – you said you did not ask for money.

WEIZMANN: Precisely. I do not want money.

ARTHUR: A title, perhaps? Baron? Viscount? Do not hesitate.

WEIZMANN: Nothing would induce me to accept a title. I should have to pay more for everything.

ARTHUR: Then may I ask, without offence, since you want none of the things that everybody wants, what the devil do you want?

WEIZMANN: I want Jerusalem.

ARTHUR: It's yours. I only regret that we cannot throw in Madagascar as well. Unfortunately it belongs to the French Government. The Holy Land belongs naturally to the Church of England; and to it you are most welcome. And now will you be so good as to hand over the microbe.

ACT III

Mr Bernard Shaw in his sumptuously furnished study reading the announcement of the Balfour Declaration.

MR B.S.: Another Ulster! As if one were not enough.

CURTAIN

Lord Janner, who would appreciate this playlet, tells me that Shaw once outlined an even shorter three-act play. A student who wanted to be a dramatist asked him for an idea. 'Act One,' said Shaw. 'Man: I adore you. Act Two: Man: I adore you. Act Three: Man: I adore you.' The young aspirant protested this was repetitively dull. 'Not at all,' corrected Shaw, 'the man would say it to three different women.'

CHAPTER TWENTY-THREE

FIRST VISIT TO AFRICA

My first visit to Africa was during the summer recess after my re-election to Parliament in 1950. I was invited to Uganda by the Farmers' Cooperative Federation and to Kenya by the African Union. Their representatives in London had become close friends. Ignatius Musazi was detained in Britain following a revolt in Uganda; although he was in London at the time of the clash a Commission of Enquiry named him, on flimsy evidence it seemed to me, as one of its instigators. He was a strange man, tall and handsome, but shy and reserved of speech. I had difficulty in persuading him to remain in England whilst I went to Uganda. He wished to defy arrest. I promised to report to James Griffiths, the Colonial Secretary, when I got back and hoped this would open the way for him.

Mbiyu Koinange, the representative of the Kenya African Union, was similar to Ignatius in some ways. He had spells of withdrawal when one never knew what he was brooding over. But he could be great fun, laughing like a hurricane. He came to London to awaken public opinion to the contrast between the land hunger of his people in the Kikuyu reserve and the great spaces reserved for Europeans in the neighbouring White Highlands. Mbiyu was a legendary figure in Kenya because of his association with Jomo Kenyatta in establishing African schools. His father, ex-senior chief of the Kikuyu, deposed by the British but retaining African loyalty, was to be my host in Kenya.

I travelled by seaplane, so much more enjoyable than today's aircraft. Jets are just a means of transport. One gets in, sits in a narrow chair, has a tray meal, sleeps, gets out. The seaplane was a house in the air. One sat on a lounge settee, wandered upstairs and downstairs, stood in the bar to chat and drink, borrowed books from the library. One got to know one's fellow passengers, played games with the children. It was a holiday. Besides, one learned something of the countries we passed through. We stayed a night on the island of Sicily and another at Luxor in Egypt, the seaplane resting on the Nile. I left it at Khartoum to spend some days in Sudan.

Sudan was a year from self-government. The Egyptians had withdrawn and the British were preparing to do so. The question was: would Sudan vote to become independent or federate with Egypt? I met the spokesmen of the two views, both religious leaders as well as political. My reception by Mahdi Pasha was fantastic. I was escorted by uniformed guards from the gate of a shining palace, guided through an avenue of thirty bowing, white-robed notables towards a majestic figure in flowing silken garments, who sat awaiting me as a king on a throne. At the subsequent banquet, however, the Mahdi became ordinarily human, feeding a pet kitten from his plate. I did not like this alliance of religion and wealth. I remembered the poverty of Luxor, the ragged children with inflamed eyes. Nevertheless, I was impressed by the dignity of my host. His story was dramatic.

His grandfather led the revolt which brought the death of General Gordon in 1885. Thirteen years later Lord Kitchener took revenge at Omdurman, killing his father. Kitchener was merciful to the son, only ten: 'He is too young to put to death.' Stripped of power, Mahdi's boyhood was spent in penury, but, when the goodwill of the Sudanese was required in the First World War, the British restored their traditional leader's fortunes by pre-enting him with a timber-rich island estate. He used his new wealth to collect the largest cotton interests in Sudan. He told me that he became pro-British and anti-Egyptian by his impression of the sincerity of Attlee and the width of view of Bevin when he was summoned to meet them in London.

His rival, Mirghani Pasha, was anti-British and pro-Egyptian. His personality did not impress me, but I responded to his simple living and his colleagues showed that they had more contact with the people by pouring out facts of the absence of education, medical attention and social services. The election of the first all-Sudanese Government did not take place until after I returned to London. Mirghani's more democratic party won, but the sequence was surprising. The Government declared, not for federation with Egypt, but for independence. I would like to know the intrigues which brought that about. A great British success.

I cannot leave Sudan without reference to the Gezira scheme. In all subsequent experience of Africa I never found anything more constructively inspiring. One million acres of land lay arid in the triangle between Khartoum and the White and Blue Niles. The desert was converted into fertile farms, growing cotton, wheat, millet, under a partnership of Government and Cooperative tenants. The income of the tenants was £39 a year in 1938. In the year of my visit, 1950, it was £600, and £75,000 had been set aside for medical and educational development with the tenants' participation. This extraordinary transformation was achieved by damming the Blue Nile and channelling its Ethiopian waters, rich in silt, across the dry earth. The genius behind it was Arthur Gaitskell, brother of Labour's subsequent leader. When I returned to London I had tea with him in the Commons. He looked at the indicator and saw that Gaitskell was speaking. 'I bet I'm the only man who has seen from a tea-table that he was speaking in the Chamber,' he laughed.

I flew on to Uganda over the swamps of southern Black Sudan. In Khartoum I had met a pathetic deputation from its people resentful of oppression from the Arab north; later I shall tell of the negotiations which led to their autonomy. The seaplane descended on Lake Victoria, a tree-banked inland sea. An English official in the customs asked my name. When I told him he said smiling, 'There are three thousand people outside to receive you.' I was astonished. The Farmers' Union which had invited me was officially suppressed. How could such a welcome be organised? But there the people were, lining the road for three miles and a thousand were outside the bungalow near Kampala where I was to stay. This was my first evidence of the irrelevance of the isolated British administration at distant and isolated Entebbe. Soon I had more. The Farmers' Executive had been hiding in the jungle – they came out for the first time to meet me – but they had planned not only my reception but my tour throughout Uganda with a thoroughness which no legal organisation could have exceeded. They had actually constructed meeting places in twenty widely divided centres, with auditoriums as large as football pitches, roofed by banana leaves stretched over crisscross frames of bamboos. In two places, where there was no accommodation, they had even erected bamboo bungalows, duly fitted with European-style lavatories, for my night's stay. A cook, a mobile kitchen and a bath accompanied me everywhere. So much for suppression!

At the meetings I listened more than I spoke. I felt I was in an occupied country. The Government was the enemy; everything it ordered had to be resisted. The collaborating chiefs, paid salaries by the British, and the Africans in the police were regarded as stooges and traitors, the same psychology as I had met in the resistance movement in Nazi-occupied France. The non-collaboration went to extremes. A Government Research Station advised on agricultural techniques and disease prevention, but the farmers would have nothing to do with it. I found on the estate of a loyalist chief that production and cattle stock had improved and malaria had been elimin-

179

ated, thanks to this official aid, but the farmers refused to cooperate. They had genuine grievances in the unfair payments made by the Cotton Marketing Board which yielded large profits to the Government and by the exploitation they suffered from Indian ownership of the processing ginneries. These were immediate grievances, but the temper of the meetings was indignation against the British occupation.

I was disturbed by the anti-Indian feeling. It surprised me to learn that there were more Indians than Europeans in East Africa, descendants of the indentured labour force which had built the railway from Mombasa on the coast to Uganda. In the main streets of Kampala one might have been in an Indian city. The graceful figures of Indian women, in green and gold saris, walked the pavements, their children about them. Indians had a monopoly of trade; the shops were all Indian. It was only when one went into the hidden alleys behind the broad avenues that the thousands of Africans crowded in mud huts became visible. I went to see the leaders of the Indian community who offered to negotiate with African representatives regarding the ginneries, and later, when I saw liberal Indians in Kenya and Nehru in London, their intervention led to fuller cooperation. Alas, not enough. I was shocked in the seventies by the brutal eviction of Indians from Uganda by General Amin, but I understood its popular support.

The Governor of Uganda, Sir John Hull, was absent in London, but I went to see the Acting Governor, who was friendly but referred me to officials. The officials were courteous but cold and distant, in strange contrast to members of the administration in Sudan. I learned the apparent reason. An African employed in the telegraphic service gave me a copy of an instruction which he said Sir John had signalled to his staff. It ordered them to supply me with information legitimate for a Member of Parliament but not – repeat *not* – to help me otherwise, and to observe my activities. When I returned to London I showed the copy of the telegram to John Dugdale, the Minister of State, and he authorised an enquiry. No trace of the signal could be found. I remained sceptical.

My interviews with the British officials were monologues. They noted what I said, but declined to comment on the ground that the absent Governor alone had that authority. I said plenty. I raised not only the grievances of the farmers, but a wide range of political and social questions. Why had Africans no elected members in their native Parliament of Buganda? Why were there no state schools for African children? What are you doing about the eleven children out of twelve who do not complete their courses at school because their parents cannot afford the fees or because they have to work to keep the family alive? Why were there no social services; no unemployment, sickness, old age or widows' benefits? Why was the medical service so inadequate? (As I found when I had a fever at a distant farm and learned that the nearest doctor was eighty miles away.) Did all this represent the mission of civilisation we were taking to Africa? I acknowledged one good provision in Uganda – the prohibition of the alienation of land which prevented white occupation.

I visited the Kabaka, the hereditary ruler of the Buganda, the dominant tribe. He lived in a mansion on a parkland overlooking Kampala. First I saw his Cabinet – Prime Minister, Finance Minister, Law Minister. I was told they were nominees of the British administration – certainly they could not have been more subservient. The Prime Minister told me everything in Uganda was perfect, that was the word he used. The Ministers followed me into the Kabaka's chamber, throwing themselves on the floor in obeisance. What was I supposed to do? To my relief the Kabaka, Oxford-mannered, stretched his hand and invited me to sit down. I did not dare to speak openly because I sensed that the Ministers had been ordered to be present by Entebbe. Later the Kabaka defied the Governor and was exiled to London, and during this visit I had the impression that he was a prisoner in his own palace. He was regarded by many Africans as a playboy. Perhaps that was his escapism.

In great contrast with the Kabaka's palace was my visit to the Central Prison where I saw prisoners, including two women, still detained for their part in the earlier revolt. They were resolute, but tears were in their eyes when I gave them messages from their families. I was angered by the distinction between the conditions of the African and the European prisoners. However light the offence of an African, he had food, clothing and accommodation inferior to those of the worst European criminal. I was still more shocked by something I had never expected to see in a British prison – in a corner of the exercise yard half a dozen Africans were chained at the ankles. I had seen this only in American films of bygone days. When I got back to my bungalow I telephoned the Acting Governor. He was unhappy, but explained that the men had attempted to escape.

When I returned to London I submitted a report of all I had seen to James Griffiths, the Colonial Secretary, whom I admired for his humanity. He could not make all the changes I suggested, but much was done. Ignatius Musazi was unconditionally released three months after he returned to Uganda, a majority of elected members were added to the Buganda Parliament, the Kabaka's three Ministers were replaced by men who had popular support, the ban on the Farmers' Cooperative was lifted, the cotton ginneries were placed under Cooperative control, the sentences on the political prisoners was reduced, and prison reforms were introduced, including the abolition of the human chains. I do not claim that all these reforms were due to my political recommendations, but I like to think that I contributed towards them.

CHAPTER TWENTY-FOUR

KENYA BEFORE MAU MAU

I had still to go to Kenya. Jomo Kenyatta met me at the airport, unchanged from our London days, aquiline features, a cloak over his shoulders, the invariable ivory-topped stick in his hand, grinning radiantly. We motored to ex-chief Koinange's bungalow at Kiambu, through the broad streets of Nairobi, thronged with Africans, Indians, Europeans and Arabs, glimpsing a beautiful flower-adorned European suburb, passing the European coffee plantations to the African banana farms. We turned down a lane and there was the Koinange picture-book bungalow, red brickwork, blue woodwork, a white door. On the steps stood an old smiling man, dressed in a pressed grey suit, and by his side five women, from old to young, in workaday clothes, with beaming faces, the ex-chief and his wives. I had been told even by liberal visitors to Kenya that I could not live with Africans. I have never been more comfortable than in this Kiambu bungalow. The sitting room might have been that of any English home, my bedroom was cosy, an English style lavatory. The only difference was the separation of the women and children, who lived in a kraal fifty yards away, a circle of tall well-conditioned roomy huts, rising like steeples. My London friend, Mbiyu Koinange, the oldest son, who had raced me from England, laughed boisterously as he hugged me. The ex-chief charmed me from the first. He was born before registration and no one knew his age. He could not read or write or speak English, but he was gentle, gracious, dignified, a Nature's gentleman. He was a sincere Christian, spiritually cultured.

If I had no doubts about my African home, I soon learned that others had. The next morning whilst I was still taking a cup of tea in bed, a journalist arrived from Nairobi's leading daily. He asked me if I realised how shocked Europeans were that I should be staying with natives. It was not done. It was

183

unprecedented for a British MP not to stay at Government House or at least in a European hotel. I sought to reassure this outraged opinion by making my first visit that morning to Government House. The Governor, Sir Philip Mitchell, was on leave, but I had the friendliest time with the Acting Governor and Chief Secretary. I told them how as a young Socialist I had been brought up on books on Kenya by Norman Leys and Macgregor Ross, and they surprised me by saying that this was also their introduction. The books were compulsory reading for students entering the Colonial Service.

I was soon to learn that the injustices described by Norman Leys persisted. The ex-chief took me round his farm with its hundreds of banana trees, Mbiyu with us to translate. We stood overlooking a European farm. The land had once been the chief's but was appropriated for alien possession with the rest of the White Highlands. The only compensation offered was the value put upon its trees which the ex-chief declined to accept; that would have been to recognise the theft. 'When someone steals your ox,' the old man said, 'it is killed and eaten. One can forget. When someone steals your land one can never forget. They are always there, the trees, the little streams, one loves.' The European farm was lined with coffee plants. 'I was the first to grow coffee in Kenya,' he said. 'My plantation was a model. The plants were uprooted and I was forbidden to grow more. Only Europeans are allowed to grow coffee.'

Kenyatta came in the evening and with the ex-chief and Mbiyu we had a long political discussion. What were the Africans to do – resort to force or exert political pressure? I urged the latter, pointing out that with a Labour Government in England there was a new opportunity. The ex-chief strongly supported and Kenyatta and Mbiyu agreed. We decided to press for elected African members of the Legislature, the lifting of the ban on the Kikuyu's political organisation, and a giant petition on land hunger which I would present to the Commons. The whole purpose was to build up an African movement, extending to all the tribes, which would take the fullest opportunity of constitutional advance. Kenyatta was excited by the prospect and wrung my hands as he departed. I have often thought back to that conversation. Jomo was afterwards charged with beginning to organise Mau Mau at this time. In fact, he began to organise political action.

Next day I drove with Jomo to see his training centre for teachers at his independent schools. We passed a woman balancing a ten-foot tree trunk on her shoulders, her husband a few steps ahead unburdened. The woman staggered and I wanted to get out, but Kenyatta stopped me – the woman would resent intervention more than the man. 'It's a women's revolution you want here,' I exploded. 'When I speak to your African Union may I say so?' 'It's dynamite, but have a go,' Jomo laughed. Then I challenged him on the Kikuyu habit of women's circumcision about which he had written in his *Facing Mount Kenya*, his degree thesis at the London School of Economics. Kenyatta did not so much defend the practice as explain. The object was to preserve virginity before marriage by eliminating external sexual excitement. The operation consisted of removing the sensory nerves on the clitoris which could incite the desire for full intercourse. It was then only by internal contact that physical reaction could be aroused. At puberty both sexes had their club huts where they went to bed together, the girls naked except for a cloth between their legs. Thus the boys could get relief, but the girls remained virgins. As I listened I was outraged. It seemed to me to be barbaric to safeguard virginity by the surgical limitations of a woman's natural physical reactions. It was another example of man's domination in Kenya.

I found the training college for African teachers in a rough and unfinished stage. A green space of several acres was dotted with wooden huts, but the students were still engaged in putting together permanent buildings. Kenyatta had his headquarters here, the most elaborate thatched construction I have ever seen, with large rooms, a library, a bedroom and kitchen, furnished tastefully and comfortably. Shelves were crowded with books, anthropological, social and political, strongly biased to Marxism. On the walls were photographs of Lenin, Paul Robeson, Nehru. On the return journey we visited one of the African schools, reasonably equipped, the teachers and children devoted, but it was the scene of the building of a new school which moved me most. Our car pulled up behind a lorry beneath a steep bank. African men and women were unloading large blocks of stone and struggling up the bank under their weight. In the field above men were constructing the walls of a large hall. This was entirely voluntary labour, revealing the enthusiasm for education. The founder of the schools was Mbiyu. He had returned from his university in America consecrated to spreading education. Later these schools were closed as nurseries of Mau Mau and Mbiyu was bracketed with Kenyatta for establishing them with this purpose. I did not see a sign of this on my visits.

It was when returning from one of these schools that I saw the most shocking thing in all my African experience. We descended from high uplands to a plain of maize crops, dotted at regular intervals by circles of smouldering black ashes. Among them sat an old man. We stopped the car and ran to him. He was shattered, crying and almost speechless, but gradually Jomo gathered his story. Police had arrived that morning with bulldozers, knocked down the row of peasants' huts and set the ruins alight. There was one armed officer still on guard, who confirmed the story and added that the police would return the following day to burn the crops. Commented Jomo, 'The old man says he has nothing in the world and that he will die with his maize.' Villagers had arrived from nowhere. We persuaded the old man to go with them; they were already caring for the other families. I wrote a report and despatched it to the Acting Governor. Three days later, sitting in the plane which was to take me back to England, his reply was handed to me. The bulldozed and burnt-out peasants were Kikuyus squatting illegally on the land of another tribe, the Masais. They had been warned of eviction.

The next day I investigated the land hunger of the Kikuyu which had led those peasants to trespass. I visited villages where hardly an able-bodied man was to be found. There was not a yard of uncultivated land and they were driven to become cheap labour in the towns. Many of the Kikuyu became 'serfs' on the extensive European farms, provided with huts and small patches of land to grow the family food, paid 2s 6d to 4s 6d a week, not allowed to leave the farms without permits. The men in the towns were paid wages which the Medical Officer of Health for Nairobi said were inadequate to keep a single person in health. Their wives and children left behind in the village went hungry.

My visit to the villages had been tiring and I begged to be excused visiting a housing estate. An incident followed when I quarrelled angrily with Kenyatta. He suggested that I should relax for a time by getting away from my persistent companions and go with him for a short quiet drive. The drive turned out to be long, and I became increasingly annoyed because I wanted nothing more than to return to the Koinange bungalow and rest. Jomo kept reassuring me, but despite my protests the car went far into the country. We drove into a drive through banana plantations and Jomo at last revealed that we were visiting his home. Outside we were greeted by a group of girls, but Jomo hurried me inside for a drink. The house was a granite fortress, the entrance hall bare and cold. I was so bad-tempered that I insisted on immediate departure. As we left Jomo asked me to say a few words to the girls; I wished the African cause well, but they were unresponsive and seemed perplexed. I did not forgive Jomo, but now I wonder whether his thought was not to relax me in female company. That would have been in accordance with his reputation.

The climax of my visit was a racial goodwill party which ex-chief Koinange arranged for thirty prominent representatives of each community – African, European, Indian. It turned out to be much more than that. According to *The Times* 30,000 Africans attended. Mbiyu suggested that this was a spontaneous expression of admiration, but my impression is that it was a contrived demonstration of African strength in the presence of community leaders. The official guests sat at tables prepared for tea on the grass which fronted the bungalow. Everyone seemed to have come; Government officials, members of the Legislature, the UN Commissioner, the Indian Commissioner, judges, religious leaders, settlers. Kenya had never before had such a representative assembly. The Africans crowded round us, packed as far as the eye could see between the banana trees, clinging to the branches of larger trees. The chief stepped to a 'mike' and described the occasion as a supreme venture to break through barriers of race to reach the human spirit in all. Sir Charles Mortimer, prominent member of the Executive Council, Dr Kalabala, the UN Commissioner, and a veteran leader of the Indian community spoke in the same vein. I delivered my speech and thought the occasion was over.

I was summoned again to the side of the ex-chief. He lifted from a large box a silk-lined cape of grey-black fur and placed it over my shoulders, hugged me and kissed me on both cheeks. Guests clapped in appreciative astonishment; the African crowds danced and shouted in mad excitement. The old man raised his hand and at last there was silence. In solemn words he pronounced me a chief of the Kikuyu tribe and his own blood-brother. Again pandemonium. African men shouted and stamped in unison, the woman danced and shrilled. This was the ceremony they had come to see.

The next morning the ex-chief brought his five wives and Mbiyu into my bedroom. 'According to Kikuyu custom you are now inseparable from me,' he said. 'These are your wives. This is your son.' Mbiyu has called me 'Dad' ever since. Two other whites have been inducted as Kikuyu chiefs: before me, Dr Leakey, the Kenya historian, and, afterwards, D. N. Pritt, who defended Kenyatta at the Mau Mau trial. My chieftain's robe hangs in a cupboard waiting to be worn.

CHAPTER TWENTY-FIVE

KENYA DURING MAU MAU

With my Parliamentary colleague and friend, Leslie Hale, I returned to Kenya shortly after the Mau Mau Emergency had been declared. Jomo Kenyatta and the officers of the Kenya African Union were already arrested. Our visit was bitterly resented by the European settlers and became front page news both in Nairobi and London. The Press swarmed about us at the airport. I read out a prepared statement: we had come on a fact-finding mission, we hoped to see representatives of the four races, we would encourage cooperation and discourage violence, we believed in the equality of all peoples and would claim that for Africans. The newspapers listened with polite indifference. They had questions to ask. Had Kenyatta paid our air fares and signed the cheque? Were we the guests of the African Union? We did not know who had signed the cheque. Was I aware that Michael Blundell, the European leader, had charged me in the Legislature with being a Communist, with attending Communist conferences all over Europe and with having been arrested in Poland as a Communist? Leslie chuckled, but we had agreed to avoid controversy. 'If it is necessary to reply to Mr Blundell I'll do so in the House of Commons,' I said.

The plane had been hot, and Leslie shocked the Europeans by descending from it with shirt open at the neck and without socks. 'A Poor White,' exclaimed a sumptuously dressed lady, using the Kenya term for down-and-outs. There was a sequel three days later. A helicopter dropped a pair of socks weighted with stones in the garden of the house where we were staying. An attached tag addressed the gift 'To a Distressed MP from Charity'.

We were startled on leaving the airport to learn that a military guard would accompany us everywhere whilst in Kenya. An African sergeant would sit with us in the car, six armed African police would follow in another car and three European officers would bring up the rear in a third. We protested but were informed that the Governor insisted. There was no attempt to hide that we were to be protected not from Mau Mau but from Europeans. The new officers of the Kenyan African Union met us – Odede, a member of the Legislature, who had replaced Jomo as chairman; Aurori, also a Legco member, the treasurer; and Murumbi, ex-civil servant, the new secretary. Where should we stay? The Koinanges wanted us at Kiambu, but I heard with incredulity that the ex-chief was in custody on the charge of being an accomplice in the murder of a 'loyalist' chief. To stay in a house over which this charge hung would bring prejudice against us; the alternative was to accept an invitation from an Indian sympathiser, Mrs Desai, in Nairobi. Friendship called. I had no doubt that the ex-chief was innocent and the family (who had been made my family) would want our sympathy and support. I put the problem to Leslie. 'Of course we go to the Koinanges,' he said. We had a moving welcome, but in fact stayed only one night. The Africans argued that we must be in Nairobi to see people.

Mrs Desai's house was in a suburb where Indians (but not Africans) were allowed to live side by side with Europeans. It, too, was a bungalow, spacious with flower-beds about it. The African sergeant placed his men with their guns round the house. From a window we could see the car with the European officers in the road opposite. Mrs Desai was the most wonderful hostess of whom I have ever been a guest. There were the armed men in the garden; Africans and journalists came from dawn to midnight; she never knew how many to seat at a meal. On one occasion, officers with guns at the ready burst in to make an arrest; messages came that European fanatics were on the way to murder Leslie and me. Her husband was absent in India; she did not speak English. Yet all the time she was serene and gracious, a slim figure in her sari, moving quietly about the house. We revered her.

We decided to talk to the Government first. We saw the Chief Secretary, who had been Acting Governor in Uganda when I was there two years earlier. He was as dumb as he had been at Entebbe. We saw the Ministers in succession, including Sir Charles Mortimer who had spoken at the Koinange party when I was made a chief. He was anxious for us. The most forthcoming was the Attorney General, with whom Leslie as a solicitor made rapport. The Law Minister acknowledged the wrongs from which the Africans suffered, but was appalled by the atrocities committed by Mau Mau. He showed us photographs of babies mutilated beyond belief. He was scrupulously fair, saying that only ten Europeans had been killed and acknowledging that one photograph at least pictured not the infamy of Mau Mau, but of thieving gangsters. (This photograph, nevertheless, was exhibited in the House of Commons library as a Mau Mau atrocity.)

After the Ministers we were received by the Governor, Sir Evelyn Baring, distinguished in appearance, charming of manner. He was liberal in approach, but we doubted if he were decisive enough for action. We faced him with an immediate test. The new leaders of the Kenya African Union, Odede, Aurori and Murumbi, had offered to broadcast appeals to their peoples to boycott Mau Mau. Following our representations, they were summoned to meet the Secretary of State, Oliver Lyttelton, visiting Kenya, as well as the Governor. The Colonial Secretary, we were told, ignored the Africans; he entered, nodded to the Governor to speak, listened and left without a word. Telling us this, the Africans laughed but I could sense their bitterness. The Governor was more courteous, but insisted on the impossible condition that in their broadcast the African leaders should repudiate Kenyatta even before he had been put on trial. We appealed to the Governor to reconsider this decision, but could not move him. Then we put to him an alternative: why should not we ourselves broadcast an appeal to Africans to refrain from association with Mau Mau? He refused; we despaired. It became evident that the Government put the isolation of African leaders and even moderates and their supporters before the need to isolate Mau Mau.

When we got back to Mrs Desai's, Odede had a brainwave. He suggested that Leslie and I should write an appeal to the African people, endorsed by Aurori, Murumbi and himself, and promised that KAU would distribute it throughout Kenya. I asked Leslie to draft it, knowing he had the human touch needed, and he did it superbly. We identified ourselves with African demands for land, wages, education, elected members of the Legislature and the elimination of discrimination, but ended with the firm declaration that those who advocated a resort to violence were the real enemies of the African people. Murumbi hurried to the KAU offices to make arrangements for translation, publication and distribution, and a few days later we heard from distant places how the appeal had been welcomed. It is an irony that soon afterwards Odede, who inspired this move to prevent violence, should have been arrested and detained and that the Kenya African Union, which implemented it, should have been suppressed.

Our visits to Ministers completed, we set out to visit what was described as Mau Mau territory. The police sergeant was squeezed in between Odede and the driver and second and third cars followed with the five

African guards and the three European officers. We were doubtful if any African would speak freely to us under such intimidation, but worse was to come. On the outskirts of Nairobi we were stopped by military police and informed that an armed escort was waiting to accompany us. Two cars with three officers each and a lorry with twelve guards, rifles in hand, lined up. What should we do? We decided on a try-out, but our experience at the first village, Fort Hall, was enough. Africans lined the road and clustered the market place to meet us. 'No meetings allowed,' warned an officer, preparing to disperse the crowd. I never felt more frustrated. I asked Odede to go among the people quietly to express our regrets and to say we would protest.

We returned seething to Nairobi. Leslie got on the phone to Government House. He began explosively, became conciliatory, reached agreement, cracked a joke. In future our immediate guard would be limited to our faithful sergeant and one officer, with five police travelling in a lorry a hundred yards behind; we would be allowed to meet Africans alone behind closed doors. We went to other tribes than the Kikuyu and, except for the Masai nomadic cattle breeders, everywhere the grievances were the same; land hunger, prohibition of coffee and sisal growing, serfdom on European farms and men forced into the towns. At a Wakamba village the complaint was against the British-paid African chief. When we sought him out he said he could not speak without permission from the District Officer. We took him to the DO who still did not allow him to speak, and who assured us that everyone in the tribe was prosperous and happy. Our interpreter was missing. 'Sorry to have inconvenienced you,' said the DO, 'but I had instructions to pick him up. Funny he should walk into my hands like that.' 'What is the charge against him?' I asked. 'No charge. He'll be screened. I suppose he's been in suspicious company.' 'He's been in our company,' said Leslie.

We arranged two meetings with the settlers. The first took place in their office in Nairobi, Kenya's leading woman farmer presiding. She was well-tailored, clear cut in features, competent, strong-willed. 'You ask us to regard Africans as equals,' she said in an even voice. 'Every African is dishonest, a liar, lazy. Their language has no word for love, gratitude, loyalty.' That was the most frightening thing I heard in Kenya, incredible, but there the words were dotted down in my shorthand. Back in the car I asked our Kikuyu sergeant the terms in his language for love, gratitude, loyalty. 'Wendo, ngatho, wathikeri,' he replied. By a mistake we failed to keep our appointment with the European farmers at Thika. We started out when we should have arrived and only an angry secretary was left. This was a disaster psychologically. I wrote apologising, but we never lived down the charge that we feared the meeting.

At Mrs Desai's we began to see deputations at 8 am and between engagements saw them until midnight. We were disturbed by the reports that many of our visitors were afterwards arrested; the European officers in their car outside the gate noted all who came to see us. On the third night we learned that they went off duty at 11 pm, and from then on those who did not wish to be identified came after hours. They included prominent liberal Europeans. Sometimes visitors were arrested when with us. One afternoon when we were meeting a deputation of trade unionists, two officers, revolvers in hand, burst in and demanded, 'that man with a beard'. When the deputation left I phoned the police. I was assured everything was all right; the man had been released. The next morning I heard that the 'man with the beard' had been interrogated for an hour on what had occurred at our meeting. I do not believe that the officers even knew the name of the man when they arrested him; they picked on anyone to learn what had been said.

There was another occasion when the motive was different. A well-known journalist was interviewing me. We were sitting on a settee, chatting, drinking, smoking. Three European officers rushed the door and, revolvers pointing at my visitor, commanded him to accompany them. On the balcony, our guard at attention, one officer searched the journalist whilst the second covered him. Neither arms nor incriminating papers were found. The senior officer apologised, explaining that they had had word from HQ that a man was on his way to kill me and his description fitted. The journalist hurried away to despatch a better story than he had expected.

The most moving of our experiences was a visit to the ex-chief Koinange in prison. We sat in the office of a prison official, a young Englishman in tunic and shorts, who continued with his papers. The ex-chief clung to me and embraced me. We sat in a group, Aurori translating. The old man was little concerned with himself, but he was broken by the tragedy of Kenya and anxious for his family. It was pathetic to hear of the pleasure which the news of our visit to his home had given him. This was the first time Leslie had met the ex-chief. He had wondered at my affection for him, but during this brief talk he was won completely. When we got back to London Leslie devoted himself to securing the best legal defence. When news came that Dingle Foot had secured his acquittal, Leslie was as happy as I was. But we rejoiced too early. The ex-chief was re-arrested under the Emergency Laws without any charge brought against him – and held in detention for six years. I will complete the story. I received a message that he was suffering

F.B. at the unveiling of a plaque on his old home in Islington

Clem Attlee presenting F.B. with a briefcase on his 70th birthday. The setting is
the Slough Labour Party dinner

from infirmity in old age. I tried to get Lennox-Boyd, at that time Colonial Secretary, to place him under 'house arrest' so that he could go home. After consulting the Governor he refused; the utmost concession I could get was permission for one of his wives to join him. Later came news that he was seriously ill and I persuaded Lennox Boyd to allow his son Mbiyu, then in London, to visit him and raised the money for him to go. The old man got worse and I begged the Colonial Secretary to allow him to return to his farm for his last days. Again refusal; then news came that he had been taken by plane and ambulance to the farm to die.

This was one of the most unforgiveable examples of Ministerial inaction I have ever known. Firm for African rights and self-government – of course Koinange was. But he loved peoples of all races, longed for their cooperation, and had a spiritual beauty which lifted him above all but a few. I bowed my head on my next visit to Kenya two years later as I stood by his simple grave under a tree on the farm he loved.

We had only three days left. We came for fact-finding and to contribute to solutions. We had got our facts, but had contributed little constructively. We were sitting, after eleven o'clock at night, with journalists and sympathetic Kenyans, Europeans as well as Africans. 'Why not a round-table conference of all races?' suddenly said Leslie. We gasped, but to our surprise two of the most distinguished of the journalists, James Cameron and Colin Legum, said they thought the idea would be accepted. Opinion had changed since we arrived. The Nairobi Press had altered its tone; the Tory papers in London wrote that we had behaved correctly; Kenya Europeans acknowledged our reasonableness. Leslie suggested that we should prepare a list of immediate reforms: higher minimum wages for Africans, extended African trade unions, reduction in the price of *posho* (the African staple food), liberty of Africans to grow coffee and sisal, cooperative farming, extended education for Africans, equal pay to all races doing similar work in the public services, the progressive elimination of racial discrimination and so on. If we could get a document on these lines signed by leaders of the four racial groups – African, European, Asian, Arab – the psychological effect would be great and might break through Kenya's disastrous conflict. Everyone became excited as Leslie spoke. Our African friends insisted that we should put everything off to pull off this exhilarating project. The journalists left to prepare the ground. Leslie and I stayed up most of the night drafting the statement.

We met at the office of the European Electors' Union, European, Asian, African and Arab members of the Legislature. We shook hands a little uncertainly. The two Europeans were Michael Blundell and W. B. Havelock.

Blundell, large, easy-mannered, summoned me into a side room. He said he agreed to meet me because I had indicated at the airport that I would reply to his criticism in the House of Commons and not enter into controversy in Kenya. He went on to acknowledge handsomely that, after checking my political record, he was wrong in describing me as a Communist. He promised to withdraw the charge before the Electors' Union. He took my arm as we re-entered, which reduced the tension considerably.

I had asked Leslie to state our case because there was less prejudice against him and he did so conciliatorily. Blundell was all out to be accommodating. Pencil in hand, he went through our document, ticking paragraphs with which he agreed, deleting items and phrases – I still have a copy of the statement as amended by him. He agreed that the African minimum wage was too low, but declined to accept early reconsideration and refused to welcome trade unions; he was ready to say that the price of *posho* was too high, but would not subsidise it; more serious, he insisted on scratching out the paragraphs condemning racial discrimination and asking for equal pay for equal work. But he actually strengthened references to African housing and he endorsed land registration and cooperative farming. Other members of the conference were almost entirely silent, but agreed with Leslie that, despite the deletions, the declaration was worth while as a basis for a united inter-racial front. With relief and hope we folded our papers.

The one uneasy face was Havelock's. He clearly felt his European colleague was going too far. He threw a note to Blundell. Leslie hastened to suggest that the revised statement should be adopted. Blundell opened the note and read it whilst we all paused anxiously. Blundell spoke persuasively. 'It has been suggested,' he said, 'that our agreement would have greater effect if it came from ourselves rather than by the initiative of our visitors. There will be a meeting of the groups in the Legislature tonight. Should we not postpone our joint statement until then?' The suggestion had force and it was reassuring that the conference agreed that Leslie and Havelock should meet next morning to draft a press statement about our meeting.

That evening we had a party at Mrs Desai's; journalists, Africans, Europeans, drinking, singing and laughing together. We took beer to our guard and, to their surprise, to the three spying officers. We were overjoyed by this unforeseen achievement of our visit. The journalists had already written their stories for despatch on the morrow of the breakthrough of racial cooperation in stricken Kenya.

Then disaster. Leslie's voice broke on returning from his meeting with Havelock. He told how when Blundell returned from our conference to his farm he found a sheet of paper with a threat from Mau Mau. The joint declaration, said Havelock, would appear to be appeasement in face of the threat. The Europeans could not sign it. The whole thing was off. Leslie and I sat silent. How near we were to success, how bitter the cause of defeat!

We left the next day. We spent three days in Uganda and I found a great change since my visit two years earlier. The previously outlawed Farmers' Cooperative held a reception for us at the exclusively white Imperial Hotel, where the previously exiled Ignatius Musazi was host to Government officials and to Establishment Africans, including the Kabaka. The Kabaka's presence meant that we could not dance despite an inviting band, but I arranged with African girls to go to a party where I drank a prohibited Ugandan spirit, after which I remembered nothing. Next morning on my pillow was a message from Leslie written on sheets of toilet paper describing how I had been his hero and how I had fallen. I have never been able to persuade him to tell me what happened that night!

We flew in a tiny single-engine plane to Toro, a distant province, where the greatest grievance of the Africans was that their land had been confiscated for a national park for animals. 'What about sanctuaries for human life?' exclaimed the Princess of Toro, who won Leslie's heart because in dress and speech she might have been a millworker from his Oldham. When our car stopped at a road sign there seemed to be something in the complaint. It read: 'Give Way to Elephants'. We spent a night in a rest house, but there was no sleep. Africans crowded the floor, the princess presiding from the one seat. Our departing car travelled under the Mountain of the Moon, where we saw the ugly excavations for Uganda's first copper mine. Our little plane rose from a field, a lark fluttering upward in front of the propeller. Leslie, with a love of birds, pointed excitedly as we crossed a mountain range to an eagle soaring majestically in the sky. The unending forests became boring and I began to snooze. I awoke with a start. *Our one engine had stopped and the plane was falling!* It lasted only a few seconds, but the silence of the immobile propeller was loud. The pilot pushed buttons, the engine began to purr, the propeller to move. I pinched Leslie's cheek and he winked. The pilot wiped sweat from his forehead. I had begun to speculate whether there would be by-elections in Oldham West and Eton and Slough.

We saw the new Governor, Sir Andrew Cohen. What a contrast with my last visit to Entebbe! We talked as friends over tea, sometimes differing but respecting one another. He was a generous person. There was a student at Makerere College, Abu Mayanja, who led a students' strike and was expelled. I knew he was brilliant and I appealed to Sir Andrew to give him a further chance. He responded by saying that he would give Abu a state scholarship to Cambridge if he would undertake three years' service to the Uganda Government on completing his course. Abu refused, he wanted to serve only the African cause. I approached Sir Andrew again and he withdrew the condition. Abu went to Cambridge and became Education Minister in the Buganda Government. I do not know what has happened to him since the Amin *coup*.

I add a postscript to this chapter. I was never scared of assassination in Kenya: I was once in London. We had had a late sitting at the House and Harold Wilson had driven four MPs and me to our homes in Highgate. At nine the next morning my wife awakened me to say that a visitor had travelled through the night from Plymouth to see me. I took him a cup of tea. He was in a long army coat and had a hand deep in a pocket. I waved to him to sit down, but he remained standing. 'I come from Kenya,' he said abruptly. 'I have some questions to ask you.' He asked me what I thought of Europeans, Africans, Mau Mau. I told him. He kept a steady gaze on me, his hand moving in his pocket; his attitude became menacing and I acknowledge I trembled. At that moment my wife opened the door, our son, young Christopher, at her side, leaving for school. I gave him a cheery 'Goodbye' and the door closed. My visitor laughed. '*Goodbye*,' he sneered and half pulled his hand from his pocket. He hesitated and paused, and then suddenly turned to the door and strode out. The next day I received a letter from 'Kenyan Cornishman' saying that he had intended to shoot me but had come to the conclusion that I was not worth hanging for. I did not regard that as a compliment.

CHAPTER TWENTY-SIX

THE CRUMBLING EMPIRES

After India, the colonial revolution of the fifties began in the French occupied territories. I was not involved in North Vietnam's triumph except through association with the Indo-Chinese in the Congress of Peoples against Imperialism and the aid given to them from our Paris headquarters, including a group of intellectuals, Sartre, Camus and others. But I am among the few who were at the Tours Conference of the French Socialist Party in 1920 when Ho Chi Minh was a delegate. Young, slim and dark, he made an impassioned speech on, 'the abhorrent crimes committed against my native land', and voted for affiliation to the Third International on the ground that Lenin was the hope of the victims of imperialism. Defeated, he was one of the breakaway group which formed the French Communist Party. I am told that I met him with other Vietnamese at a Marxist club in Charlotte Street, London, when he was employed as a kitchen hand at the Carlton Hotel, but of this I have only the vaguest recollection. In later years, as I shall tell, I took a leading part in the British campaign against American intervention in Indo-China; in these earlier days I was more concerned with Africa.

Leslie Hale and I, notorious after our visit to Kenya, were invited to Tunisia for the 1951 trade union conference. En route I went to Switzerland on an exciting project. My friend, Joseph Kruk, was then secretary of an international Jewish medical organisation, OSE. His council was considering taking over a wartime Nazi hospital at Davos in the Swiss Alps for tubercular Jewish refugees still lingering in German displaced persons' camps, and he asked me to report on it. My visit to 'Mon Repos' at Davos made me enthusiastic. It had bedrooms opening on balconies over snow-clad mountains bathed in sun and contained all the necessary medical apparatus, including the most modern X-ray. The proposal also appealed to my sense of justice. The Nazis had made 'Mon Repos' their secret Swiss HQ for radio activities during the war; the hidden broadcasting rooms were shown to me. I became secretary to a committee in London to raise funds for Joseph Kruk's project, and I was confident that the historical irony of converting a Nazi hospital into a centre for the treatment of Nazi victims would bring response. Then to my disappointment Kruk wrote that his council had decided to concentrate on sending money to Israel. An historic opportunity missed.

At Davos I caught a chill and at the Tunisian trade union conference I was drowsy, though the debate was on the lively topic of affiliation either to the Communist-dominated World Federation of Trade Unions or to the Con-federation of Free Trade Unions. The latter got the vote. I was awake enough, however, to be captivated by the personality of Ferhat Hached, the secretary. That afternoon, despite my tired protests, we visited the Bey of Tunisia, old, gracious, reserved. Nominally he was the King, but a French high official was present and showed us who was boss. I threw off my listlessness to spend the next day at Carthage, heir to the Phoenician empire. And the following morning I made a dull farewell speech to the conference and said goodbye to Leslie who was going to Rome. As I climbed the steps to my room my body ached and I threw myself fully dressed on my bed. I did not wake until five the next afternoon when a doctor came to take me to an OSE clinic which I had promised Kruk to visit. I have only the dimmest memory of its clean rooms. The doctor insisted on taking me to see also the Jewish quarters. Were they really the confusion of chalk-baked caverns which I saw as in a nightmare? At the doctor's home I collapsed over dinner.

It was four days before I returned to consciousness, and I stayed in the hospital of the White Sisters for three weeks. It was touch and go, so much so that Leslie and a dozen Labour colleagues – bless them! – met the cost of sending my wife to Tunis by air. I chose well the place of my collapse. The OSE doctor was the leading specialist in North Africa on lung diseases and I had virus double pneumonia. The care by the White Sisters was wonderful. The sister who looked after me postponed her holiday in France until I was through the crisis. My other memory is of Hached's kindness, not only to me but to my wife. One sometimes needs to be ill to know how good people can be.

After a stay in the South of France under medical care, Edith and I returned to our Highgate home. I was still convalescing when Habib Bourguiba, leader of Neo-Destour, Tunisia's all embracing independence movement, came to see us. He gave the impression of a diplomat from a great power rather than the head of an African rebellion: immaculately dressed, exquisitely mannered, precise in speech. He foresaw repression, negotiation, victory. Three years passed. Bourguiba's forecast was in its first stage. He was imprisoned, Neo-Destour and the trade unions outlawed. But then Mendès-France came to power in France. At the Geneva Conference he brought to an end (to be renewed by America, alas) the fighting in Vietnam. His first step in Tunisia was to allow the trade unions to resume, and to release some leaders from prison, though Bourguiba was kept under house-arrest in France. I was invited to their revived conference.

Tunis had one heavy sorrow for me. Hached had been assassinated by the French 'Red Terror'; I went to see his wife and children. For the first time I met his successor, Ahmed Ben Salah, who had returned to Tunis from three years' training at the Brussels headquarters of the Free Trade Unions. We sat late in a café the night before the conference and discussed in depth the policy we should advise. He was about thirty and had a lively personality, strong features, flashing eyes. Irving Brown, representing American unions was with us, calculating, suspicious of me, anti-colonial but even more anti-Communist. I had given thought to policy in the plane coming over. Mendès-France gave Tunis a new opportunity. I decided I would do all I could to influence the conference to provide the new Prime Minister with an opening to reverse French policy. To my delight Ben Salah and Brown took the same view, Salah coining the slogan 'No Violence and Negotiate Peace!' It was agreed that I should open the discussion, but it was not easy because I had to follow reports of French repression, telling how 1,600 Tunisians had been arrested and detained for long periods without trial. I began with a tribute to exiled Bourguiba which aroused hysterical cheering and then addressed Mendès-France directly. He had appealed for an end to violence in Tunisia; he would give an example by ending the violence of the regime. That won sympathy and the delegates listened intently to proposals for a settlement. To my relief the response was good and Ben Saleh sounded the call for 'No Violence and Negotiate Peace'. There were a few dissentions, but he got an overwhelming vote.

Back in my Highgate home the phone rang from Paris. A secretary of Mendès-France said the Prime Minister had been interested in reports of my Tunis speech and would like to have my suggestions in full. I sent them and I had a second call expressing appreciation. Developments followed quickly. Mendès-France released more prisoners (though he kept Bourguiba in France) and offered negotiations if Neo-Destour would declare a truce. The party did so and delegates came to Paris for peace talks.

At first they threatened to break off the negotiations unless Bourguiba were freed, but Bourguiba himself urged that irrespective of his position they should seek a settlement. I happened to be in Paris attending a conference of the War Resisters International, and two of the Tunisians came to me for advice. I paid tribute to the sacrifice of Bourguiba and argued that if peace were concluded his return to Tunis would be hastened and with self-government he would soon be Prime Minister. Peace was concluded, Bourguiba was soon released, and within a few months he was Head of State. With my wife and son I attended the celebration of independence.

There was an unexpected and breathtaking sequel. Bourguiba came to London and invited my wife and me to have dinner with him at the Ambassador's residence. We expected an informal meal, but at a long table several Tunisian Ministers were present as well as their chief. Coffee served, they gathered in a circle and Bourguiba asked me to step forward. He made a little speech referring to my contribution to the peace settlement and then presented me with the Order of the Republic of Tunisia, attaching a large gold cross to my jacket with a gold clasp and colourful ribbon. This is the one governmental honour I have had (unless one counts nomination to the Lords) and I appreciated it, but I have never worn the decoration, disliking the self-advertising practice of displaying Orders on one's chest. The Tunisian Ambassador, Taib Slim, at whose residence this presentation took place, was already one of my best friends. I had visited his brother Mongi when he was under house arrest in Tunis. The two Slims have since had distinguished international careers.

In 1954 I flew to distant Madagascar. Ever since the Puteaux Conference which established the Congress of Peoples, when spirited Malagasy delegates were present, I had followed their struggle for independence. In 1947 there was a rebellion, crushed with severe repression by the French. When the leaders were sentenced to death I cooperated with Jean Rous in Paris in mobilising influential international pressure and the sentences were reduced to exile for life in France. Only when Madagascar's right to self-determination was recognised by de Gaulle in 1960 were prisoners allowed to return as free men. Every New Year's Day I received cards from the exiles, and one of my prized possessions is a coloured cartoon drawn in a Malagasy prison showing Jean Rous and myself destroying the 'chariot of imperialism'.

I had a family reason for interest in Madagascar. My grandfather was a pioneer missionary there, my father, though born in South Africa, spent his first years there, and an aunt and uncle were also missionaries in Madagascar. This was of some political significance, as I learned on my visit. My family were Protestants and were often in conflict with the Catholic regime, and to my surprise I found they were honoured by resisters to the French Establishment. When I visisted a prominent trade unionist his family welcomed me by singing a hymn my aunt had written.

I found that Madagascar was a police state. Two detectives watched me day and night, staying at my hotel at Tananarive, sleeping in an adjoining room, eating at the next table, noting every visitor, following my car whenever I visited nationalist leaders, some under house arrest. Early one Sunday morning I evaded them. With the British Consul and his family I spent the day picnicking by the side of a mountain lake. I could scarcely believe my eyes when at midday I saw on the road above us the detectives watching from their car. I hated those police eyes. I preferred the open military escorts in Kenya.

I visited the French Governor. He was icy cold. I fell ill with a fever and desired nothing more than to return to London, but I could not be moved and missed the plane. The next flight was beyond my permit. Enclosing a doctor's certificate, I requested the Governor to be allowed to stay. To my astonishment he refused. Fortuitously a cable came inviting me to Mauritius, only an hour's flight away. The next day, though still weak, I left. My one consolation when I think back to this visit is the fact that six years later many of the nationalists I saw became members or ambassadors of Madagascar's independent Government, and we renewed contact.

I felt better the moment I set foot on Mauritius and Dr Ramgoolan, soon to be Prime Minister, who was my host, treated me, so that I was fit next morning. In Mauritius I felt I was in a paradise of freedom after the police oppression in Madagascar. The Labour Party was like the best in our Party at home, warm in fellowship, inter-racial. The chairman was a Creole, a widower who carried his little daughter everywhere. Dr Ramgoolan, an Indian, was leader of the group in the Legislature. Another leading member was French. The majority of the population was of Indian descent, but there were many Creoles of mixed races, as well as a community of Chinese traders and the French master class. I had lunch with two of the French leaders at the table of the Governor. Unlike the extrovert French of Paris, they were distant, aristocratic, belonging to a cultural élite. I found they were typical of their race in Mauritius.

I travelled all over the little island, meeting generous comrades of the Labour Party everywhere. Mauritius is now independent with a Labour Government, too moderate for some of the Socialists. It has great difficulties to face, an overflowing population and a one-industry economy – sugar. The thought occurred to me that in a sensible world its people would seek an outlet in the empty spaces of Madagascar, but French and British colonialism has left the steep barrier of separate sovereignties.

Flying back to England I spent a night with the Desais in Nairobi and addressed a large meeting under Indian auspices. I was happy to find that the racial fears of the Mau Mau period were melting away, but an incident on my journey to London showed how strong prejudices still were. During an hour's wait at Rome two BOAC officials approached me apologetically reporting that an English family from Kenya had learned I was on the plane and had refused to continue the flight unless I was excluded. The officials made clear that I had the right to remain and said they would ask the family to leave rather than me if I insisted, but they were anxious about the nervous grandmother who had had a heart attack before reaching Rome. I took another plane to London.

My next African visit was to Ghana on the invitation of Kwame Nkrumah, with whom I had maintained a cordial association since his London days. I remained close to him until his fall, but I never fathomed what happened to his personality, at first one of tolerance and kindness, ending in weak dictatorship. Before leaving for Accra I called at the Colonial Office and I understood why Kwame wanted consultation. He had won an election overwhelmingly on the issue of independence, but the Chief Secretary told me that there were serious difficulties. At Accra I was surprised by the modest conditions under which Ghana's Head of State lived. The house in an unpretentious suburb was old, the walls unkempt, a rough grassy foreground alive with children and their mothers. Kwame explained that according to Ghanaian custom his relatives had descended upon him and taken occupation. One relative he was glad to have there, his mother; she was sitting under a tree in a garden chair. Kwame himself, still a bachelor, was living in two rooms with a balcony where we had an evening meal. He told me the British Government was hedging about independence because of threats from the Ashanti, the cocoa-growing inland tribe. The next morning we met at his office in an airy modern block, the woodwork streamed red, white, green – Ghana's colours. We walked arm in arm in the surrounding gardens for an hour. He was frank about the corruption of some of his colleagues. 'But what can I do, Fenner?' he asked. 'They gave me food when I was hungry, a bed when I was homeless, they visited me in prison.' This was an indication of his human generosity, but perhaps also of his weakness.

That evening I saw Sir Arden Clarke, the Governor, in Christianborg Castle rising like a white rock over the sea. From here in bygone days kidnapped slaves had been dropped into the holds of ships, many to die on their way to the West Indies and America. The Governor praised Nkrumah for his dedication, but said he was too soft with less honest colleagues. 'He has not learned Lloyd George's truth that a Prime Minister must be ruthless.' Sir Arden was worried about the Ashanti and feared civil war. He said the best service I could do was to see the tribal leaders and dissuade them from violence.

I travelled to Kumasi, the capital of the Ashanti, next day and saw the Asantehene, the spiritual and political chief. He was in white robes, face hidden, withdrawn; he resented the idea that the Ashanti should be sub-servient to 'the Coast'. When I met the resistance leaders I understood why the Governor was worried. I have never been in the presence of more emotional violence than I was for an hour. I let it flow until sheer exhaustion brought calm. Finally they agreed to refrain from initiating violence if Nkrumah would agree to an election before independence.

Joe Appiah, husband of Peggy, daughter of Sir Stafford Cripps, was at this meeting. We were London friends and I spent a late night at their flat, a jolly time, refraining from politics. I met a group of cocoa planters, en-thusiastic for Nkrumah because he had ended the exploitation of landlord chiefs, and then visited another London friend, Dr Hastings Banda, later to be Prime Minister of Malawi (Nyasaland), who gave me a balanced view. The Ashantis should be given considerable autonomy; there was no con-stitutional reason for an election, but better an election than civil war. Returning to my hotel at night I had evidence of the dangers – British troops were at every street corner. I found a courier from Nkrumah awaiting me. I kept him an hour whilst I wrote my report.

The next morning I left for the Northern Province, the most undeveloped, offenders squatting before a chief, his hut in the background, and went on for Togoland reflecting its previous German occupation in its ordered tidiness. I asked a woman drawing water from the village tap what she thought of Nkrumah. 'I love him,' she replied. 'He has brought water. Before we had to carry it three miles from the river.' Early next morning a note arrived from Nkrumah insisting on seeing me that evening at Takoradi on the coast. How my driver got me there, across river ferries and mud roads, I do not know. Kwame resisted the idea of an election. Why, when he had just had one? I argued better this than civil war and the postponement of independence indefinitely. Eventually he took a sheet of paper and wrote: 'I agree to an immediate election on condition that Mr Lennox-Boyd will guarantee, if I get a majority, we shall have independence within six months.' I took the next plane to England and reported to the Colonial Secretary. When Lennox-Boyd addressed the Commons the next day he added only one word to Kwame's formula: the majority should be 'reasonable'. There was no civil war. Nkrumah got his majority, it was held to be reasonable, and Ghana had its independence in 1957.

A good deal of the spirit of violence remained. Two of those who were at my Kumasi meeting were arrested, charged with conspiracy and detained without trial. I wrote to Nkrumah urging a trial; he replied saying he wanted to save the prisoners from the death penalty in which a public trial would result. That was perhaps acceptable, but towards the end of 1960 I became deeply disturbed when more Opposition leaders were rounded up. They included Appiah and Dr Danquah, Ghana's prominent politician before Nkrumah. I had interviewed Danquah and had found him reasonable. It was impossible to believe that either he or Appiah were plotting a violent coup d'état. I wrote to Kwame urging an amnesty. Commented the Ghana *Evening News*: 'We thank you, Fenner, but we just can't take your advice.'

A strange incident led to my second visit to Ghana. One day a Welsh businessman, a city merchant and an African visited me. They wanted me to use my influence with Nkrumah to obtain for them a London agency for Ghanaian diamonds. I refused, saying I would be interested only if the industry were organised on a Socialist Cooperative basis. I did not see the city merchant again, but the Welshman (son of a miner and working himself in the pit as a boy) was attracted to my idea. From then on Willis Griffiths devoted himself to establishing a diamond Cooperative for all Africa north of the apartheid South African Republic, and I helped so far as I could. It was on the invitation of the local diamond winners that I returned to Ghana with Griffiths, who put to them a plan, as an alternative to subservience to De Beers, to have their own processing, their own valuer and their own agency in London under Cooperative control. Nkrumah, as well as the winners, endorsed the project. Willis went to Tanganyika and met African representatives from the diamond countries. They agreed to a conference in Accra to which Willis and I went, though African self-consciousness excluded us from the discussions. The conference was supposed to be secret so that De Beers would not know what we were up to, but every delegate wore a diamond badge in his lapel and everyone was aware of what was afoot. A working committee was appointed to carry out the Willis plan, but characteristically, with national pride still ascendant in Africa, no inter-state organisation was set up. Our initiative did contribute, however, to many countries nationalising their own diamond industries.

I will conclude the Ghana saga here. Kwame began with great idealism. He insisted on Ministers surrendering their business interests and incomes and living on their salaries only; members of the Goverment were even required to reject the residences which the British Government built for them so that they could live with the people. But when I visited Ghana afterwards I was surprised to find Nkrumah's colleagues dwelling in luxurious mansions, and I could not reject entirely allegations of corruption. Nkrumah himself was living in large park-surrounded Flagstaff House and a Chequers was built for him in the mountains, but when I visited him hospitality was simple and his retreat in the highlands remained empty.

He had been for a time the leader of independent Africa. He had the vision of a United Socialist States of Africa, and he had the invaluable help of George Padmore until the latter's death. His All Peoples Conference in Accra was the occasion which decisively stimulated the triumph of the national movements in the Congo and East Africa. He was the first African leader to warn against the economic imperialism of neo-colonialism and he led for non-alignment. He had a world view of peace and was actually in Vietnam seeking an end to its prolonged war when he was overthrown by the military *coup d'état*. His achievement of reconstruction in Ghana was remarkable – universal education, dispensaries and hospitals, new roads. In the beginning he inspired a people's revolution, with widespread enthusiasm to end illiteracy, to build schools, clinics and roads in the jungle. He socialised industry and property and lessened dependence on cocoa production by collective plantations for other commodities. His constructive work was remarkable. An English civil servant told me he had been more creatively active during one year under Nkrumah than in twelve previous years. Kwame worked all hours, day and night. I was staying with Geoffrey Bing, the President's legal adviser, when the phone rang at 3 am Geoffrey answered it in his pyjamas. It was Kwame, concerned to settle some intricate point. Geoffrey told me it often happened.

Why did all this promise disintegrate? Despite wide support among the peoples all over Africa, his Pan-Africanism was defeated by the love of power of those who ruled within the nation-states. In Ghana he lost the cooperation of moderate but able Ministers and dissent began among prosperous sections of the people, like the cocoa growers, who were compelled to sacrifice profits for his social projects. An economic crisis developed, partly because of heavy national expenditure and partly because of the withdrawal of foreign investment. Strikes, encouraged by political opponents, spread and there was resistance to increased state control of the trade unions. Corruption became rife in national corporations, particularly in the Cocoa Marketing Board, as well as among prominent Ministers. Nkrumah's Party members who officered the trade unions and state projects became bureaucrats, alienated from the rank and file. The spirit of the revolution was destroyed.

Nkrumah became an isolated man. I visited him a year before his fall, he invited me to an open-air lunch with his advisers at Flagstaff House. I was shocked by their unrepresentative character, and most of them were second rate. One incident interested me. As Kwame led me across the garden a stream of children approached and he explained they were from the nursery school he had established in the grounds for his children and other under-fives. Among them was the daughter of the American Ambassador, surprising in view of Washington's distrust of Ghana. After lunch Kwame and I walked the lawn. He told me of his dedication to a book he was writing on neo-colonialism. I got the impression it was an escape from the mounting difficulties of holding Ghana together and that already he was seeking an alternative.

I saw Nkrumah again only a few weeks before his overthrow, when accompanying Willis Griffiths, still keen on his diamond project. I was shocked by Kwame's protected hideout. He had moved to Christianborg Castle, guarded by soldiers, and we had to mount narrow winding stairs to his isolated room on the topmost floor. After he had seen Willis and a deputation of diamond winners I asked for a few words with him alone and pleaded once more for the release of untried political prisoners, some of whom I was convinced were innocent of inciting violence. It might be so, answered the President, but when a conspiracy was planned it was better that a few innocent victims should suffer than that the conspiracy should succeed. I told him that his actions were making our support in England for African freedom more difficult. 'Perhaps you, too, Fenner, are a necessary victim,' Kwame said with an excusing smile. Those were the last words I heard from him.

I was invited to Lagos for the independence of Nigeria in October 1960. I had the feeling all through the celebrations that the star was offstage. The crowds had one word on their lips – Z-e-e-k', the hero of the national struggle, Nnamdi Azikiwe. He was kept in the background because he was the prospective Governor and it was against protocol that he should be seen competitively until the British Governor retired. I had known Zik over the years, championing him in the Commons when colonial secretaries were denouncing him. A giant in body, he was still bigger in mind, a credit to his American university. He was also in the best sense of the word a statesman, indicated by his deliberate postponement of independence for Southern Nigeria until the North was ready. I was chairman of the excited meeting of Nigerians in St Pancras Town Hall when he announced this decision. The audience, almost entirely southern, were disappointed, but Zik's commanding personality gained their consent that the unity of all Nigeria should be their overriding aim. At the independence celebrations I stayed in the home of a Minister whom, like many of Africa's leaders, I had first known as a student in London. Zik spent a late evening with us, speaking like a philosopher, recognising the difficulties Nigeria had to face – the tribal differences, the illiteracy and poverty – but outlining plans for co-operation, education and the social development of rich natural resources. He lectured us, but he was not merely a scholar. I have a happy memory of his gaiety at a meal at the Charing Cross Road Chinese restaurant of Freddie Mills, the boxer, to which he invited my wife and me on one of his visits to London.

In 1958 I set out for Morocco to attend the conference of the National Union of Popular Forces (NUPF), the democratic Opposition, but there was a strike at Orly airport and I arrived at Casablanca when the meeting was over. However, I was able to meet the leaders in the evening and probably learned more than if I had listened to conference speeches. Morocco had had independence for seven years without a single election. The Sultan had courageously led the national struggle and had been exiled to Madagascar, where on my visit I had asked in vain to see him. He returned triumphantly on independence and his devoted people accepted him as a feudal king. When he died demands arose for an elected Parliament, but his son refused, where-upon leading trade unions, a few progressive peasants and a number of intellectuals formed the NUPF, which declared not only for democracy but for Socialism. Among the leaders I met was Ben Barka, trade union head, a man of great dynamism and sincerity. We became close friends, going out together on his visits to London, sharing rooms at Labour Party conferences which he attended as a fraternal observer. Our friendship ended tragically. One afternoon I received at the House of Commons a telegram from Paris. It reported that he had been kidnapped and was missing. He was never heard of again. There was evidence that the Moroccan security forces with accomplices in the French police were responsible and I went to Paris to give evidence at the trial which in fact found the head of Moroccan security and French police officers guilty. My sense of personal loss, and still more of the loss to Moroccan Socialism, remained a long time.

Thus in Africa, north, east, west and south, I saw the Empires crumbling. I was still to see them crash.

CHAPTER TWENTY-SEVEN

THE MOVEMENT FOR COLONIAL FREEDOM

We move to the last British efforts to maintain dominance in Africa. The attempt began with the old-time imperialism of Oliver Lyttelton, Lennox-Boyd, and, on Suez, Anthony Eden; it concluded with the conciliation of Iain Macleod, the 'winds of change' speech of Harold Macmillan in South Africa, and the new deals of James Griffiths when he became Labour's Colonial Secretary. During this period I devoted most of my time to supporting the struggle of the colonial peoples.

Immediately on my return from Kenya I took up the injustices I had found there. I was amazed by the violence of Tory reaction – I was regarded as fomenting sedition, stabbing in the back our white kith and kin, and even called a traitor. Within the decade what I urged was gained – an elected African majority in the Legislature, African farms on the exclusive White Highlands, Africans allowed to grow coffee (and winning prizes for their plants). I had been shocked when Mau Mau erupted but I was also critical of the Government. We received disturbing reports, smuggled out, of conditions in the detention camps, confirmed by Eileen Fletcher, a Quaker welfare officer who resigned from the prison service to tell what she had seen. The worst event was the beating to death of eleven detainees at the Hola camp, which Barbara Castle exposed with splendid courage. It was not easy to voice criticism of British action. We had to meet the lofty condemnation of the Colonial Secretary Oliver Lyttelton (now Lord Chandos), and his successor, Lennox-Boyd (now Lord Boyd). It was not until Iain Macleod followed that I felt any human contact with the Colonial Office.

I did much speaking on the injustices I found in Kenya. Lord Parry, whom

I welcomed to the Lords in 1966, reminds me of an amusing incident at the unlikely meeting place of Tintern under the ruins of the Abbey – I loved its outline, was outraged by the surrounding commercialism for the tourists. Gordon Parry presided over a remarkably well-attended conference in the barn of a farm. I remember how impressed I was by the speech of the then unknown Clive Jenkins. Just as I was about to speak a cow thrust her head in the doorway and bellowed, 'Moo, moo'. 'No,' I am alleged to have commented, 'not moo, moo – Mau Mau.'

Britain's administration in Kenya was not critically threatened by Mau Mau, but troops could not dislodge the insurgents from the mountain forests and after three years the government offered an amnesty, pledging no prosecution of those who laid down their arms. When later this was accompanied by acceptance of equal African representation in the Legislature with an anticipation of full self-government, I made a public appeal to Africans to end the fighting. It did not appear to have much impact, but when my family was invited to the Nairobi celebration of independence in December 1963, I was given a vivid account of a forest meeting of Mau Mau fighters where my appeal had been influential in the decision to accept a truce. That was a little reassuring.

In 1953 I had got together with a group of MPs to oppose Central African Federation which we saw would mean Southern Rhodesian white domination of the Africans of Northern Rhodesia and Nyasaland. Leslie Hale was chairman of a broad-based committee which later became part of the Movement for Colonial Freedom (MCF). I came into stark conflict with Lennox-Boyd over Nyasaland, now Malawi, during the 1959 Emergency in the Central African Federation. From the start I did not believe his story of an African plot to massacre the Europeans and Asians. I knew Dr Banda, the African leader, like a brother. I had seen the devotion of his English working-class patients when he was a doctor in Willesden. I had been touched by his sympathy with an African woman in Kumasi, her dead baby in his arms. That man could not plan a massacre. He was also politically wise. I had been with him in his home in London when Nyasaland chiefs had come for advice; he was authoritative and kindly at the same time. In Ghana, as I have already written, he gave me the most balanced survey of a country in crisis. Now he was vindicated. In response to much pressure, the Colonial Secretary agreed, after imprisoning Banda and many African leaders, to appoint a commission to examine the facts. Under Lord Devlin's chairmanship it rejected the massacre charge. Sadly, afterwards Banda became authoritarian and compromised over South Africa.

Arrests took place in Southern Rhodesia simultaneously with those in

Nyasaland, and there is little doubt that there was a concerted plan of repression in Central Africa. Joshua Nkomo, the Rhodesian leader, was at a conference in Cairo. His instinct was to return to his people, but I received a message from his colleagues, smuggled out of prison, begging him to put their case in London. I cabled him to come and he impressed us all greatly. Nkomo has since become a central figure in the Rhodesian controversy, but even in the fifties his eminence was evident. He was physically dominant, dignified, deliberate in thought and speech, a natural leader. He could also be great fun. I remember a meeting at the Westminster Central Hall which Fascist violence threatened to break up. Joshua had the audience laughing, and only chairs, not heads, were broken.

I have called Kenneth Kaunda (the leader in Northern Rhodesia) the Gandhi of Africa. I have met few men more inherently pacifist and instinctively tolerant. I became close friends with him when he visited London, always a little startled by his black hair standing on end as though he were permanently shocked. I wondered then whether Kaunda was strong enough to meet the problems of what is now Zambia, but he has proved that he is. About this time there was trouble in the northern province from which Kaunda was banned. 'Let me go there and I will stop it,' he said. When I made the suggestion to Iain Macleod, then Colonial Secretary, he agreed, though a little sceptical. Kaunda succeeded. Becoming Head of State, Kenneth had to modify his pacifism. There was a religious community which declined to accept State Law and shot police instructed to arrest them. Kaunda had to authorise force by troops, more difficult because his mother had belonged to the sect. Later, when conflict arose with the Ian Smith regime in Southern Rhodesia, he recognised that pacifism was not enough.

The first warning of what became known as the Suez Crisis of 1956 was given by Anthony Eden before the summer recess. Hugh Gaitskell was equivocal in response, some sentences good, some ambivalent. The crisis grew and nothing was done. Left MPs and officers of the Movement for Colonial Freedom got together in Sydney Silverman's office. We arranged an immediate Caxton Hall meeting; it was so crowded that we packed all five halls in the building at one of which I chaired. I particularly remember the stinging speech by A. J. P. Taylor. The MCF planned a Trafalgar Square demonstration. The announcement brought the most widespread response I have known. Not only was the Labour movement stirred: letters from leaders in the academic, literary and art worlds poured in; from my own constituency protests came from five shocked Eton College masters. Within a few days Suez became the biggest issue since the war.

By now the Labour high-ups were stirred and the MCF handed over Trafalgar Square to Transport House. Seventy thousand people attended. Gaitskell was now clear-cut and of course Nye Bevan was.

The Suez invasion became world humiliation, one of the blackest spots in British history. Subsequently it was revealed that there was a secret conspiracy between Britain, France and Israel. The explanation? Partly concern for British and French shareholdings in the nationalised Canal, partly fears that oil supplies would be stopped (hysterically exaggerated by Eden), and partly, I am convinced, by the nervous breakdown of the Prime Minister. Eden, who earlier had impressed me, was ill.

South Africa represented everything to which we were opposed. Though independent it was an occupied country, a white minority denying the non-white majority any political rights. The distinction between its racism and the rest of the world was that, though many nations practised some discrimination, most were ashamed of it, whilst South Africa on the other hand boasted of apartheid, applauding it as a basic precept of her political philosophy. The Bill which the Government introduced when South Africa withdrew from the Commonwealth was half-hearted, maintaining imperial preference, sugar subsidies and defence arrangements. We obtained one concession – South African refugees would not be deported from this country. During the debate I made a proposal which received some international attention. I suggested that refugees should be granted a Nansen passport. I had a letter from Pandit Nehru welcoming the idea and American, Canadian and other delegates to the United Nations promised support

I took the view that white South Africa could be influenced by two very different pressures, the first from the British Protectorates, the second from, strangely, sport. If we made the three British territories, Basutoland, Swaziland and Bechuanaland, models of African advance and inter-racial equality, I believed the effects would penetrate South Africa. A beginning was made by representation of both Africans and Europeans in the Legislatures, but in social progress the Protectorates became Britain's forgotten colonies. I do not know how many Parliamentary questions I put down demanding action. With the aid of Felicity Bolton, I published a widely circulated pamphlet exposing Britain's indifference. A further issue arose. Many of the political refugees from South Africa crossed to the Protectorates. I became involved in the famous case of Ganyile. He and two Africans fled to Basutoland (now Lesotho), and we were able to prove that South African police had crossed the border to kidnap them. They were threatened with death, but we made such angry protests that the Government was led to intervene. Jeremy Thorpe and I, after pressing hard in the Commons, were seen by the Minister, and Ganyile and his companions were returned to the Protectorates.

Sport was crucial because to white South Africans rugby football and cricket are a religion. The Movement for Colonial Freedom initiated a committee against racial discrimination in sport, arranging a deputation to the High Commissioner of New Zealand, to which a rugby team from South Africa was going. It was a high-powered deputation, including the Dean of Westminster, Michael Scott and Jimmy Hill, then playing for Fulham, now the celebrated TV commentator. The MCF handed over the campaign against South African racialist sport to the Anti-Apartheid Movement, and later under the leadership of Peter Hain, Young Liberal, it became a massive protest, national and international, preventing many South African tours.

The situation in what was Belgian Congo (now Zaïre) was tragically disturbing. The Belgians left without doing anything to prepare Africans to take over and chaos ensued, involving defiance by the Belgian–British mining monopoly in Katanga, renewed Belgian intervention, the presence of a United Nations force and American–Soviet conflict, finding climax in the murder of Patrice Lumumba, the national African leader, and the death of Hammarskjold, the UN Secretary General, in an unexplained air crash. I was attracted to Lumumba by all I heard of him. He had a record of serious study in youth, was granted a scholarship to Belgium, devoted himself to social service on returning to the Congo and endeavoured to bring about Belgian withdrawal by goodwill and agreement. He had little response and, influenced by events in Ghana, Nyasaland and Rhodesia, realised that Africans must rely on themselves. He became Pan-Africanist and Socialist, against tribalism, and established a strong all-Congo nationalist movement. His party won the pre-independence election and he became Prime Minister but, with Belgium and the USA intriguing against him, he was ousted by a military *coup*, imprisoned and sent to his death in reactionary Katanga—there is no doubt that the American CIA planned his murder. I shall never forget the memorial meeting which the MCF held in Trafalgar Square attended by tens of thousands, nor the march of thousands to the Belgian Embassy. The dignity of the occasion was spoiled only by a few hotheads who clashed with the police in Eaton Square.

Cyprus was a major crisis. I do not know how many times we protested against Britain's repressive policy. I visited both Cyprus and Greece. The saddest thing in Cyprus was the animosity created between the previously friendly Greek and Turkish populations – I was given pictures of families from both communities resting together during the midday heat under the shade of trees whilst their children played about them. Some of the Greek prisoners who were brought to Britain complained of ill treatment in Cyprus. Jennie Lee and I went to see them at Wormwood Scrubs, and in the presence of the Governor and Medical Officer they stripped their bodies to show wounds and scars. I got the impression that to impress us some of the bruises had been made worse by self-infliction, but I had no doubt brutality had occurred. Jennie and I sent a detailed report to the Minister and in the House demanded an enquiry. The only investigation granted was by officials in London; their whitewashing report was necessarily limited and unconvincing.

The Greeks in Cyprus had considerable responsibility for alarming the Turks by demanding union with Greece. I decided to go to Cyprus to meet the leaders. This was not difficult to arrange because the Cypriot representative in London, Spyros Kyprianou, was a close friend, young and able; when independence came I was delighted to find him Foreign Secretary, although only thirty-two. In talks in Nicosia and Athens I urged independence as the alternative to union with Greece. I had meetings first with Clerides, the Greek spokesman, reasonable and conciliatory, and then with Archbishop Makarios in his Nicosia palace, where he invited my son and me to a friendly tea, and again across the water at the Athens Foreign Office. He was impressive with a calm serenity that was above bitterness; it was clear that he would not insist on union with Greece. In Athens with two Labour MPs, Kenneth Robinson and Lena Jeger, I met the Greek Prime Minister and other Ministers, who also told us they would agree to independence if it were the wish of the Cypriots. The substance of these talks was conveyed to the British Foreign Office and perhaps contributed to the coming of a peace (temporary, alas) based on independence. The treaty which nominally ended hostilities was, as events unhappily proved, superficial in its treatment of the relations between the two communities. I was also disappointed that the large British bases, a repudiation of genuine independence, should remain. In Cyprus I had been astonished to find that five miles of the main road from Nicosia to Famagusta, the largest port, was British territory.

One incident on a visit to Cyprus I remember with peculiar pleasure. In the white temple at Pynka above steep cliffs to the sea I stood on the stone from which Pericles first pleaded for democracy twenty-five centuries ago. I felt the hand of history on me as I pleaded, to a wondering audience of tourists, for the extension of democracy to the world.

Another Mediterranean island with which I became involved was Malta. The courage of its people during the Second World War was recognised by the presentation of the George Cross to the whole population. On my visit

I made the precipitous descent into one of the crude shelters, hacked from rock, where they crowded during the continuous air raids. For three years the island (or accurately group of islands) was ruled directly by the Governor and the Colonial Office. On the invitation of the Maltese Labour Party I flew there and was impressed by the popular support for Dom Mintoff, its uncompromising leader. There were 70,000 at the May Day demonstration, proportionately to the population of 300,000 unique in size. I stayed with Dom and his family in their white cottage. He was boisterous and volcanic, but relaxed with charm. We discussed how his conflict with the Catholic Church, a major obstruction to independence, could be resolved. The population was almost entirely Catholic, and Dom himself was nominally a member of the Church. With the support of his wife I overcame his reluctance to my seeing the Archbishop. When I did so I hoped I had arranged a meeting between him and Dom, but it did not come off. In the 1960 election the Archbishop declared it a mortal sin to vote Labour and Mintoff was defeated. Back in England I tried to get leading Catholics to influence the Pope to intervene. Results were not immediate, but negotiations between Rome and the Archbishop began, and a few years later the dispute in Malta between the Archbishop and Labour's leader was settled.

Malta illustrated how closely colonial policy was linked with military strategy. On several visits I had the impression that the island was under military occupation. There were the largest barracks I have seen, RAF airports, a coastland ideal for tourist development reserved for military training, the deep harbour lined with British and American warships, and in the centre of Valetta, the capital, the Mediterranean headquarters of NATO. Iain Macleod, sincerely seeking a solution, discussed privately with me the difficulty of reconciling military necessity with the democratic right of self-determination. Mintoff regained power and by tough ultimatums, which made him unpopular here, finally won independence with controlled military presence.

Another crisis in which I played some part was in far away British Guiana on the north coast of South America. Elections were won by the People's Progressive Party led jointly by Cheddi Jagan, engaging young Indian, Communist inclined, and Forbes Burnham, large impressive African, Social Democrat. Burnham led the descendants of African slaves, urban workers, and Jagan the descendants of Indian indentured labourers working on the sugar plantations. Their inexperienced government had little help from British civil servants, and their radical measures without technical administrators brought some chaos. Suddenly a state of emergency was declared by the Colonial Office. Troops poured in; the Constitution was suspended.

The Government's White Paper explained that petrol had been stored to set alight the Governor's house and public buildings, but I was able to force the admission in Parliament that this alleged plot, evidence for which was very flimsy, was 'discovered' only after the emergency had been announced. Disastrously a split took place between the Indian supporters of Jagan and the African supporters of Burnham. The two leaders came to London and met a group of MCF MPs. We begged them to instruct their Parties to heal the breach and, though it became clear that differences were great, they consented to send a cable which I drafted and which with some hope I despatched from the Commons post office. Alas, the reconciliation was only temporary.

When the Constitution was restored, Jagan won with a small majority. He took over a bankrupt administration, but when he appealed to Britain and America for loans, had little response. His only alternative was a stern Budget, raising stiffly the taxes on property and profits but also imposing compulsory savings on workers' wages. Then a fantastic thing happened. There was a strike by Burnham's urban trade unionists supported by the employers and (as admitted later) encouraged by the American CIA. That was an unholy alliance, but it was followed by something equally ironical. When rioting and arson occurred, Jagan, the Communist, had to call for British troops. Guyana, as the territory was called after independence, continued to be bedevilled by the conflict between the Jagan and Burnham Parties. Fearing Communism, Britain and America supported Burnham, electoral changes prejudicial to Jagan were imposed, and there was convincing evidence of election malpractices within the territory. Burnham's declared object when he became Prime Minister was to establish a Co-operative State, and he has won popular support for measures contributing to its realisation. Recognition should be given also to his notable leadership within the Commonwealth for the Third World's New International Economic Order. There is still some hope of reconciliation between the two leaders.

I visited Israel twice, taking my son on one occasion because I had two air tickets. I was deeply impressed by the almost miraculous transformation of the desert into farms and towns. I stayed in kibbutzim where equality in work and life maintained the idealism of the early settlers. I was interested in the pooled care of infants during the day whilst mothers worked, families united in the evening. I could not make up my mind whether this was the solution of the mother–baby problem. The comprehensive authority of the Histadruth, the trade union organisation, was something new to me; it dealt not only with working conditions, but actually administered the main social services – a vast expression of workers' power. The Government itself controlled the major industries, and altogether Israel was the most radical example of social democracy I had seen. When I stayed in a kibbutz under the Golan heights I understood the Jews' fear of the insecurity of their frontiers. Although there was no immediate crisis, the children slept regularly in underground shelters.

I had a memorable discussion with Golda Meir, then Prime Minister. I have rarely heard anyone more convincing, and she did me the honour of saying it was the best exchange of views she remembered with the exception of an evening with Aneurin Bevan. My visits to Israel were arranged by the Left wing in the Coalition Government, Mapam, and by the monthly journal, *World Tomorrow*, which over the years has sought Jewish–Arab co-operation. My views were not changed fundamentally – I remained opposed to Zionism – but I realised that if Israel ever becomes politically integrated with the Middle East her people can make a contribution to its well-being. Alas, her subsequent oppressive occupation of Arab lands makes this hope dim.

Behind all these activites was the Movement for Colonial Freedom. It was formed in 1954 by the union of many committees, but from the outset the MCF was much more than a collection of MPs and experts. It became in Britain a mass movement, including representation of more than three million in trade unions, Labour Parties, peace and liberal organisations; and at the same time it gained the trust and cooperation of the national leaders in most of the occupied territories of Africa, Asia and the Caribbean. In the mid-fifties there was great interest in the emerging anti-colonialist struggle, but little knowledge. For some time in the Commons I drafted questions with briefs for a long list of interested MPs – so many in fact that the Government conceded a second day in the week to the Colonial Office. Very soon, however, Members became so well informed (as Barbara Castle did on Kenya and Stephen Swingler on Rhodesia) that they could take the lead. The MCF supplemented this information service to MPs by an educational campaign in the country, leaflets, pamphlets, meetings, and by marches and great demonstrations in Trafalgar Square and elsewhere. We arranged speaking tours for African leaders, among them Joshua Nkomo, the Southern Rhodesian leader to whom I have referred; Mainza Chona, afterwards Prime Minister of Zambia; and N. Chiume, afterwards radical leader against compromise in Malawi. This united campaign by the powerful African movements in the three territories involved had a considerable effect in convincing opinion in Britain against the maintenance of the Central African Federation.

Our association with Africa was reflected by an invitation from newly independent states in East and West Africa to John Eber, our secretary, to cement cooperation. We had a remarkable series of secretaries, among them Douglas Rogers, who had been my assistant on the *New Leader* and who became a devoted champion of Nkrumah; Joseph Murumbi, able representative of the Kenya African Union and afterwards prominent in independent Kenya; and Barbara Haq, best of all, for her knowledge and extraordinary dedication, her genius in winning trust and her constructive practicality. More than anyone in Britain, for example, she was responsible for ending the conflict between Arab Sudan and its black southern territories. We had working committees on all spheres of the Third World with Tony Wedgwood Benn chairing South East Asia, Judith Hart the Middle East, John Stonehouse East and Central Africa, Dr Leon Szur Latin America and myself Southern Africa.

The MCF was wise in recognising that on certain issues, such as apartheid in South Africa, defence funds for political offenders, Third World Poverty and the American war in Vietnam, still broader organisations could win wider support, and we participated in the foundation of the Anti-Apartheid Movement and John Collins's Christian Aid, as well as taking the initiative in establishing War on Want, to which our treasurer, Frank Harcourt Munning, transferred, the British Council for Peace in Vietnam, of which I became chairman, and the Chile Solidarity Committee.

Although Harold Wilson was among our sponsors and Anthony Greenwood became our treasurer, the MCF got into some trouble with the Labour Party because we had members, including Liberals and Communists, who belonged to proscribed organisations, and affiliates not associated with the Labour Party. Twice Transport House warned us of the danger of proscription, and I had a solemn meeting with the Chief Whip of the Parliamentary Party. I replied by warning in turn that any disavowal of the MCF would alienate African sympathy with the Labour Party, but agreed that, whilst continuing to accept individuals, we would not accept affiliations from proscribed organisations.

The Party Executive then adopted another tactic, setting up the British Overseas Socialist Fellowship to divert activities to a controlled organisation. I welcomed the Fellowship and became a member of its committee. It did valuable work, holding university seminars and summer schools for British and overseas Socialists and acting as host to visitors from Africa and Asia, among whom I remember Ben Barka from Morocco and Jayaprakash Narayan from India. The idea of competing with the MCF failed, however, particularly when the chairman, Kenneth Younger, resigned to become head of

Chatham House and I replaced him. The Fellowship withered away when many, including Dr David Pitt, later West Indian chairman of the Greater London Council and now Lord Pitt, resigned in protest against the Labour Government's 1965 White Paper on Immigration. Years later I was reminded of the Fellowship in the unusual circumstances of listening to a television interview with the general manager of Jaguar, Geoffrey Robinson. For an industrialist he was extraordinarily Socialistic – and then I recognised him as one-time secretary of BOSF. Transport House used to provide secretarial help from its research staff, of which Geoffrey Robinson was a member. On Maurice Edelman's death in 1976, Geoffrey was elected Labour MP for Coventry.

These years saw the independence of most of the larger British colonies. My family and I were invited to the celebrations in Uganda, Kenya and Tanzania and, as I have written, I went to Ghana and Nigeria. They were fantastic occasions, hysterical rejoicing as the Union Jack was lowered and the new national flag raised, followed by pictorial fireworks. In Uganda we stayed at a hotel in Entebbe. This small garden city by Lake Victoria symbolised the change more clearly than anything I saw. Previously Uganda Entebbe's delightful white houses were entirely occupied by British civil servants. Now not an Englishman was to be seen; their African successors had taken over. In Kenya President Jomo Kenyatta invited us to his farm, not the cold fortress of older times, and I was delighted to meet again his first Sussex wife and their grown son, both happy to be invited from England and neither embarrassed by the presence of the second, African, wife. I introduced Edith to my five Kenya wives, widows of ex-chief Koinange, who were allotted to me when I was made his 'blood brother'. There was no cause for embarrassment on this occasion! As always, 'son' Mbiyu greeted me as 'Dad'. He was now a Minister.

My warmest memory is of afternoon tea in the garden of the house where Julius Nyerere, shortly to be President of Tanzania, was staying. He had also invited Leslie Hale, my wife and son and we had rarely been so won by a man. I had admired Julius from afar, his dedication to at-the-roots Socialism and we had corresponded, but this was the first personal contact. His eyes lit as he told of his aims. Socialism to him was much more than an economic system; it was a way of life, making demands on personal conduct like a religion. No sincere Socialist could be rich in a poor country, he would be robbing others. He told us that no member of his Cabinet would be allowed involvement for gain in industry and that Socialism would begin in the villages, cooperative communities sharing their incomes, voluntarily building their schools and clinics. When I went to Tanzania's independence I visited these villages. It was not easy to change old habits, but Nyerere's enthusiasm was infectious. He took part himself in building the walls of schools and clinics.

I visited many other countries in anti-colonial activity. I went to the All African People's Conference at Cairo, welcomed by President Nasser, a dominating personality, urging Arab–Black unity. I was impressed by the ability of Tom Mboya, the builder of trade unionism in Kenya, leaning towards America where he had been a student, but outstanding in his balanced, constructive contribution. Except for the colour of his skin Mboya might have been an English civil servant, his clothes neatly pressed, his manner coolly courteous. I met him several times, at first unable to pierce his distant reserve, but, seeing him off at Heathrow on one occasion he suddenly became warm and genial, appreciative of MCF cooperation; and on our visit on Kenyan independence he invited Edith and me to his charming bungalow and he and his wife welcomed us like intimate friends. It was a terrible loss to Kenya when he was assassinated.

I went to Rome to a conference representing Mediterranean territories and was welcomed with conviviality by Nenni, veteran Socialist leader, renewing our comradeship of forty years ago. I went to a conference at Belgrade where I had a dramatic confrontation with Marshal Tito. The Yugoslavian Government had brought from Highgate Cemetery the body of Dusan Popovoc who had been secretary of the Serbian Socialist Party during the First World War. I told Tito of my friendship with him in the struggle against the war and how deeply moved I had been to see the procession of men and women passing his coffin in tribute. The Marshal gripped both my hands saying: 'Thank you, comrade, thank you.' Our hands still locked I voiced a challenge. 'Wouldn't it be a still happier tribute,' I said, 'if you released from your prisons his two comrades, Alexander Pavlovic and Bogdan Krekic?' Tito dropped my hands and stepped back, his face white. Then he recovered and said distantly: 'We are considering the matter.' Pavlovic, founder of the Serbian party, and Krekic, founder of the trade union movement, were both over seventy years of age and had been in prison since 1958. In fact they were released a few weeks later, due probably to international pressure which Walter Padley MP, organised, but I hoped I had a little to do with it. Walter, I should have written earlier, was the most brilliant of the young enthusiasts in the ILP. I had affection as well as admiration for him. He was a witness when Edith and I married. He became chairman of his union, member of the Labour Party Executive and a Minister, but, handicapped by asthma, to my disappointment, he was never able to fulfil his promise.

Activity on behalf of political prisoners was one of my priorities. Whenever I went to a country where they were persecuted I appealed for an amnesty. I did so with Nkrumah in Ghana, with Nasser in Cairo, with Gomulka, First Secretary, in Poland and with Karamanlis, Prime Minister, in Greece.

Another Communist country I visited was Poland. I had been there before the Communists took over, in very different circumstances. My Netherlands friend, Peter Schmidt, and I had been invited to address a meeting for the Polish ILP in Warsaw. We were taken aback when the first twenty minutes were spent in a fierce fight between Socialists and Communists, the chairman, unperturbed, remarking that meetings always began like that. The Communist rioters thrown out, he controlled the rest of the proceedings authoritatively, but Peter and I were embarrassed to learn that his name was 'Comrade Penis' and to have to address him thus. On the way back we sent him a picture postcard from Ostend congratulating him on his chairmanship; we could not refrain from adding our hope that he was still strong and erect. Before returning to London I addressed a great anti-war demonstration with Peter in Holland and, repeating Keir Hardie, urged an international general strike if war were imminently threatened. My speech received press attention and the Government ordered my immediate departure, and informed me that I would not be allowed to return. In fact, I have visited Holland several times since and have not been challenged.

This second visit to Poland also had its surprises. Somehow the American Friends Service Committee got the Government, perhaps liberal among Communists, to allow them to hold a three weeks' seminar for students from both West and East. Each of the three lecturers, a liberal professor from Paris, a woman economist from the Moscow Academy of Science, and myself, a democratic Socialist, were asked to lead discussions for a week. A curious thing happened. We met at the headquarters of the Warsaw ballet, a large disused military establishment. Seventy students met in a lounge but, when news reached university students that one of the lecturers believed in a libertarian form of Socialism, they poured in on motor cycles and bicycles, and we had to move to the dance hall. I won support by insisting that poverty was the greatest affront to liberty, but I was interested in the freedom which was the concern of the students and urged that liberty of thought was the only guarantee of the good evolution of society. It was clear that Polish youth were not rigid-minded.

At the seminar I met an unknown historical hero. The caretaker was aged but of statuesque figure and head. He brought me two illustrated biographies of Rosa Luxemburg and astonished me by saying: 'You were a friend of

Rosa.' I found he knew because he had been her close associate and he had seen my letters to her. Then I learned something more remarkable and important. He revealed that he was secretary of the Sailors' Committee which organised the Kiel mutiny, an event which some historians have said did more to bring the First World War to an end than the defeat of the German army on the battlefield. There was no doubt that he was speaking the truth, the details of his story were so vivid. It is one of my regrets that it was impossible to take a recording. He had helped to change history.

My activities had not embraced the East. I was interested in the Communist revolution in China and the economic power of Japan, both changing the balance of the world, but the ground I already tried to cover was enough. I was similarly inactive about Latin America, victim though it was of economic imperialism. On these areas I left action to others. I was, however, active about the British territories in the West Indies. Norman Manley, Prime Minister of Jamaica, a leader of outstanding presence and ability, reminding me of Ramsay MacDonald at his best, always had a meal with me at the House when he came to London. Eric Williams, Prime Minister of Trinidad, was associated with the MCF before achieving independence. I remember him sitting crunched up on the floor at a crowded committee meeting in an interview room at the Commons, nevertheless orating to us for half an hour, my chairman's efforts to stop him quite in vain. Afterwards he became famous for his detailed speeches, occupying pages in the Trinidad papers. Edith and I were invited to the independence of Barbados, startled to find we were accommodated in the holiday bungalow of Mr Edward du Cann, chairman of the Tory Party, leased to the Government in his absence.

By chance I became involved in South East Asia. When the federation of Malaya, Singapore and the British colonies in Borneo was proposed as Malaysia, the Parliamentary Labour Party sent a deputation composed of Arthur Bottomley, afterwards Minister for Overseas Development, my brother-in-law, Reg Sorensen and myself to investigate and report. We were charmed by Tunku Rahman, the Prime Minister of Malaya, who received us as friends in his home (I had met him in London when he had released political prisoners at our request) and were impressed by the ability of his Deputy, Tun Abdul Razak, his successor. We met the leaders of the Opposition, young and radical, who were opposed to federation as an imperialist device. In Singapore we had long talks with Lee Kuan Yew, the dynamic Prime Minister, and attended a conference of the Left Opposition, repressed as pro-Chinese.

I was in two minds about Lee Kuan Yew. We had cooperated in anti-colonialist days when he showed great courage, and he was now constructive, able and sure of himself. I went with him to a forest village and was moved by his friendship with the people and their response. Although Chinese himself, he was obsessed with the fear that the large Chinese population would become more loyal to their Communist motherland than to Singapore, and he repressed ruthlessly those in the trade unions, the schools and the university whom he suspected of being Communist inclined. I was shocked by the prison conditions of many of those arrested and protested angrily, with the support of Arthur and Reg, against the inhumanity of solitary confinement. Lee Kuan Yew was then favourable to Malaysian Federation, though later he broke away. Singapore left on me the contradictory picture of achievement and oppression.

We flew to Borneo, meeting in Sarawak a lively Opposition as well as the Government, were received by the autocratic but benevolent Sultan in oil-rich Brunei, and conferred in Sabah with the élite politicians, little related to the primitive existence of its people. We had exciting journeys, in army helicopters to Sabah, protected only by a chain from dropping into the sea, and in a crude army transport plane on our return, thrown about violently in a storm. Arthur Bottomley and Reg Sorensen reported in favour of Malaysia, I against. I did not believe that there was sufficient political consciousness to justify a union extending to the distant territories of Borneo. In the event, Brunei declined to join, Singapore subsequently withdrew and Sarawak and Sabah remained uneasy partners. My main opposition, however, was to the strategic intention of Malaysia. The idea of the Federation was thought up in Whitehall to kill a plan for a wider confederation including the Philippines and Indonesia, unanimously endorsed by the Foreign Ministers. This would have neutralised the whole area, a great contribution to peace; but Duncan Sandys was determined to thrust his Western spear of defence across the body of Southern Asia. How long will it last?

CHAPTER TWENTY-EIGHT

TEN YEARS' REACTION

When Labour was defeated in 1951 we did not expect to be in Opposition for three Parliaments. After the 1945–50 revolution and the retreat the following year came uninhibited reaction. The decade of Tory Government undermined steadily both the Socialist achievement and psychology of the post-war resurgence. Public enterprises and social services were throttled and the motive of each man for himself replaced the tentative emergence of each for all and all for each. I took some part in Labour's campaign, both in the House and in the country, but my specialisation on colonialist issues and on peace meant that more often I cheered on others than spoke. Sometimes, however, constituency experience enabled me to particularise the general case.

With the coming to Slough of workers incited by its factory development, housing was the great problem. A Tory Act increased rents exorbitantly and when tenants were unable to pay they were evicted. The Slough Tenancy Committee reported to me twenty-four eviction cases in one month. I could not read them without emotion – families broken up, the father dossing with friends in one house, the mother in another, the children taken to a council Home. There was the problem of newly-weds, crowded with in-laws or renting one room. I wrote to each couple as their marriages were announced in the local papers, sixty-seven in a month, and had answers from thirty-three, of whom only three had obtained a house and they had to go outside Slough. I appealed to the Government to make a national enquiry about the circumstances of newly-weds. When this was refused, the *Sunday Pictorial* did so. It found that fifty-three per cent were living with in-laws after five years of marriage. A Catholic priest, Father

Eamonn Casey, joined me in action. Together we established an association of Slough newly-weds who by pooling their resources could meet the cost of mortgages in succession. The priest later established the Catholic Housing Association on a national basis which did valuable work, and then reverted to his Ireland as Bishop of Kerry.

Slough had its non-white immigrant workers, mostly Indian and West Indian, and I became disturbed by the prejudice against them. Nine years in succession I introduced a Bill to make racial discrimination illegal. At first my Bills included Northern Ireland and religious discrimination and housing and industry. To all of these I returned later, but at the moment I was concerned to get the principle accepted and limited the scope of succeeding Bills to public places. The change of opinion was extraordinary. My earlier efforts were backed only by Leftist colleagues, Leslie Hale, Barbara Castle, Michael Foot, Sydney Silverman, Stephen Swingler and others; before the end the Labour front bench, Jo Grimond for the Liberals and even back bench Tories gave support. In the Upper House, also, Lord Walston introduced the Bill, not expecting success. I tried to convince the Tory front bench and had talks with Ian Macleod and Selwyn Lloyd, whose opposition seemed to me disingenuous. They argued that a law against discrimination would give statutory recognition to races as separate sections of our society. To anticipate: before the 1964 election Harold Wilson announced that a Labour Government would legislate on the lines of my Bill and when it finally became law the Tory leaders withdrew their opposition. The Lord Chancellor, Gerald Gardiner, did me the honour of saying I was the real author.

This endeavour to outlaw racial discrimination aroused vicious antagonism from people obsessed by colour prejudice. I had streams of abusive letters and phone calls which got me out of bed at all times of the night, ending with advice to remove children from our house because it was about to be bombed. The house was not bombed but it was assaulted. The occupant of the flat above was a Jewess who had escaped Hitler's gas chambers in Germany. On a Sunday morning, up before us, she went to the front door to collect the milk. Imagine her shock when she saw on the glass panelling two large swastikas painted in glowing white! She cried out and when I reached her she was slumped fainting on the floor. There were swastikas not only on the door but on the broad steps and the pavement, whilst on the walls were large slogans, 'Keep Britain White'; it took two workmen eleven hours to remove the paint. The threats became so continuous that the police placed our home under guards; for twenty-four hours a day they patrolled. I would have them in for coffee when returning late

group family photograph: surrounding F.B. l. to r. are his wife Edith, his married daughter
Olive, son-in-law Jim Wood, daughter Audrey (married to Wood) and on the floor, Olive's
daughter Carol. Inset, the author's daughter Joan. Both Audrey and her husband have recently
ied

ascist slogans daubed on the author's house

With the widow of
President Allende of Chile
at a Trafalgar Square
demonstration

The author aged eighty-eight,
photographed by his son,
Christopher

at night from Parliament and Edith would start them off with cups of tea in the morning.

What followed was more cruel, not to us but to non-white victims. We got phone calls from coloured people asking about rooms to let. One night I returned home to find my wife providing coffee for a West Indian family who had walked five miles to enquire about accommodation. Several times during the day coloured people would call and women would be in tears when they heard there were no rooms. The explanation? 'Keep Britain White' fanatics had placed advertisements in newsagents' shops all over north London announcing furnished rooms to let at our address, adding 'coloured persons welcomed'. We took particulars of the shops and phoned the police. They had the advertisements removed within an hour, but they could not get sufficient evidence to identify those responsible.

Once there appeared to be a plan to kidnap me. I was chairing a meeting on an Immigration Bill at the St Pancras Town Hall which was attacked by a swarm of Fascists; our stewards kept them out with some casualties and arrests. A note was brought to me on the platform saying that a Daimler was at the door to take me home safely. I was suspicious and did not respond. Three times the Daimler returned, the driver stating that the car had been hired to collect me; the stewards again sent it away. When I got home my secretary phoned to say that the BOAC had been on to her to confirm a booking for me on a plane to New York. I knew nothing about it. Had the Fascists really planned to get me in the Daimler to Heathrow and on to the plane? It seemed fantastic.

How often one felt useless in Parliament! One pressed cases or pleaded for wider justices only to be defeated by a stone wall of evasion. These failures are too many to mention. There was a memorable occasion, how-ever, when I succeeded, thanks to support from both sides. News reached me that a young Spaniard named Joaquim Perez-Selles had escaped from Franco's navy and reached this country as a stowaway, and that an order had been made to deport him back to Spain. His father, who had fought in the civil war against the Fascists brought up his son in libertarian ideas and when called to the navy the lad three times deserted. On the first occasion he was arrested in France, but after a short period in prison was recognised as a genuine refugee and released. He got a job on a Norwegian boat which had engine trouble off the coast of Bilbao, and he was picked up by Spanish police and sentenced to two years' imprisonment. On discharge he was again conscripted, deserting in New York, where the Americans handed him over to the Spanish authorities, who sentenced him to thirty months. At the end of his term he was sent to a disciplinary battalion, but escaped again and contrived to hide in a ship to London. He was arrested at Tilbury, tried and ordered to be deported and placed on a boat returning to Spain. On board he declared he would throw himself overboard, and the captain declined to take responsibility for him and he was escorted back to prison. There he was when I heard the story.

With Gordon-Walker, the Shadow Minister, I saw R. A. Butler, the Home Secretary. He was adamant, rejecting the view that Perez-Selles was a political refugee, saying he was guilty only of 'refusal to comply with the normal Spanish obligation for national service'. In the House I asked for an immediate opportunity to discuss a motion which a hundred Members had signed. When Butler refused there was an uproar. From the Labour Front Bench Hugh Gaitskell and Nye Bevan demanded time for discussion, and John Dugdale got in with a motion for a debate the same evening. The Speaker turned it down. I was in despair. 'The boy goes tomorrow, perhaps to his death,' I shouted. The Speaker looked at me enquiringly and changed his ruling: 'Accepting what is said by the Hon. Member for Eton and Slough I think I should allow the motion.' A great roar of cheers came from the Labour benches.

The debate was one of the best I have heard in the House, everyone realising that not only was the lad's fate at stake, but also the traditional principle of British asylum; it was one of the very rare occasions when the mind of the majority was changed. The House was crowded and tense. R. A. Butler admitted my facts but insisted that Joaquim was not a refugee. I had the impression that Tories as well as Labour Members were uneasy, and in fact the decisive speech came from a Conservative, John Foster, barrister and ex-Minister, who urged that the boy should be given the chance to go to a country other than Spain. Maurice Macmillan, son of the Prime Minister, supported him; Labour MPs, front bench and back bench, weighed in and Butler gave way to what had evidently become the wish of the whole House. He would give the deserter a fortnight to find a country other than Spain to which to go. I went round the Embassies and Mexico agreed. I raised the fare from sympathisers, and I think I was nearly as happy as Joaquim when I saw him on the plane at Heathrow. The case became a precedent for other refugees.

I came into conflict with the Government and my own leaders, even at the end with Nye Bevan, on the issue of nuclear weapons. Bombs which could destroy all mankind seemed to me a blasphemy against creation, and Britain's possession of them and acceptance of America's bases I regarded as inviting national suicide, no real deterrent in view of the nuclear strength of the two super-Powers. In 1954 I initiated the first movement in Britain against nuclear arms. After the announcement of the hydrogen bomb, I called a meeting in a large Commons committee room of the House of Commons and there was an impressive response, including Lord Beveridge, Canon Collins, the Rev. Donald Soper, George Thompson (at the time of writing European Community Commissioner), and a number of Left MPs. Six of us walked the length of Whitehall bearing posters; these pioneers of CND marching were Anthony Greenwood, Tony Wedgwood Benn, George Thomas (now the Speaker), Richard Acland, George Craddock and myself. We organised an Albert Hall demonstration, but it was not successful and left us with a debt of £600. This sank us. Then came the CND and the Aldermaston marches. The first was from London with the first stop Slough. We arranged tea in a public park, but there was a deluge of rain and we resorted to the Wesleyan Church, the minister of which was sympathetic. I welcomed the drenched procession from the pulpit. On that first march there were only six hundred. Four years later we had to sleep in Slough schools twelve thousand marching from Aldermaston, among them my son, Christopher.

The CND had become the most powerful Youth movement the country had seen, and support came from local Labour Parties and trade unions like the Transport Workers under its new secretary, Frank Cousins. Then came disaster. At the Brighton Labour Party Conference, 1957, Nye Bevan, whom we all accepted as the leader of the Left, declared that if he became Foreign Secretary he would not be prepared to go naked into conference with the super-Powers. The implication was that he required nuclear clothes. Nye defeated us. The initial effect was shattering. In Parliament the Left group was temporarily destroyed. We used to meet in a corner of the smoking room, Nye dominating every discussion. We had debated nuclear weapons and, to be fair to him, Nye had always opposed unilateral disarmament, though I do not remember his extending this to nuclear arms. The Brighton speech broke up this grouping; Nye sat alone in the smoking room with a few faithfuls, Michael Foot, Leslie Hale, Harold Davies. I was in two minds. I was distressed by his disavowal of nuclear disarmament, but I was excited by the prospect, obviously part of his détente with Gaitskell, that he was destined to be Labour's next Foreign Secretary, certain that he could lead us to better relations with the Soviet Union and cooperation with the un-aligned world.

The boycott by his old associates hurt, and I went down to his small farm at Amersham to spend a weekend. Nye showed me round with pride, but he talked little about politics; he was brooding and perhaps the illness which brought his early death was already upon him. It was all tragic. Something went out of Nye's life; he lost his power of magnetic oratory. He became depressed, encouraged only by his wife Jennie. Nye had come to know Jennie when she joined ILP talks at the MacNulty rendezvous during the fatal 1929–31 Labour Government, and following MacDonald's desertion they became companions in rambling the countryside which they both loved. I used to say mischievously that I slept in Jennie's bed the night she was married. So I did – I was staying with her parents at Lochgelly whilst on a Scottish speaking tour. Nye and Jennie were married in London.

It says much for the spontaneity of the CND that it grew despite this setback. The Aldermaston March became a wonder and more trade unions and constituency parties were won. A year later at the Scarborough Conference we carried the vote against the leadership, Nye absent in his fatal illness, but I do not think even he could have defeated us. Then came Hugh Gaitskell's dramatic defiance. 'I will fight and fight again,' he declared, and at the Blackpool Conference a year later he triumphed. He carried conference on the unilateralist issue, but at the cost of Left victories against the Polaris base, the training of German troops in Britain and nuclear arms by whomsoever made. The nuclear controversy was preceded by a conflict on German rearmament. Here Nye had been our leader. At party conference we were defeated by the last minute defection of a trade union whose own conference had been on our side. In Parliament seventy-two of us sat in the Chamber during the vote, a public demonstration.

When the Government allowed the Americans to use Christmas Island for nuclear tests the CND MPs decided we must protest on the air estimates. Should we satisfy ourselves by voting once on the major section, or should we push our opposition to the point of voting against each clause? Twenty-four or us decided on the one vote, but five, including Michael Foot, Emrys Hughes and Sydney Silverman, voted every time. The leadership exploited the split; the twenty-four were reprimanded, the five were expelled from the Parliamentary Party. At times I envied them – they were no longer subject to the tyranny of the Whip – but it was not long before I myself was in trouble. When some of us voted against the training of German troops in Britain we were summoned before Hugh Gaitskell, George Brown, the deputy leader and Herbert Bowden, the Chief Whip, one of the most formidable trials of the many at which I have been an offender. We were reminded that the Standing Orders had been suspended in the hope of Party loyalty, but in view of our conduct they would have to be reimposed. The new code did at least include my phrase, inherited from Maxton, that expulsion would be restricted to serious and persistent breaches, but it required that Members should never vote against any decision of the Parliamentary Party. How persistent was this conflict between discipline and conscience!

The conditions of work for back bench MPs were ludicrous. We had no room, not even a desk. I sat on a settee at a low table in a corridor, my consolation good neighbours, John Mendelson next, Barbara Castle opposite, Judith Hart and Laurie Pavitt near. The telephone was fifty yards away and one's secretary had to be summoned from her files a quarter of a mile away. MPs now occupy desks in a string but are still accommodated like sixth-form pupils. We had moments of relaxation, a television room on the top floor, to which I escaped to watch an England versus Australia test match, and the Harcourt Room where we could bring friends for a drink whilst awaiting the ten o'clock division. There was a good story about the Harcourt Room. An MP's last train left shortly after ten and we always pushed him to the front in the division lobby so that he could catch it. On one occasion he caught his train only to find his home in darkness. Opening the door, he called for his wife – and then remembered he had left her in the Harcourt Room!

I got on well with the staff. If the House adjourned after 11.45 pm they were taken home by car. One night a barmaid expressed concern because the debate was likely to end just before that time. I went into the Chamber and the Minister, concluding his reply to a Welsh Member about some local grievance, sat down at 11.43 pm. The Speaker rose to adjourn the House when to his surprise I rose to continue the debate. Enthusiastically I supported the Welshman's case; to this day he does not know why. Big Ben struck 11.45. The staff had their cars home.

MPs are social workers as much as legislators. Indeed, I found that most spent more time on grievances of constituents than on consideration of business in the Chamber. One who did not and got away with it was Jimmy Maxton. 'I'm a Parliamentarian,' he would say, 'not a bloody aunt.' I could not be so logical. I suppose I spent about half my time on Slough cases, 5,000 in all, ten a week, each involving about five letters, visits to Departments and Ministers, sometimes questions in the House. A real problem arises here. Constituents have a right to approach MPs, and MPs, thinking of the next election, want to be good constituency Members. Perhaps allowances for competent assistants would contribute to a solution.

One had some extraordinary cases. A matronly woman startled me by saying that the passport authorities insisted she was a man. The registrar of birth certificates had mistakenly recorded her as a boy and she had failed to convince umpteen officials that she was not. Fortunately I found the midwife who brought her into the world and an affidavit from her finally gained recognition of the woman's sex.

Slough is cosmopolitan and had an exceptionally large number of refugees from countries the other side of the Iron Curtain. I gained the nickname 'The Scarlet Pimpernel' by my efforts to reunite families. There was a thirteen-year-old Czechoslovakian girl whom her parents had not seen for ten years; the foster mother of a Jewish child whose parents had both been gassed; two Yugoslavian girls who had become engaged during the war to Ukrainian soldiers resident in Slough; the baby daughter of two Hungarians who fled during the rising; the Romanian wife of a prominent Slough industrialist.

The most remarkable case was that of the Russian mother of a girl who had been kidnapped by the Nazis. The family had lived in a Polish village and the daughter, when eighteen, was literally snatched from a tree in the orchard and carried to a waiting car. For five years she was compelled to act as an interpreter for the Germans, threatened with a concentration camp if she declined. At the end of the war she became a member of the staff of the American HQ in Vienna and married the correspondent of a well-known Paris paper, who – incredibly in her eyes – was arrested as a spy for the Communists; he escaped to Canada where he was killed in a car accident. Meanwhile, the Americans sent her to London in charge of refugees. She stayed when the appointment was over and somehow brought up three children and reached a position where she could invite her mother, growing old in Russia, to join her. For three years she failed to move Moscow, and when she approached me I got no further for several months. Then I wrote a personal appeal to Khrushchev, and a month later mother and daughter met at Heathrow after twenty-two years. I wish I could end the story there. In fact, the mother proved a martinet, treating her grown daughter like a child. They had to separate and to the distress of the daughter the old lady died. Even that was not the end. One of the sons got into trouble with the police and, broken and in despair, the girl who had been kidnapped by the Nazis thirty years before had died in tears – a tragic theme for a novel which someone might write. What happened gave some strength to the Russian argument that the reunification of families after long separation is not always a good idea.

There was a better ending to another remarkable case. A young man begged me to get his finacée from Czechoslovakia. He was a constituent of R. A. Butler, who asked me to act as he was a Member of the Government. The young man had been a war prisoner in Czechoslovakia, escaped, and fell in love with the daughter of an anti-Nazi farmer who had hidden him. At the end of the war he returned to England, the girl joined him and they married. After a year she went to stay with her father for a holiday – and did not return. The young husband, eager to get her back, entered Czechoslovakia illegally, jumping from the train before the frontier station. He was arrested, and after some days in prison was taken to a People's Divorce Court to hear his wife ask successfully for an annulment of the marriage. Deported to London, he wrote an angry book charging the Communists with intimidating his wife into breaking with him.

I did not know all this. When he came to me his request was that I should get here another Czechoslovakian girl whom he had also met whilst in hiding and to whom, I learned later, his thoughts turned when his wife divorced him. He had written to her, had met her when on a sponsored tour to Czechoslovakia and later had contrived a tryst at a frontier station where they became engaged. On his behalf I went to the Czechoslovakian Ambassador who with a smile handed me the young man's book, remarking, 'Your friend seems to have a flair for Czech girls.' Entirely ignorant of the former marriage, I was flummoxed. Not for a moment did I believe that the Czechs would help the young man in view of his violently anti-Communist allegations. But eventually they allowed the girl to come to England and I went to the wedding; the marriage has been successful. Another, happier, novel for someone to write.

I was outraged by the Soviet Government's overthrow of the Dubcek Government of 'Socialism with a Human Face' in Czechoslovakia. One of its Members, whose name it is still unsafe to mention, was an old friend. He had been a delegate at the 1931 Vienna Conference of the Socialist International and put to me his difficulty. He was opposed to the authoritarianism of Communism, but in Czechoslovakia the Communist Party was the only hope of the working class. I sympathised with his decision to join the Party and to work for liberalisation within it. That is what he and his friends did with success. I was deeply disillusioned by Moscow's intervention. Stalinism had gone only to be followed by a new form of imperialism.

Because of my earlier experience I became concerned with the rights and wrongs of prisoners. There was one prison tragedy which concerned me for over forty years. I have told how, after I finished my three years' imprisonment as a conscientious objector, I went to the ILP conference at Leicester and a young delegate moved a resolution on prison reform so impressively that I was impelled to second him. That young man spent most of his adult life in prison. He could not keep his hand off money and was repeatedly sentenced, but he was otherwise of generous character, dedicated to good causes, brilliant as a thinker and orator. He spent his time in prison reading law and proved shrewder in advice than most lawyers. I tried again and again to redirect his life; he would begin psychiatric treatment but never kept it up. Ethel Mannin and I met him in prison during his last term to tell him that our appeal for his release on licence had been rejected. We knew that that was the end. He suffered from diabetes, refrained from taking the insulin and died. This tragic misfit was the brother of a famous MP who was acknowledged to be among the cleverest in the House. In my view the prisoner was more brilliant even than the MP.

My happiest occasion in this Parliament was when, as chairman of the Keir Hardie Memorial Trust, set up by the ILP, I presented a bust of the father of the Labour Party to the House of Commons. The ceremony was in the crowded Grand Committee Room, the largest of all, tributes being paid by Lord Samuel, Walter Elliott and Hugh Gaitskell; the Speaker, W. S. Morrison, accepted the bust on behalf of the House. The bust was an extraordinarily fine work by Beuno Schotz, Esthonian by birth, Scot by adoption. It was first placed in a remote spot outside the Members' tea room, but Manny Shinwell made such a fuss that it was transferred to the inner lobby which it shares with Oliver Cromwell. We gave a copy of the bust to Old Cumnock, Hardie's home, where it stands beneath a tree-beautified slag heap.

A non-Parliamentary activity in which I became engaged was the establishment of a hostel for Indian students under the sponsorship of the Tilak Memorial Trust. The dynamo behind this was Datta Tahmankar, an Indian journalist and biographer of Tilak, whom he idolised as the pioneer of Indian nationalism. We bought the house where Tilak had lived in London and divided it into attractive flats where students nominated by Indian universities and the Indian High Commission could reside. I visited Lord Mountbatten to ask him to open the hostel. He was ill in bed, but even so the authority of his personality came across. My recollection of his bedroom is of the exquisite drawings of his wife which hung along each wall; her death was a great political and personal loss. Lord Mountbatten opened the hostel and was the first of many distinguished visitors. The LCC agreed to place a plaque on the building commemorating Tilak's residence; there was fierce Tory opposition on the ground of his 'sedition', to which the best answer was a speech by John Strachey at a luncheon in the House of Commons. Strachey's grandfather was the judge who sentenced Tilak to imprisonment, which led John to say that the sedition of yesterday is the patriotism of today. Madame Pandit, the Indian High Commissioner, and President Nkrumah of Ghana unveiled the plaque, a happy recognition of India's precedence in the liberation of colonial peoples. Almost all of India's leaders have visited the hostel. When Jawaharlal Nehru came he gave us a surprise.

Looking round he exalaimed: 'Why, I lived here, too! During my vacations from Cambridge I had a room here.'

I was nominated for the Nobel Peace Prize, surprised by the sponsors, who included Earl Attlee, Harold Wilson, James Griffiths, Iain Macleod, Lord Boothby, R. H. Tawney, A. J. Ayer, Presidents and Prime Ministers from many Third World countries, sixty-seven Indian MPs, Walter Nash from New Zealand, Dr Evatt from Australia, and European Socialists such as Pietro Nenni of Italy, Erich Ollenhauer of Germany and Madame Bodil-Koch of Denmark. I learned that Chief Luthuli, pacifist president of the African National Congress in South Africa, was also nominated and of course I withdrew. I went with others to Heathrow to meet Chief Luthuli on his way to Oslo. His bearing united strength and gentleness, a memorable figure. He lived and died before his time. Events have destroyed the pacifism of the ANC.

Thirty and twenty years too early I had wonderful birthday parties – when I was seventy and eighty years of age. Leslie Hale chaired a House of Commons dinner, and I am glad at least that Nye Bevan could speak – it was one of his last utterances. Michael Foot, James Callaghan and Barbara Castle took part, Jimmy causing amusement when he told how even Rhodesian whites had shown respect for me when they learned I had played rugger for Blackheath. This dinner, however, fades in my memory as I recollect the party at the St Pancras Town Hall on my eightieth birthday. It was arranged by the Movement for Colonial Freedom, and was fantastic in its attendance and spirit. Everyone came and Ray Fletcher, a Labour MP, had written a biographical sketch which was read by Sybil Thorndike, Constance Cummings and Andrew Faulds. Even more moving was the appearance of Lewis Casson on the stage, nearly blind and feeble on sticks. I was scarcely able to speak in reply, vowing that there would be no more parties until I am ninety.

One unique recognition I had. The Islington Borough Council decided to place a plaque on the house at Myddelton Square where I had lived sixty years ago. I understood such plaques were attached only twenty years after a person's death, but Islington set a precedent. There the plaque is, perhaps appropriate, after all, as a memento of pioneering Socialism and for the distinguished guests, Keir Hardie, Bernard Shaw, Edward Carpenter and others.

I should record that we had two General Elections during this period. In 1955 Eton and Slough were reasonably loyal: Labour, 20,576; Conservative, 18,124. But in 1959 we had a shock. My majority was only eighty-eight – 20,851 against 20,763. A warning of things to come.

CHAPTER TWENTY-NINE

BECOMING A LORD

At the General Election of 1964 I was defeated at Eton and Slough by eleven votes. It was partly my own fault – I did not fight with sufficient concentration. The reason for my indifference I cannot explain; perhaps it was due to an absence of united support in the local Party, some disagreeing with me on coloured immigrants, some thinking I was too old. Our organisation was deplorable. Only on polling day itself did I learn that in one of the biggest wards, with a large Labour vote, no election committee had functioned because the secretary did not like my views on race. Another reason for our defeat was the rain which descended from 5 pm until polling closed, the period when workers vote. I received a sad letter from six workers at a gravel pit who were soaked on returning home and they and their wives did not go out – they had thought, 'Fenner is safe'. If they had voted, I would have had a majority of one! On the Tory side the organisation was more efficient than it had ever been and the candidate, Sir Anthony Meyer, and his dynamic wife were adventurous, driving through the streets all day and waving to their supporters. They deserved to win.

Undoubtedly the determining issue was the invasion of Slough by Commonwealth immigrants. I was angry with the Home Secretary, Henry Brooke, who was reported prominently in the local press as saying that he had never heard me speak in the Commons except on colonial issues; in fact, my last speech before the dissolution was on the notorious Hanratty case centred on Slough, and it was Brooke who replied. (I was convinced Hanratty was not guilty of the A6 murder and for some years I pressed Home Secretaries to hold an enquiry but all refused.) When my election defeat was announced I was sorry for friends who worked unsparingly, but personally I was not depressed; Labour had done well in the rest of the country and somehow I felt I had finished a stage of life. One strange thing lingers in my mind. Before the election I had listened on the radio to the prophecies of Old Moore's Almanack for the year. They included an exceptional election defeat for a 'prominent Left Wing Socialist in the South of England'. A consolation for my rejection by Slough was the return of Joan Lestor at the subsequent election. She was a better MP than I could have been. I maintained associations with the constituency. The Council honoured me by naming a splendid block of flats 'Brockway House'.

Tony Benn phoned urging me to think of the House of Lords. This was curious because he himself had refused to become a Lord when his father, Viscount Stansgate, died and had won the right of hereditary peers to opt out. Tony gave his father as an example of what a peer could do and I was impressed because I had seen him in radical action. Nevertheless, I was against the existence of the undemocratic Chamber as a legislative body and debated with myself whether it would not be too compromising to join. When, however, Harold Wilson summoned me to 10 Downing Street I did not hesitate. 'You will take the Labour Whip,' he said. 'Yes,' I replied, 'but I shall use the House primarily as a platform for Socialism and Peace.' Harold smiled; 'That we should expect,' he commented.

So I became Baron Brockway of Eton and Slough; there was some Tory muttering that I had included Eton. In residential Totteridge where I now live there were amusing consequences. A friend in the north addressed a letter to 'The Lord Brockway' without including the number of the house. The letter was returned with the explanation that there was no public house of that name in the street. When the Press announced I had become a Lord, women in the neighbourhood vied with each other to give me lifts in their cars, but most of them stopped doing so when they learned my views. My wife declined to be called Lady Brockway, anti-Establishment and egalitarian to her finger-tips.

It is sometimes thought that peers permanently wear ermine robes. I have done so only three times: when I was introduced; when I sponsored the introduction of Lord Wells-Pestell, now a Minister, who insisted that one of my books had converted him to Socialism, and my Left colleague in the Commons, Tom Driberg, who became Lord Bradwell (but died tragically soon). The introduction ceremony is an ordeal – dignified or amusing according to taste. Headed by the Garter King of Arms in heraldic dress of red and gold, followed by two sponsors and the new Lord robed in long ermine, a procession marches the length of the Chamber and back, bowing to the empty throne every few yards and, mounting to a top bench where, obeying the muttered instructions of the Garter King, they rise and sit three times, doffing black hats to the throne, the Lord Chancellor doffing his is acknow-ledgement. Finally the new peer kneels and takes the Chancellor's hand, whilst supporters welcome him with a roar of 'Hear, hear'.

This was all a game to me, but I was disturbed when the long Command from the Queen was read. It required me to defend the Monarchy, the State and the Church – the function of Parliament in mediaeval times before social problems, thanks mostly to the emergence of the Labour Party, were recognised as relevant. I had some doubts about allegiance to the Monarchy. I am theoretically a Republican, though many Presidential privileges do not please me and I do not regard the issue, as my friend Willie Hamilton does, as a priority. When first elected to Parliament I had put my problem to the Speaker who assured me that a Republican could conscientiously de-clare allegiance, regarding the Monarch as the embodiment of the State. That interpretation eased my doubts and ever since I have accepted it, affirming rather than taking the oath, in accordance with my Humanist be-liefs.

There was an incident involving the Monarchy and the wearing of ermine robes. When the Queen opens Parliament the Lords are expected to be in ceremonial dress. I believe the Standing Orders used to insist that the garment should be the property of the peer, though in fact most are hired from Moss Bros. for the occasion. I decided to claim the right to attend without wearing a robe and found in fact that I could not be excluded. Having gained the point, I have not troubled to attend the State opening since, but I do not think anyone has followed my example.

I have sat on both sides of the House reflecting Labour in Opposition and Government, always below the gangway, behind the Liberals or the Bishops, indicating a certain independence. The most effective way of intervention is by questions. At first I put down one every day until Tories complained that I was hogging the limitation to the four questions allowed for all peers. After that, I restricted myself, except when something very urgent arose, to two questions a week, only to find that very often fewer than the daily four questions were tabled by others. With some regrets I decided to follow the advice of Charles Trevelyan to specialise. I was deeply interested in the issues raised by Britain's economic crises, taking the view that inflation, unemployment and wage conflicts are reflections of capitalism and that democratic Socialism alone is the answer, but generally I disciplined myself to raise issues of peace and racialism. Once, however, I got the Party to agree to my initiating a debate on Capitalism versus Socialism, the only time, I think, that Parliament has considered the fundamental alternatives since Philip Snowden promoted a similar debate in the Commons in the 1920s. It is a trifle ironical that such a debate should have taken place in the House of Lords.

I did not limit myself to questions. Back benchers in the Lords have greater opportunities than in the Commons. In the elected Chamber a back bencher never knows whether he will be called in a debate. In the Lords, if one indicates a wish to speak, there is a certainty. There is another unique opportunity. In the Commons if one wishes to raise an issue not within the business of the day, time is usually limited to half an hour on the adjournment at 10 pm. In the Lords one can put down what is called an 'unstarred question' and the debate is timeless, often with many speakers, and sometimes develops into a major occasion. I became known for the frequency of my unstarred questions, but I sometimes wondered with what effect. Ministers and civil servants told me their departments took notice, but the media in Britain, and thus the public, pay little attention to the generally irrelevant Upper Chamber. However, I often heard from distant parts of the world that issues I raised had received mention there.

One also has opportunities in the Lords to introduce Private Members' Bills. I did so four times with some results. I sponsored a Bill to amend the Race Relations Act so that it would cover discrimination in housing and employment in addition to public places. I had a favourable response from the Government, which subsequently passed an Act on similar lines. I was dissatisfied with the limited functions of the Race Relations Boards which could act only on complaints. When the Board asked for powers to prevent discrimination by investigating practices in industry I introduced a second amending Bill accordingly. I had known Sir Geoffrey Wilson, the chairman of the Board, as a boy. He is the son of A. C. Wilson, a Quaker who was of great help to conscientious objectors in the First World War and with whom I had spent a seaside summer holiday. Happy recollections remain of playing on the sands with Geoffrey and the children. I saw Roy Jenkins, the Home Secretary, about the Board's functions; he was entirely sympathetic, and indicated that he would include in his Sex Discrimination Bill powers which would serve as a precedent for a Bill to reconstruct the Race Relations administration. This he did.

Three times I introduced a Bill for a Charter of Civil Rights in Northern Ireland. I became convinced that a basic Charter was the first answer to the discrimination from which the Catholic minority had suffered for fifty years. It seemed to me more important in the long run than power sharing, though I welcomed this temporarily. We were opposed to a Coalition Government in Britain; why should a joint Government of Loyalist Big Business and Social Democrats, many of whom are sincere Socialists, work more effectively in Northern Ireland? My Bills were received with sympathetic purrs by both front benches, and action was taken to prevent discrimination in public housing, but little was done on a broader scale until 1976 when a Commission to study the question, with Lord Feather as chairman, was appointed. Unhappily Victor Feather died before conclusions were reached.

An extraordinary feature of the House of Lords is that it has no chairman to maintain order. The Lord Chancellor sits on the Woolsack, seemingly equivalent to the Speaker's Chair in the Commons, but he has no authority to discipline us. His duties are limited to announcing business and, after quaintly stepping aside, speaking on legal issues. Amazingly, proceedings are conducted like a Quaker meeting with a Leader of the House gently expressing the consensus of opinion when a Lord intervenes irrelevantly or exchanges on a question are overlong. Lord Windlesham and Lord Shepherd both served admirably as our Quaker Elders, and uniquely this somewhat anarchistic arrangement works.

Except for the front benches and Committee chairmen, peers are not expected by tradition to be immersed in Parliamentary duties. When I entered the House, there were less than twenty desks for the thousand back benchers and accommodation for only five secretaries. Immediately I sought a working place and found an unused desk which had been Earl Attlee's. He told me he was served by an office in the Temple and when I enquired about the papers which cluttered desk and drawers he said, 'destroy them'. I did so, but I have wondered since what historic documents went to waste. Later more accommodation was provided for peers but it is still inadequate. The truth is, however, that few Members of the Lords regard it as a place of work. There is the call for Committee service, but, as I have noted, we do not have the continuous demands from constituents which MPs have to handle. I was told in the Commons that I had more letters than any back bencher, and the postal officials in the Lords tell me the same. They still come from all parts of the world.

Many people came to see me – members of pressure movements, visitors from overseas, and, in astonishing numbers, students who wanted information for their theses. I suppose Manny Shinwell and I are the only pre-First-World-War Socialists still active politically, and students seeking material write to us for interviews. Manny, older than I am, cannot be troubled, but I have a natural feeling for youth and think of it as a worthwhile service, so I used to see as many as two a week. From two American girl students I had a visit which gave rise to one of my favourite stories. After tea they wished to go to the toilet and I guided them to the rest room reserved for peeresses. Visitors were not allowed there; worse still they had a pocket flash-light colour camera, also forbidden in the House. They had never seen anything like the peeresses' toilet – steps up to the throne, the bowl beautifully decorated with blue flowers, a great plunger at its side – so they took a photograph. I heard subsequently from America that they sold it to a press syndicate and that it appeared in so many newspapers that they paid for the whole cost of their journey to Europe from the proceeds. I was scared that I would be discovered as responsible for this breach of Upper Chamber privacy, but I never was. The girls gave me an attaché case to commemorate the occasion.

I got committed to an adventurous effort to end the army occupation of a South Dorset region at Lulworth and Tyneham. It was patriotically surrendered to the Forces in preparation for D-Day and in acknowledgement Winston Churchill promised that it would be returned at the end of hostilities, a letter going to each tenant with this assurance. I was asked to intervene by a veteran Quaker ILP-er, Mavis Caver, who was chairman of a local committee, with Ronald Legg, editor of the attractive *Dorset Magazine*, as secretary. The members were typical of the radical new generation, taking no notice of the 'Trespassers will be Prosecuted' notices which surrounded the army land. Somehow they got hold of a master-key which opened all gates and when I visited them they took me on a guided tour, ending with a cheese and wine party round a bonfire on a prohibited hill above the coast. This was the first time since my years as a conscientious objector and my forged passports for refugees from Nazism that I had knowingly broken the law, but the spirit of these young people was so gay and infectious that I could not resist. With Tyneham I fell in love. There are places more distinctively beautiful, but nowhere in Britain have I seen such harmony of varied beauty, the bay with its white cliffs, the rolling hills, the mystic wonder of Thomas Hardy's Egdon Heath. The village was in ruins, but one could still sense the charm of its white-stone cottages, its Elizabethan manor house and exquisite little church. A Government Commission reported in favour of evacuation by the army, but the Ministry of Defence insisted that it must remain. I did everything – spoke in Dorset, wrote to the Press, saw Ministers with deputations, which included an original tenant who produced the wartime pledge, and raised the issue again and again in the Lords, where I got considerable support. Our efforts were not all in vain. Under this pressure the Defence Ministry agreed to provide enjoyable facilities for civilians on land and coast and there is even a hope that a huge clay pit which has outraged Egdon Heath may be turned into a lake. My friends in Dorset are now asking that the area shall be designated a National Park, which would not be inconsistent with army control.

There was another coast which I loved, the Gower peninsula near Swansea in South Wales. Edith, my son Chris and I went often for holidays, captivated by its cliffs and coves and wild ponies, above all by the magnificent Rossilli Bay. On one occasion the bus carrying us to Swansea on our return to London stopped at Rossilli and Chris and I jumped off for a last sight of the bay. When we got back the bus with Edith and luggage on board had gone, but the driver of a second bus, not destined for Swansea, rescued us. He gave chase for two miles down narrow lanes off his route and we rejoined Edith. Where else than in Western Wales could that have happened? I was made a Freeman of the Gower for influencing the Minister of Agriculture to prohibit the destruction of trees along the coast. The honour brought no privileges, but I appreciated it.

It was the Immigration Bill of 1971 which first led me to think that there might be some value in a Second Chamber. I had moved the rejection of the Immigration Act of 1968 and nearly defeated the Labour Government. To my surprise I had been supported by prominent Tories, including the Marquis of Lansdowne, Viscount (Lennox) Boyd of Merton, Earl Perth and Lord Windlesham, who felt in honour bound to keep an understanding at the time of Kenyan independence that Asians who opted to remain British citizens should have passport rights. I was deeply impressed by this display of integrity and was a little dismayed to find Lord Windlesham, for whom I had high regard, introducing the 1971 Bill which depreciated still further the status of British Asians. I have no doubt he felt differently and he went out of his way to be conciliatory, doing his best to meet the many proposals I made, particularly on the issue of police intervention and, later, the right of a man living abroad to join his wife if she was resident here.

A second issue made me realise the value of a revising Chamber. Some years earlier I had travelled from South Wales with a naval officer and three young boys. The lads had been in a strict orphanage and were excited by the prospect of life in the navy to which they had been recruited. A year later one of the boys wrote to the House of Commons begging me to get his discharge. He found existence in the navy more distasteful even than in the orphanage; with great difficulty I got him out a year later on compassionate grounds. When a Defence Bill came before the Lords I found that juveniles had to serve thirteen years after enrolment, and won the sympathy of the House by telling not only of the Welsh boy but of others reported to a continuing Committee which the Control Board for Conscientious Objectors had set up to advise those in the Services who developed misgivings. The result was amendments to the regulations allowing boy recruits to reconsider their enrolment after six months and to decide at eighteen whether they wished to remain in the Forces. I was chairman of the CBCO Committee. We only had two or three cases a year, but to defend liberty of conscience was imperative to me, however few the cases.

I had innumerable instances of threatened deportation under the Immigration Acts. With the maximum of inconvenience they came mostly at weekends, when I would hear that individuals and families had been stopped at Heathrow and were to be sent back on the next plane. Weekend cases meant ringing the duty officer at the Home Office, in charge during the absence of the Home Secretary and his staff, who would then phone the Minister's private secretary at his home, who would in turn have to contact me. If a Member of Parliament questions a deportation, it is delayed until representations are considered; this involved urgent instructions from the Secretary to Heathrow. I wondered if senior civil servants were ever free of their duties.

Two things I must add. The Ministers, Lord Windlesham in a Tory Government, and Alex Lyon in the succeeding Labour Government, made their decisions with humanity, stretching rules to the limit when personal hardship was involved. I could cite many cases, but one must do. A young nurse told me she was to be married in three days' time, but her fiancé had been picked up by the police for overstaying his permit and was to be deported that day. There was no doubt he was at fault, but the Home Office allowed the couple to be married, and as the husband of a lawful resident the boy was permitted to stay. The second thing I must add is that I would never have been able to act in these cases without the initiative of Mary Dines, the secretary of the Joint Council for the Welfare of Immigrants. It was she who received the information from Heathrow, it was she who sorted out the complicated facts, and it was she who drafted my letters to the Home Secretary. She is incidentally the only person I have ever permitted to sign a letter in my name without seeing it. I have known no one who so combined sympathy and efficiency.

The John Stonehouse tragedy was a great shock. I write tragedy because twenty years' association indicated that he had both dedication to good causes and an unusual ability. I knew him first when the Congress for Peoples against Imperialism shared offices off Victoria Street with the Socialist Students' International of which he was secretary. He left that post after some dispute and I nominated him as organiser for the Uganda Farmers' Cooperative whom he served well until conflict again occurred. He was elected to Parliament, was prominent in championing African liberation causes, particularly the right, of the majority in Rhodesia. He went there, was arrested and declared a prohibited immigrant. I admired this and we cooperated closely, but he began to aim at personal power and our courses diverged. He devoted himself to finance, taking the view that a successful politician must have security, but about that I knew nothing. Nor did I become involved in a controversy which arose about his chairmanship of the London Cooperative Society, though my political sympathies were with his critics, by no means all Communists. We lost contact and I was surprised when he insisted on a dinner with MPs on my seventy-fifth birthday. About all that happened afterwards I need not comment, but I had great sympathy with his wife Barbara and his daughters, wonderfully loyal, with whom I had been friendly over the years.

The House of Lords is one of the friendliest places I know. There is rarely bitterness in debates and outside the Chamber all of us, Labourists, Tories, Liberals, cross-benchers, mingle. For meals the Oxbridge and Temple tradition of one prolonged table is followed, each newcomer joining the sitting queue, not knowing who will be his neighbours or opposites. In the bars one exchanges drinks with whomever is standing by. I was on amicable terms with many political opponents, among them, my Leftist friends may be shocked to hear, Lord Hailsham, a hangover from the days when we both championed Seretse Khama. He joked whenever we met. When I was putting questions every day he solemnly told me that at the opening prayers the Bishops beseeched the good Lord 'to deliver us from the daily Brockway'. I told him in 1975 that I expected to be on the Front Opposition Bench before long. 'Why?' 'There'll be a Coalition Government.' 'Then I'll be with you,' he laughed, 'they won't have *me*.' (The coalition did not come but coalition policy did.) Other Tory friends were Lady Tweedsmuir, though we came into continuous conflict at question-time, and Lord Mowbray and Stourton, Tory Whip, with whom one night I went in search of the fourteen bars in the Houses of Parliament, finding only eight. This social contact with Tories was a contrast to the remoteness I had experienced in the Commons. I had only two Tory friends there, Hugh Fraser who cooperated in the campaign for peace in Nigeria and – hard to believe – Margaret Thatcher. She lived in Hampstead Garden Suburb not far from my home in East Finchley, and she and her husband sometimes drove me back when the Commons sat late. She was charming and was shrewd in political comment, but it did not occur to me that she would become leader of her Party. She did not seem to me to have the stature of Edward Heath. I was in the Lords when Winifred Ewing, the Scottish Nationalist leader, was elected. Her parents were members of the Glasgow ILP and I used to hold her on my knee when she was little more than an infant.

Among Liberals in the Lords I was friendly with Lord Avebury, previously Eric Lubbock of Orpington fame, a colleague on all racial issues; Lord Foot, the fourth brother of that extraordinary family, alert on personal rights; Lord Beaumont, who helped generously in our campaign for peace in Nigeria. I once remarked in the Chamber that another Liberal, Lord Gladwyn, aroused my political hostility whenever he rose to speak. It was typical of the House that he immediately invited me to tea. Among cross-benchers, Lord Boothby and his 'golden girl' wife always joined me if I was alone in the guest room, and I had some accord with young Lord O'Hagan, who was at Eton College when I was its MP. Among Bishops, I admired specially Mervyn Stockwood and the Bishop of Durham.

I was troubled sometimes whether this climate of friendliness – everyone called me 'Fenner' – was undermining my principles. I do not think it did so – I expressed them forthrightly – but admittedly the conflict between the opposing parties was much less pronounced than in the Commons. We were ostentatiously polite; there were never the scenes which frequently characterise 'Another Place'. Some more militant Labourists, acclimatised to the Commons, revolted against these gracious habits; I cannot say I did. Perhaps I *was* succumbing! Yet I became more Left every day, convinced that radical participatory Socialism is the only answer to mounting economic ills. I said in the House that I was far to the Left of Communists. They wanted one revolution; I wanted two – social revolution in the West, a libertarian revolution in the East.

My closest associates were, of course, Socialist colleagues, too many to mention. I revered Boyd Orr, world citizen in spirit as well as conviction. It was a great joy to welcome Leslie Hale, comrade since Kenya days. I enjoyed getting to know Ritchie-Calder, whose writings on the technical possibilities of the future fascinated me. Lord Carradon, another Foot, whom I had admired as British representative at the United Nations, embarrassed me by saying I was his leader in the Lords. Donald Soper, of golden voice and speech, made me responsible for his presence in the House: 'if it's good enough for Fenner, it must be OK for me'. Harold Davies, friend for many years, had his desk next to me, teller of good stories; sitting next to me in the Chamber was Tom Maelor, comrade of prison, Parliament and Palestine. I rejoiced in Bill Blyton, a working-class Geordie, blunt, uncompromising, and learned much from Wynne Jones, also a Geordie, a university lecturer. For Manny Shinwell years meant affection, despite our differences on arms. For Gerald Gardiner, ex-Lord Chancellor, I had great respect, a Quaker with the spirit and practice of tolerance. Among women, there was Jennie Lee, outspoken as ever, Dora Gaitskell, though she always challenged me in the House, and Pat Llewellyn-Davies, Chief Whip, who was once told off by her leader for glowing approval of one of my Leftist speeches.

My attitude to the Labour Government was one of amicable scepticism. I did not believe they could solve our problems within capitalism. They held that they could not adopt Socialist alternatives because their majority in the Commons was only one and, still more, because they had only one-third of the electoral support. Meanwhile, they were protecting the workers more than a Tory Government would have done, so I gave them qualified support. That became opposition in the spheres of unemployment, armaments and many aspects of foreign policy, as I have indicated. Except for Barbara Castle, comrade in African struggles, Michael Foot, who reminded me in many ways – not only in his oratory – of Jimmy Maxton, and Tony Benn, most far-seeing in his advocacy of participatory democracy, I had little warm feeling for Members of the Cabinet. Harold Wilson had always been kind – when leader of the Opposition he used to drive Barbara Castle and me to our Highgate homes after late sittings, and at Slough he said I was more responsible for colonial liberation than any man: but one never got close to him. He did a unique job in keeping the Party together and was head and shoulders above his opponents. Jim Callaghan, becoming Prime Minister in April 1976, had always been friendly – he once sounded me out as to whether I should follow him as Opposition speaker on the colonies – but that was the only time I had a cup of tea with him. Denis Healey I never really knew, very able, convincing on TV, but one would never guess he was a Socialist. I admired Shirley Williams (daughter of my revered friend, Vera Brittain) a moderate but combining with exceptional competence a human touch which wins all who know her as well as thousands of TV watchers.

Even in the Lords I was a member of the *Tribune* group, admired immensely the mind of Ian Mikardo, penetrating through all confusion, delighted in the forthrightness of Eric Heffer, remembering the fellowship of his ILP home in Liverpool many years ago, and valued the devotion of Stan Newens, indefatigable, the only man I knew who did more work than I did. Outside Parliament I had the friendship particularly of Jack Jones among Trade Unionists and Alf Lomas among Cooperators, both not only good in Home affairs but of world Socialist vision.

Let me scotch one allegation about peers. When we overwhelmingly passed the Bill to legalise homosexuality among adults, it was rumoured that there were many 'gays' among us. There was actually a story that whilst in the Commons the custodians cried at the end of a sitting, 'Who goes home?', the farewell in the Lords was 'Who goes homo?', but I saw no evidence of the practice, except for one peer who slipped poems into my pocket. Let me scotch, also, the fiction that all Lords are rich – 'living like a Lord' is the phrase. It is true we have millionaires, but others found life difficult. Attendance allowances for expenses are at a maximum of £13.50 a day, but the Upper Chamber meets only for about a hundred days a year. I was among a group of Lords who regularly took modest evening meals in the Commons public cafeteria to avoid the cost of the Lords' dinners. I was astounded to be told by a Lord of distinguished name, reflecting the public service of his ancestors, that he was sleeping in the library until he got his allowance at the end of the month. He acknowledged that he had even slept on the Embankment because he could not afford to stay at an hotel. An unhappy and almost certainly unique case, unsuspected by those who sat with him in the Chamber.

The introduction of life peers changed profoundly the character of the Upper Chamber. It was no longer dominated by the sons of the aristocracy, though they remained the great majority. Women were admitted for the first time and made their mark: Lady Young among Conservatives, Lady Seear among Liberals, Pat Llewellyn-Davies, Jennie Lee, Alma Birk, Edith Summerskill, Barbara Wootton and Nora Phillips among Labourists, and many others. The Labour life peers brought not only direct challenging speech but a knowledge of the living conditions of ordinary people which had been absent. The House of Lords remained undemocratic in composition, but it became far more democratic in complexion.

This invasion of democratic voices in the Lords was used to defend its existence. When, in November 1975, a conflict arose betwen Commons and Lords on Michael Foot's Bill establishing closed shops, Lord Carrington, the Tory leader, even cited me as a reason for maintaining the House of Lords. Typical of Lords' courtesy he came to me and said he intended to be mischievous about me; of course I said I did not mind. His reference turned out to be delightfully funny. He said he suspected that some Labour Lords were glad that the House had not been abolished, 'for how on earth would the noble Lord, Lord Brockway, operate?' He proceeded: 'The noble Lord, Lord Brockway, fires questions at a rate and with an accuracy and penetration scarcely exceeded by the general-purpose machine gun. How could he continue? Picketing the Foreign Office each day with a different placard would hardly be a substitute, and even he might find it both colder and more fatiguing than your Lordships' House.' Similarly, Lord Carrington teased Lord Shinwell and Lord Milford, our one Communist, an unlikely hereditary peer. The humour was light, but it was also piercing. I think it is true that it would be easier to end the Lords if there were not radical voices within it.

My prejudice against the House was modified by the quality of many of the debates. Among those who had been made peers for distinction in different spheres – industrial, scientific, educational, medical, administration, colonial service – there was a wealth of experience which gave contributions of knowledge. This was less evident when social conditions were discussed, but very often indeed the debates were of a higher standard than in the Commons. There was another reason besides knowledge. In the Lords there is much less party pressure; there is no intimidation from Whips. One can speak freely the truth as one sees it, with the consequence that debates leave an impression of collective sincerity. Views, of course, reflect backgrounds and the undemocratic character of the House means that the point of view of the Establishment rules, but as I listened I began to feel that a really representative House could serve valuably as a political British Association, a forum of knowledgeable and experienced representatives from all spheres of administration and from industrial and social life.

My thoughts grew from the idea of a forum to the possibility of a Second Chamber which would reinforce rather than repudiate democracy. Earlier I had thought that a Commons Select Committee could serve to revise Bills and to give the Government the opportunity for second thoughts, but I came to feel that party partisanship and Whips' control would not provide the conditions for the necessary consideration. The House of Lords at present is obviously incapable of fulfilling the task because of its unrepresentative character. It is incongruous that we should have a revising Chamber of no less than 1,139 Members of whom 817 are hereditary Peers. A clue to the solution was suggested to me by Joan Hymans, a conscientious Councillor at Camden with an unusually active mind. 'Why not a Second Chamber of representatives of the grass roots of the people?' she asked. Why not? Not only the TUC and the CBI, trade unions and managements, but also the professions, the Churches, women's organisations, consumers, students and others, a reflection of the vital democratic activity of the nation. To these could be added a limited number of persons of experience and distinction nominated by the political parties through Government appointment as now. This would involve elaborate consideration to secure equitable representation and would be, let us face it, a concession to the idea of a Corporate State, but the Assembly would be advisory rather than legislative, an extension of the Government–TUC relationship on incomes policy in 1976, the House of Commons dominant with the right to reject proposals and to apply legislation without the one year's delaying power now allowed to the House of Lords. The revised Second Chamber would represent a development of participatory democracy, enabling the regionally-elected Members of Parliament to be aware of dynamic cross-section opinion and inviting the cooperation of all who matter in our society.

CHAPTER THIRTY

THIS MAD WORLD

In the Lords I became more involved than ever in issues of freedom, world hunger and peace. As I have stressed, a peer does not have to spend the hours demanded by a constituency and this gave time to read and research the problems of conflict which mounted over the world. Near at hand was Northern Ireland. I have already described how I introduced Bills for a Charter of Civil Rights. Soon I became more involved. This was not intentional; one thing led to another.

The Northern Ireland Civil Rights Association, a body which held aloof from violence, invited me to address a meeting at Londonderry. It was to be on the same day as an illegal march and I went only on the assurance that it would be held independently. I travelled with Councillor Joan Hymans to whom I have just referred, who represented the Movement for Colonial Freedom in which she was active. She was utterly dedicated to human equality and liberty, working constructively against racialism not only in this country but particularly in Southern Africa. For eighteen devoted years she has done the great personal service of driving me everywhere in her car, named 'Uhura' (Africa's Freedom call). We were surprised to be driven south from Belfast airport to the Republic, our Irish friends explaining that the car would be stopped if we drove direct to Londonderry; they were proved right by the experience of observers from the National Council for Civil Liberties who were allowed to enter Derry only when everything was over. Before we had gone far we were held up by armed soldiers who searched us and the car thoroughly though with a friendliness which did not suggest tension. At the border to the Republic I was astonished to find troops and customs officers occupying a caravan at the side of the road – the IRA had blown up their headquarters. Control was surprisingly light; we were waved on without being searched or questioned. After lunching at the first town in the Republic we took a direct road to London-derry with easy inspection at the frontier and an amicable search outside the town. So far there was no evidence of conflict.

In Derry itself things were different. The Catholic march was to be to the City Square for a demonstration. Our driver stationed the car in a side road where we could observe the procession as it descended from the high-lying Creggan, a Catholic stronghold, to the centre of the city. It was like a holiday outing. Men and women, the children left behind, strolled laughing and carefree in broken ranks as though to some festival; I did not see anyone carrying arms or even a stick. At the bottom of the hill they were to be joined by a similar march from the other Catholic stronghold in Bogside. We watched as thousands passed and then followed down the hill, well behind. The road mounted to the city centre, and not far up we could see a barricade manned by soldiers. The organisers repeatedly instructed the marchers, 'Don't be provoked to violence. Turn back when you reach the barricade.' But this proved impossible; those in front were jammed against the barricade which threatened to collapse. Army batons lashed out and youngsters retaliated with stones. Inevitably violence grew. We heard the different sounds of exploding tear-gas shells and rubber bullets, and marchers streamed by us, red-eyed and weeping from the gas. 'We had better get to the meeting before further trouble,' our driver said, turning down a side street.

A lorry serving as a platform stood in front of a wall inscribed 'Enter Free Derry'. It faced a long open space; about two thousand gathered around. As I began to speak hundreds of people came running as for their lives from the distant right, followed by a fleeing crowd from the main roadway at the far end of the open space. I caught a glimpse of army vehicles behind them; shots rang out; those about me dragged me down flat on the lorry. At my side was Bernadette Devlin who with mike at her lips took command. 'Get down on your knees and crawl away,' she told the crowd, and they did so towards side streets, a remarkable sight which I just glimpsed. I wanted to lift my head to see what was happening further away, but I was roughly pulled down. I heard the sound of running people as they fled past to the protection of Bogside houses. Then the firing broke out again, first far to the right and then nearer. For a shattering moment or two bullets struck the wall behind us. Then came quiet, and Bernadette ordered us to slide to the ground, and, bending low, to follow her to a near-by friendly home. My last memory of the scene was of a priest, waving a white handkerchief, tending to a wounded man in the empty square. Thirteen were shot dead on 'Bloody Sunday'.

We talked little as our car to the airport zigzagged through darkened, barricaded streets bristling with the guns of soldiers. We left a Derry that had added understanding to our knowledge. I told the story, as I have told it here, at the subsequent enquiry at Coleraine. The only part of my evidence reproduced in Lord Widgery's white-washing report was my acknowledgement, already made to the Lords, that the troops had not fired deliberately at our meeting.

On the anniversary of 'Bloody Sunday' I attended a memorial meeting in Derry, again accompanied by Joan Hymans, who on this occasion represented among others the Borough of Camden; an unusual gesture even for a local authority with a large Irish community. I dug the first sod for a statue in memory of the thirteen dead, since beautifully completed. I ventured a new line in my speech. Since it was accepted that Ulster should join the Republic only with the consent of the people, I urged that the frontier issue should be put in the background for a time and, as the best evidence of cooperation between Protestants and Catholics for the ultimate realisation of a united Ireland, all effort concentrated in securing joint action on common demands by the workers of both communities. Later, I repeated the appeal at a Civil Rights meeting in Tyrone and was surprised by the response; but, alas, this approach has made as yet little, though some, progress.

There were two exceptional women at these Derry meetings: Bernadette Devlin, whom I have already mentioned, and Vanessa Redgrave, the gifted actress. Bernadette was young, in her early twenties, and her first speech in the Commons captivated everyone. She came to see me in the Lords to get tips about Parliamentary procedure, and I was attracted by her political attitude, basically Socialist, calling for a workers' front across the frontiers of Ireland. When unmarried she became pregnant she was courageously unashamed, later marrying her man, but prejudice against her private life probably contributed towards her defeat in her constituency. She decided to go back to her university studies, but she identified herself with an extreme revolutionary group, isolating herself from serious politics. I hope she may return to the main stream.

Vanessa Redgrave came to the Derry memorial meeting. I had met her before – she was treasurer of the Movement for Colonial Freedom – but this was the first opportunity of real companionship. We all stayed with the same working family, and I was delighted to find her a helpful, caring and jolly girl without a trace of a star's temperament. Driving back to the airport we all needed drinks, denied by Northern Ireland Sabbath prohibition. Our driver put that right, finding an inn which forgot this particular law. Vanessa made friends with all the customers, singing and dancing among them for sheer fun. I was not surprised, though sorry, when later she became candidate for the Revolutionary Workers' Party. She is by nature a rebel against all the snobbery of society.

Whilst I am writing about Ireland I should mention my involvement with the Price sisters sent to twenty years' imprisonment for their part in bombing outside the Old Bailey. I received a letter from a Civil Rights group in Britain asking me to intervene because they were hunger striking and reported to be near death. These young girls were very much in the public eye and I realised that if they died all hell would be let loose among the Catholics in Northern Ireland and also in the Republic. Roy Jenkins, the Home Secretary, agreed that I should see them and I went to Brixton prison. I had repeatedly seen photographs of the girls in newspapers and on television, police portraits which made them hard and tough. I was astonished when they entered the small cosy room where, in the presence of the chief wardress and a woman note-taker, we talked. They were delicately beautiful, almost spiritually, no doubt because their bodies were frail from weeks of starvation. They were also calm and responsive. Dolours who spoke most was in her early twenties, Marian, also alert, under twenty. I established contact by saying how James Connolly was a hero of mine sixty years ago, and their eyes lit up with appreciation. When I told them I did not approve of their bombing, they were at pains to assure me that they had taken part only on a pledge that sufficient warning would be given to prevent casualties and how deeply hurt they were that, owing to a delay in communications in London, a death and injuries had occurred. That gave me my opening. Did they not realise that if they died from hunger striking many more people in Northern Ireland would be killed from the violence that would break out, and that they would be responsible? I saw this shook them. Their reply was that they accepted the twenty years' sentence and their only object was to be transferred to a prison in Northern Ireland, which was their homeland and which would enable their parents to visit them. Their mother found the long journey by boat and train beyond her strength.

I reported this conversation to Roy Jenkins, who immediately made arrangements for the parents to travel by plane and promised to consider transference to a prison in Northern Ireland. Meanwhile, Jock Stallard, MP for St Pancras, and Paddy Devlin, Social Democratic Member of Stormont, had also been active. Roy Jenkins authorised us to tell the girls that he hoped to be able to transfer them to Ulster by the end of the year, four months away, though this would depend on the security situation. Jock, Paddy and I saw the girls, now much weaker, in their prison hospital ward. They were impressed and promised a decision after they had seen their parents, for whom the Home Secretary arranged a flight from Belfast the next day. Dolours and Marian then ended their hunger strike.

I was abused by some of the Press and in many letters and telephone calls for my intervention; people jumped to the conclusion that I sympathised with the bombing crime. I was reassured by the reaction in the Lords, particularly from Lord O'Neil of the Maine, ex-Prime Minister of Stormont, who congratulated me on saving Ulster from a bloodbath. The story did not end there. The situation in Belfast worsened and the girls were not transferred by the end of the year, which led them to renew hunger striking. Roy Jenkins assured me he would keep his promise as soon as conditions allowed, and I went to the girls again. I had learned that their mother was seriously ill and it was this, confirmed by a visit from their father next day, which led them to stop fasting. Their mother died shortly afterwards.

I had a strange relationship with the girls. Despite my humanism my role became something of a confidential priest's. I argued the rights and wrongs of bombing. They were sincere Catholics and they acknowledged that when they were nearly dying (the Medical Officer gave them ten days before loss of consciousness) they seemed to be near to their God and realised He would not countenance violence, but in a world of violence they had acted within prevailing conditions. I was impressed by their dedication to the cause of Socialist unity in Ireland and by their ability, and suggested that they should write a book addressed to Young Ireland describing the New Ireland they wanted. Dolours was enthusiastic and promised. My whole object was to turn the minds of the girls in a constructive direction, and in this I think I succeeded. When at last they were transferred to Armagh prison they enrolled as students of the Open University and frequent letters which I had from Dolours indicated how they were devoting themselves positively to the future.

Many months later I received from Dolours the poem that follows. I had said to them, 'You are gloriously young,' and that prompted her to write this.

> He is old,
> Gloriously so,
> (He will know the meaning of that)
> Yet, there is no fear in his old shoulders
>   of heavy burdens.
> He has borne his share,
> And part of mine.
>
> When it was not 'Politic'
> He came to us.

When we were not 'News'
He came to us.
When only humanity mattered
He came to us.

Like us he told them –
Sticks and Stones . . .
They did not try to break his bones,
Just his heart.
He has forgiven them –
For me, forgiveness is not my part!

We have not heard the last of Dolours and Marian.

I was distressed by what was happening in the new nations of Africa and Asia. Democracy was a weak plant amidst illiteracy and poverty, and national unity grew with difficulty amidst tribal divisions. One of the problems was that the ruling élite belonged to a different world, European–American educated, living in European and American comfort whilst those they governed existed in primitive destitution. Among this élite, which included army officers, government was often a competition between rival groups – during the first decade I was in the Lords there were fifteen *coups* in Africa. In colonial times the habit of 'dash' had been endemic, an extension of the tipping system, becoming corruption, and in the new business and political circles corruption became rife. Politicians and their families amassed fortunes in Nigeria and Ghana and I was disillusioned when some of those who had denounced land hunger in Kenya acquired vast estates at the expense of the still exploited peasants. There was at the same time an absence of tolerance and the ruthless imprisonment of political opponents. It was a disheartening picture, but I never doubted that it had been right to extend independence to the new nations. The military *coups*, violence, persecution and corruption in Europe when empires gave way to nation states were even greater. There were also encouraging facts – the work of disinterested men and women everywhere and countries like Tanzania and Zambia where Nyerere and Kaunda gave an example of high principle.

I was stunned by the civil war in Nigeria, which we had regarded as a model of democratic federation. When the troops began to march, the Movement for Colonial Freedom took the initiative in forming a Peace in Nigeria Committee, of which I became chairman. It was widely representative, including two former Governors, Sir James Robertson and Sir John MacPherson, Tories from Lords and Commons, including Lady Elliot and Hugh Fraser, MP, Labour and Liberal, Lords and MPs, representatives from all the Churches, Anglican, Catholic, Nonconformist, the Salvation Army as well as Africans from both sides.

The Committee asked James Griffiths and me to go to Biafra and Lagos to explore the possibilities of a truce followed by negotiations, and, hearing from both sides that we would be welcome, we went, accompanied by Dr John Wallace in case of medical need. Dr Wallace was my local GP and had volunteered for service in Biafra with the Save the Children Fund. As the war closed in he had been evacuated, but readily agreed to return. We travelled from the island of San Thome in an illegal relief plane, the floor piled high with bags of milk powder, a uncertain journey because we had to cross Nigerian territory and the air force attacked incoming craft. As we neared the mainland lights were put out and Jim gripped my hand whilst John tuned his portable recorder to music. The airstrip was in a narrow valley, rocks and trees on either side. For a moment before touching down it was brilliant with light, extinguished as soon as we stopped.

Ogoja, the headquarters of the secessionists, was under siege and the streets had road blocks, and lorries packed with soldiers passed in procession. In his bungalow crowning a deep shelter we met Colonel Ojukwu, the commander – he had been Governor of the Eastern Province before the declaration of Biafran independence – greying, rounded, hairy in face, quiet-spoken, a comfortable professor rather than a military chief. We urged a truce over Christmas and the New Year, and negotiations. To our delight Ojukwu accepted, insisting, however, that Biafra must be a nation-state, perhaps confederated with the rest of Nigeria. We also saw, in a large schoolroom, Biafra's provisional Cabinet. Its members were a little suspicious, thinking we might represent the British Government which was supporting Lagos, but we won their confidence by telling how we had opposed the sending of arms. Outside the school building was a large excited crowd. I addressed them and once more our independent sincerity was realised.

My most vivid memory of Biafra is of a visit to a Catholic relief centre. Supplies of food had been cut off by the blockading of Port Harcourt, and starvation was already the enemy rather than military defeat. We were driven at dawn (bombs would fall later) to a village where in large compounds hundreds of women and children and the old were given their one meal of the day, provided by the relief planes from San Thome, distributed by Catholic Sisters. The atmosphere diffused by the Sisters was extraordinarily cheerful and I became popular with the children by leading them in singing. A different memory remains of a visit on our journey home. We were taken to a jungle village of a few huts which had been bombed and we stood by the mounds of earth where two women had been buried. We were shocked to see small sharply-pointed needles which had been scattered by the bomb. They were the same as the Americans were using in Vietnam: explosives packed with piercing splinters to kill and maim those around. Who supplied Lagos with these sophisticated weapons? We were shown at Ogoja captured arms which came not only openly from Britain and the Soviet Union (strange allies), but from six other countries, mostly through the black market.

Shortly after we reached the airstrip it was bombed, fortunately with no damage to persons or the plane, but we had to wait two hours for repairs. Dr Wallace could not accompany us to Lagos because he would be a prohibited immigrant, having aided Biafra and, as there was no direct communication, James Griffiths and I had to travel all the way back to London before continuing our mission. In Lagos we were received by General Gowon, young, direct and soldierly, with his Cabinet, and I made the plea for truce and talks. Two interesting things happened which showed Gowon's authority. As I concluded, a messenger rushed in and handed a note to the General. He read it and turned to Jim and me. 'This is to report,' he said, 'that the insurgents are preparing a major attack.' Our hopes of a truce vanished. Gowon smiled, put down the note and remarked, 'Let us proceed.' Then came a second interruption. Chief Enahoro, a controversial figure in the West and now Minister for Information, rose and made a slashing attack on me, alleging that I was an agent of Ojukwu. I was appalled because Enahoro was responsible for the intelligence services. I need not have been. General Gowon brushed aside the interruption and assured us that we were welcome, even inviting us to prolong our stay. More important, he went on to accept a truce, though he insisted any talks must be on the basis of the integration of the East with Nigeria.

I cannot continue without saying how much I owed to Jim Griffiths on these visits. We had always been friends, though sometimes differing, but during this experience we became brothers, not only in the comradeship of what we were seeking to do, but in our oneness of attitude to it. Jim had been a Cabinet Minister, with responsibility for much of Africa, and it would have been natural for him to take the leadership. He declined, insisting that I was chairman of the London Committee. He supported me unfailingly in the negotiations and his advice was wise in our evening discussions. Jim died in August 1975. No one served the Labour movement more selflessly or with greater loyalty, almost religious in its dedication.

The world map had three black blots – the hostility in the Middle East, the war in Vietnam and the racial conflict in Rhodesia and South Africa. I was active in all three. To my surprise the Inter-Parliamentary Union asked me to lead a delegation to Jordan. My companionable colleagues included John Page, Conservative MP, whom I had earlier defeated at Slough, and Tom Maelor MP (now Lord Maelor), a religious conscientious objector of the First World War, concerned to visit neighbouring historic Palestine. In Jordan we visited the UN camps for refugees – sand and small huts without comfort – and hearing their case I became a fervent advocate of the creation of a Palestinian State.

To the American invasion of Indo-China I was among those who immediately responded, initiating the British Campaign for Peace in Vietnam and repeatedly criticising in the Commons and Lords the Labour Government's support of the USA. I had a curious experience. A letter came from professors at Ann Arbor University, Michigan, inviting me to a week's seminar of 'world intellectuals' on Vietnam. I repudiated the designation but joined academics from all over America and Europe, the only one among them who had not been to a university. At the end of the week there was a demonstration of four thousand students, who proceeded to occupy classrooms all night to discuss their problems. I went to a discussion by boys who expected to be called up. It was just like a meeting of COs in the First World War, a minority of religious objectors, others objecting on political grounds. American law allowed exemption with alternative service to religious objectors. Should they accept? No, they decided, they would demonstrate solidarity with their political comrades who had decided to tear up their draft cards. This visit was before the mass movement against the war developed in America. When I remarked that the students seemed isolated in their opposition I was told, 'Wait until we get home and arouse our parents.' Nearly one hundred thousand young men in the USA either refused service or deserted; one-tenth of the Forces, an amazing phenomenon. I acted for a group of resisters in Britain, objecting in the Lords to any deportations to America, helping others to get to Sweden.

The military *coup* in Chile in 1974, and the murder of Salvador Allende, the democratically elected head of state, in which the CIA was involved, outraged and angered us. Within twenty-four hours the MCF organised a vast demonstration in Hyde Park and a march to the Chilean Embassy where the Ambassador, not yet deposed, was deeply grateful for our support. Austen Williams allowed us to hold a memorial service in St Martin's, but the occasion I remember best was a massive Trafalgar Square demonstration addressed by Señora Allende. I presided and, placing my arm across her shoulders, said that her husband would share immortality with the Socialist martyrs, Jaurès, Karl Liebknecht and Rosa Luxemburg. She was moved to tears.

The problems of Black oppression in Rhodesia and apartheid South Africa were always with us. I greatly appreciated a warm note I had from Judith, daughter of Rhodesia's Liberal ex-Prime Minister, Garfield Todd, suffering years of house arrest. I also harried the Government on the Simonstown Agreement with South Africa, which was said to be necessary because the Soviet Navy was in the Indian Ocean – but so was the American navy with bases leased from Britain. The answer surely was the neutralisation of the Indian Ocean as demanded by the bordering Asian and African States. The Southern African scene was completely changed by the Portuguese withdrawal from its colonies, particularly by the African victory in Mozambique. One was shocked by the conflict between the three nationalist movements in Angola, but further north the transition in Guinea was happier, even though their African leader, Amilcar Cabral (young, realistic, constructive, who, like many others visiting this country, came to see me in the Lords) was murdered before they gained their independence.

I would like to add here a personal note. There were few persons to whom I have been more politically opposed than Lord Fraser of Lonsdale. He stood for the old order and supported South Africa. Yet, when I was in difficulties about an African in this country who wanted his repressed family in Johannesburg to join him, Lord Fraser, to whom I turned in despair, wrote a personal letter to his friend, South Africa's Prime Minister, Mr Vorster, as a result of which the wife and children were permitted to come. Lord Fraser and I established a human accord despite somewhat acid exchanges in the Chamber. He was blind, but did not have to ask who it was when I met him in corridor or stairs. He knew my voice.

Earlier I had paid a second visit to India on the invitation of the Government, travelling from Bombay to Delhi, Calcutta, Madras and Bangalore. I was impressed by its advance in industrialisation, but shocked by the continuing poverty of the mass of the people. The contrast between technological advance and life was dramatically seen at the atomic power-station near Bombay. I was awed by its white cathedral-like incarnation of power – the new age either of liberation or destruction – and yet its entrance roadway was being repaired by the fingers of kneeling women, justified as a means of providing more employment than machinery would have required. In the capital I saw the contrast between the spacious New Delhi of Lutyens mansions and the hideous overcrowding of Old Delhi. As I drove from Calcutta airport I wondered whether India had any pride; we passed through narrow streets bordered by stinking sanitation channels; any other Government, perhaps hypocritically, would have hidden them. I had the bad luck to be ill on the one day I was to return to my childhood village of Berhampur, but in Madras I was able to visit the teachers' training college of which my sister Nora had been Head. She started it with twelve students in 1923; now it had nearly two thousand. I liked Bangalore, well planned without evident poverty though I am sure it was there.

In Delhi I had tea in her bungalow with Indira Gandhi, the Prime Minister. I first had tea with her and her famous father when she was a student at Cambridge and we had met at Kenya's independence as I have described. It is difficult to reach Indira's personality; though friendly, she does not unbend and gives an impression of hidden strength and decision. I had admired the way she began her premiership by excluding the old reactionary guard from the Congress Party, and her leadership during the Bangladesh war was supreme, but it came as a great shock when in 1975 she arrested her political opponents, particularly Jayaprakash Narayan, and destroyed the liberty of the Press and the judiciary. I understood her difficulties. Some of her opponents were undoubtedly conspiring to overthrow the administration and 'JP' was conducting a formidable civil disobedience campaign, which, whilst challenging India's greatest evils, corruption and the exploitation of peasants, was also challenging the existing representative democracy. Indira's condemnation by the courts for electoral malpractices was, as *The Times* wrote, for trivial technical offences; she was above suspicion of corruption. Moreover, she used the Emergency to good purpose, reducing the cost of living for the poor, stamping on corruption. All this was consistent with the strong person she is, but nevertheless it was a terrible blow to the expectation that India would progress to social justice through liberal democracy. When Narayan was imprisoned I wrote to him suggesting that he should offer cooperation with Indira against corruption and peasant exploitation. I do not know whether he got it – he was not allowed letters so I sent it to Indira, asking her to let him have it. I received no reply from her. I was hurt.

I planned a two-day stay in Algeria on the return journey to England. At the independence celebrations there in 1963 I had met Wendy Campbell-Purdie, who surprised me by saying she was growing trees in the Sahara. Later in London she set up a committee, under the chairmanship of the Rev. Austen Williams, the progressive vicar of St Martin-in-the-Fields, to support her project. I decided to see what she was doing. Wendy drove me to the little Arab town of Bou Saada, the scene of her tree-planting, on the edge of the Sahara desert. The next day I fell unconscious with a heart attack. Wendy nursed me through the crisis under the care of two Czech doctors, who as part of their country's aid scheme worked at the local hospital. My two-day visit became two months. It was some time after my return to London before I fully recovered.

I was deeply impressed by Wendy's project to which she took me often by car. Her theory was that in the no-man's-land between fertile soil and desert it is possible to grow a wall of trees which would prevent the desert expanding and which could become a point of advance into the desert itself. At Bou Saada she was proving it – after three years the trees were taller than herself. I was intrigued by the possibilities. The desert was extending by a mile each year; a wall of trees round it would save good land. I read Wendy's textbooks, which told how there were rivers and lakes under the Sahara which the Romans had reached with wells. In Israel they had proved that by irrigation the desert could be made fertile in three years. Great hopes arose in my mind. Here in the Sahara and other deserts (one-seventh of the area of the earth) was the potential fertility which could meet the danger of the hunger of millions through world population growth.

A desire arose in me to put on the map of reality Wendy's discovery and its expansion to other deserts. That would mean the participation of the surrounding Governments, of the World Food and Agricultural Organisation and of the Special Development Fund of the United Nations – an immense political task. The snag was that Wendy was not a politician; she held too much to principle, leaving the Rome headquarters of FAO disillusioned by its caution, leaving Morocco where she began tree-planting because of the persecution of her Socialist friends. It would have been difficult to find a government in this mad age with whom she would have been happy to cooperate.

I was tempted to give up all other political work and devote myself to the task of convincing the world of the opportunity which Bou Saada had revealed. I wished to do something constructive in my last years; so much of my life had been a protest. I returned to England doubtful about my future, but finally decided to remain in British politics. I gave my spare time from the House of Lords to writing *The Colonial Revolution*, a tome on the national struggles of peoples everywhere. My mind was still in the Sahara, but I had the consolation of knowing that the Governments of Algeria and Senegal had adopted Wendy's scheme and were planting their walls of trees all along the borders of the desert.

The implications of the wasted deserts grew in my mind. I became increasingly depressed by the failure of the West, including Britain, to respond to the needs of the Third World. Governments had a series of conferences dealing with pollution, population, food, the seas, and at each there was confrontation between the developed and developing countries. Pollution – the worst pollution was of human life through poverty. Population – the best way to prevent uncontrollable growth was to extend civilised standards of life which promoted lower birth rates. Food – the answer was international coordination of grain distribution and fertilisation of the deserts. I raised all these issues in the Lords and particularly the Law of the Sea conferences, which reflected the fundamental divergence. Who should exploit the mineral wealth under the oceans? The West suggested that an international authority should issue licences but these would be seized by the multi-national companies. The Third World proposed that the wealth should be regarded as the heritage of mankind to be developed directly in the interests of all by the international authority. Here was a direct confrontation between multi-national capitalism and international Socialism; the British Government modified its position a little under pressure, but not enough.

I became increasingly convinced that economic relations between the developed and developing nations would dominate the coming years. Under the chairmanship of President Boumedienne of Algeria the unaligned nations proposed a new international economic order based on national possession of natural resources, control of multi-national companies and, importantly, the coordination of the prices they received for their raw materials with the prices they paid for manufactured goods. The Commonwealth Heads of State became involved and the United Nations devoted a session to the subject. Here was an opportunity to begin to bridge the gap between the rich third of the world and the poor two-thirds – a great challenge. Liberation (the successor to the Movement for Colonial Freedom) agreed on my suggestion to promote a representative conference in London and Stan Newens, its chairman, and I went to Algeria to receive Third World cooperation. We became, with Judith Hart – the splendid Minister for Overseas Development, unhappily sacked by Harold Wilson – co-directors of the project. To contribute towards ending world hunger had become an obsession with me.

I was against going into the European Community. I am not anti-European. I was a foundation member of the Movement for a United Socialist States of Europe, but resigned when it became instead the Socialist Movement for a United Europe, allying itself with Churchill and Duncan Sandys. I regarded the European Community within the Treaty of Rome as a capitalist set-up, but at the same time I could not agree with anti-marketeers who argued that Britain must retain its sovereignty; in our shrinking interdependent world national sovereignty must be severely qualified. The real problem here is the difficulty of relating national and multi-national authorities to the needs and wishes of the peoples they represent. Even within a nation a citizen often feels he has little contact with his Parliament; the gulf would be much greater with a multi-national Parliament. A difficult problem of participation.

Most of my time in the Lords was devoted to issues I have described, but I became known primarily as an advocate of peace. Perhaps I did feel most deeply about this; I was conscious all the time of the massed nuclear weapons which could destroy mankind. I put the chances of world genocide at more than fifty-fifty and urged not only disarmament but every proposal which would decrease the danger of war – the reform of the United Nations, a Geneva Conference on the Middle East, UN intervention to settle the conflict in Cyprus, constitutional talks in Rhodesia, the neutralisation of the Indian Ocean, the termination of the military alliances of SEATO (achieved in 1975) and CENTO and, most of all, every possible step to further the détente between the two super-Powers. I despaired of the futility of the millions of words spilled out at the everlasting Disarmament Conference at Geneva. I came more and more to see that the arms race would end only when there was positive association in daily life between the people of all nations.

This conviction incited a new enthusiasm. Ten years before, I had read of a proposal by the Soviet Union and the Communist countries for a European Conference for Security and Cooperation with the aim of ending the military functions of NATO and the Warsaw Pact Alliance. That was my fervent desire, but I dismissed the sincerity of the Communist appeal because it was an appendix to a violent attack on the USA and Western Europe, scarcely attuned to a response. Two years later, however, the Soviet Union changed its approach and spoke in conciliatory and realistic terms. There seemed to me no doubt about the sincerity of Mr Brezhnev and the Kremlin. For six years, almost alone, I pressed the case in Parliament. Both front benches were at first lukewarm, but détente was in the air and, despite misgivings, NATO finally agreed. The first conference of Heads of State, held at Helsinki in June 1973, appointed commissions which after two years' discussion made comprehensive recommendations, and in August 1975, a recalled Summit Conference endorsed them. The decisions were breathtaking in scope, transforming the earlier negative coexistence of East and West into positive cooperation. *The Times* remarked that if implemented they would transform the pattern of Europe.

Here was the opportunity for the living identification I believed to be the doorway to disarmament and peace. I devoted myself to it, persistent in the Lords, securing support at the Labour Party Conference, writing pamphlets, attending international conferences at Liège and Brussels. I was encouraged by personal letters from President Kekkonnen, the host at Helsinki, Chancellor Willi Brandt, Senator Edward Kennedy and others. I was excited that the peace forces of Europe had achieved so much, but doubts remained.

Would the recommendations be implemented? Would the expectations of radical disarmament voiced at Helsinki be realised? I was fearful that the conflict between the structures and prejudices of Western capitalism and Communist authoritarianism would once more destroy our hopes.

The spring of 1976 was unusually wonderful, the world of nature a shining rainbow of blossom and leaf, but the human world showed signs of moving towards a new cold war. In America and Britain the sceptics attacked the Soviet Union for expanding military power and for denying the Human Rights provisions of the Helsinki agreement. I was not competent to judge the balance of military forces, but I noted that the Pentagon said that USA strength was not inferior. I had sympathy with the critics of Soviet treatment of dissidents (in the Lords I said that dissidence today was the condition of progress tomorrow), but the specific Helsinki pledges of family reunions, facilities for journalists, acceptance of Western papers and Western observers at military manoeuvres were fulfilled. What concessions had the West made? The core of the Helsinki Act was economic integration. Here the initiatives were taken by the East. I pressed again and again for action by the West, but there was frustrating delay.

The real test of Helsinki will of course be disarmament. Discussions on partial reductions got bogged down, but Mr Brezhnev offered drastic measures, including the outlawing of nuclear weapons and progressive steps to full disarmament. Bluff, said the sceptics. Then let us call the bluff, I urged. Goronwy Roberts the Foreign Office spokesman in the Lords, sympathetic, sincere, the most selfless of Ministers, welcomed Mr Brezhnev's proposals but insisted on international verification which the Russians had refused. In April a momentous change took place. On his London visit Mr Gromyko, the Soviet Foreign Secretary, accepted international inspection and the Soviet agreed to it in Moscow negotiations with the USA. It is true the topic was tests for peaceful purposes, but the important fact is that the principle of verification was endorsed. The significance of this change did not seem to be recognised by the statesmen of the West, but surely it provides the greatest hope of our time. It is up to the Soviet Union to make clear their intention beyond all peradventure. It is up to all devoted to peace to demand that the opportunity be seized.

CHAPTER THIRTY-ONE

UNFULFILLED

I have lived a full life and have been involved in most of the social and political changes in Britain, and many of those abroad, during the last seventy years. If I had to live it again I would not change it much except in seeking cultured leisure and perhaps in personal relationships. I have been a political animal and missed the fulfilment of culture. Literature and the arts have been incidental in my life and only in later years have I appreciated what I have missed. Like Beatrice Webb, I have come to love music by listening to it on radio and television, but I know little about it. I am awed by Gothic architecture, its avenues and heights, though again I am ignorant. I feel at one with creation among the beauties of nature, but I know the names of only the most familiar trees. I an uneducated: a full life but an unfulfilled life. I have also sacrificed personal relationships to my political obsession. There is some truth in the saying that one can love humanity and be less than considerate to individuals. I have been unfair to others. These deficiencies I hope I would change if I had to begin again. One cannot even be a good politician if one is less than a complete human being.

Another thing has been borne on me. Politicians are amateurs compared with artists and technicians. I revere the genius of the composers of the classic symphonies. I marvel at the efficiency of scientists and engineers; how is it possible to send men to the moon and robots to Mars? Where are comparable politicians? We are untrained and even our techniques of presentation are less then competent; think of the boring political broadcasts. Artists have contributed works of beauty which lift us to the stars. We politicians deny them to most of mankind. Scientists have produced a source of energy which could transform the life of the world. We politicians use it for destruction and death. We are a poor lot. When will a statesman arise with the voice to arouse people to a sense of the world's stupidities and possibilities?

My children, and their children, have helped to keep me young. I was fortunate in my four daughters, all Socialists in life as well as mind. Audrey, the eldest, was elected astonishingly to the Council of Churchill's Westerham more than twenty years ago and became its leading citizen. She and her husband, Jim Wood, devoted themselves to the Sevenoaks Labour Party. Margaret, born while I was in prison, was all love and laughter, tragically killed when a newly-wed in the Second World War. Joan, the third, is active in the Woodcraft Folk, the youngsters' community in the Cooperative Movement, officiating in Socialist Youth camps all over Europe. One of her boys gave me my first great-grandson. Olive, a nurse, has lived for others, taking a course in cancer care when Audrey became ill, tending her to the end. I have a son, Christopher, a computer consultant, whatever that may be. I am hopeless with figures and money. He inherits mathematics from Edith, who alone saves me from empty pockets, forgotten debts and tax misdemeanours. I have two and a half sisters. Nora, Indian college head, rare in spirit and mind, to whom I have referred; Phyllis, teacher, living in retirement with Nora at Stratford-on-Avon, local preacher and Labour Party member; and step-sister, Nellie-Frances, married to a Reverend, mother of John Roper, Labour MP, and active pacifist Christopher. All three are in the Brockway tradition.

I confess I have an obsession other than politics – sport. Most weekends I spend watching rugby, soccer, cricket, tennis, athletics, gymnastics on television. I revel in it, my relaxation, perhaps my escapism. Karl Marx said that religion was the opium of the masses. The mountainous thousands overlooking a soccer match make one ask whether today football is not the opium. Political meetings are considered successful when the audience is two hundred. Fifty thousand attend Manchester United (my team since Munich). The partisanship of the fans stimulates violence; for most of them football is a relief from the drabness of life. If clubs and public authorities provided more facilities for sporting activities and encouraged fans to participate, not only would interest be added to existence but a physical alternative would be given to violence. I hate the increasing commercialism of sport; a reflection of the profit motive inherent in a capitalist environment. Another personal habit. I have been a vegetarian for seventy years, proving that one can be healthy. Flesh eating has two evil consequences. It cruelly exploits animals and it spends money on grains which could feed thousands of malnourished humans. I have faith that a distant day will come when many will feel identity not only with all people but with all life.

My generation was silent on the subject of sex. No adult ever said anything to me about it in boyhood and teenage. I went to a boys' school and knew no girls, except for a brief time my sisters. Sex education would have been regarded as indecent and there were no books on the subject. Even when I lived in a community with fellow late-teenage Socialists, the taboo remained; we never discussed sex nor exchanged more than a puritanical kiss with a girl when saying goodnight. I grew to manhood regarding sex as a pleasurable relief, but not appreciating that it should also give equal physical satisfaction to the woman. Of very many young men of my time that was typical and most young women were similarly uneducated, regarding it as their duty to submit to the appetite of men. Perhaps Nature made sex teaching irrelevant in many marriages, but the inhibitions and ignorances of Victorian times had a disastrous effect on my generation. Only later did I realise the frustration suffered; it meant marriage unfulfilled for many women – and for men, too, because they lost the mutuality of sex. A contemporary confessed to me that he learned to give comprehensive pleasure to a woman only when he grew too old to give it completely. Today we talk much of Women's Lib. Marie Stopes with her pioneer books on sex brought as much liberation to women as did the suffragettes.

It is good that we are now frank and open about sex. Sex education in schools is still a subject of controversy, but we are passing from the age when physical love was considered as an unmentionable indecency. Of course, merely stating the facts of life is not enough; one must inculcate a sense of social responsibility and in games provide the facilities for physical activity and in the arts for expression. Although I do not agree with Lord Longford's obsession about pornography, I realise that it can be bad in effect. Some publications are sheer exploitation for profit and represent, as someone has said, 'the obscene face of capitalism'. The audiences at cinemas showing blue films and at striptease shows are almost entirely men and reflect the male domination of sex which we must outgrow. I welcome the freedom of uncommercial sex when a woman and a man willingly come together from mutual affection. I favour trial marriages; if companionship is to endure it is desirable that the partners should know each other intimately. It is only when sexual intercourse is more than physical enjoyment and is part of a deep spiritual union that a man and a woman are ready to establish a home and think of children. The family with loving parents and children is the ideal human unit, but look at all the broken marriages around us, so often due to youngsters uniting from physical attraction without the basis for continuing sympathy of mind and spirit. Wider experience would allow for more mature judgement. The pill has made all the difference. The old morality was based largely on the fear of pregnancy and the disintegration of relationships which illegitimate children cause. That fear is now being removed but we have not yet adjusted ourselves to the new facts of life and the new moral code which they necessitate.

I am a Humanist, though I am not sure that some of my fellow agnostics would accept me as such. I am not an atheist. I do not know if there be a God or an after-life. As I have tried to describe earlier (Chapter Two), I have had experiences which seemed to link me with a spiritual presence expanding personal consciousness to universal. In the silences of nature, in great music and art and in deep human love, one can experience the feeling of being part of an all-embracing life, uniting the past with the present, identifying one with all creation. I had this experience most completely when young, but it remains deeply within me, a continuing reality, often ignored, sometimes abused, but returning. Does this mean a belief in God? I have no sense of a personal God; in that respect I am an agnostic.

It is the same with after-life. One has seen a friend near death and his personality has been more vital than his body. Does it die with the body? Within the space of a few weeks I lost my eldest daughter, a wonderful person, and my best male friend, a comrade in thought and activity, and for some time after their deaths they were intimately present, but gradually the sense of closeness passed. Was this just a question of memory? I have had personal experiences where my personality has seemed separated from my body, and spiritualist friends have told me extraordinary stories. I do not know. Except for the desire to meet again those one has loved, I am little concerned. We are here, let us do our job here, not worrying about what is in store for ourselves in the future. I have no fear of death. I often think it would be marvellous to sleep and not wake up. I like Bertrand Russell's verdict – born in a spring, flowing in a river, joining the boundless ocean.

Bernard Shaw converted my teenage spiritual experience to activity in life when he advised me to 'find out what the life-force is making for, and make for it, too'. But each one of us must decide what the life-force is indeed making for. Nietzsche and Hitler believed in a life-force, the latter with disastrous consequences, but I had no doubt that the creative force which I experienced aimed at human fulfilment and fellowship and I became conscious of working with it as I served that aim. Is this all delusion? I am not a philosopher and theoretically it may be. I know only that it gave a meaning to life for me.

My break with Christianity came with the realisation that my beliefs had no connection with the theology of the churches or the consciousness of the presence of God through the person of Jesus. Rationally I dismissed the conception of God coming to man through a son by virgin birth, performing supernatural miracles and physically rising from the grave. I appreciate that many liberal Christians now reject this theology, but they still recite it in their creeds. I found myself more in sympathy with the pantheism of Eastern religions than with traditional Christian theology. There was a time when I declined to go a church service, but I learned to be more tolerant, realising that many Christians renew their spiritual experience in worship and recognising that they are often foremost in the service of peace and justice. In particular, I have the greatest admiration for the contribution which the Churches, Catholic and Protestant alike, have made for freedom and racial equality in Africa and Latin America. I revere Jesus, his life and ethical teaching. I know of nothing more exquisite in all literature than the description of the incident when the Pharisees confronted him with a woman found in adultery. Jesus did not look into her face; he went on making marks in the sand and then faced the Pharisees: 'Let him who is without sin be the first to accuse.' No humiliation of the woman; her accusers hurrying away ashamed. Perfect. The pundits may say that the incident never occurred. No matter. Even if the Gospels were proved to be a myth, we should be poorer without their picture of Jesus. His ethical teaching is eternal truth. Love felt and applied contains all the answers.

I once urged that it is the duty of Humanists to rescue Jesus from the image presented by the Church. It has the right to claim him as its own in his religious teaching of the reality of God and the heaven to come, but it systematically misrepresents his life. As I watch on television the ornamental processions, the imperious pomp, the rich robes and elaborate rituals of Church ceremonies, I ask myself what they have to do with the simple man who went from village to village in Palestine, the companion of the poor. I feel it most of all when I see Bishops blessing regiments and weapons of war in contrast with his gospel of love. The processions and ceremonies are often splendid spectacles, dignified and beautiful, exemplified in the Coronation, but how can they be symbolic of a Jesus born in a stable, exiled in a foreign country with refugee parents, growing up in a carpenter's cottage, choosing fishermen as his disciples, speaking to mass gatherings on the mountainside, turning the money-makers from the synagogue doors, denouncing the rich who would reach heaven only through a needle's eye, riding into Jerusalem on a donkey, undergoing arrest as a rebel against the Establishment, refusing to accept the jurisdiction of the Court, sentenced to death and executed as a traitor with thieves as his fellow victims? Jesus was a revolutionary, a revolutionary with love not hatred as the dynamic. Admittedly he did not campaign against the political wrongs of his time or

the imperial power of Rome over his people. He was concerned with principles for all time. It is for us to apply those principles in our own time.

And so we come to the world today. First let us consider Socialism. I will
put the economic case first, though Socialism is much more than that to me.
We have no reason to assume that capitalism will endure. Man has passed
from tribal communism to slavery, feudalism and the class-dominated
industrial revolution: development cannot end there. The injustices and
cruelties of capitalism are too great to be tolerated: the poverty, the unemployment, the homelessness, the ugliness, the unfulfilled life of millions, the
wars for exploitation and power. It is argued that these evils can be remedied
within capitalism and much humanising is possible, but the non-Socialist
alternative of spreading personal ownership is against all economic trends.
The irreversible course now is towards monopolisation in industry, increasingly on a multi-national scale. To speak of shared ownership, except
through insignificant shareholdings, in such a system is an obsolete view
and – except for individual promotion within the engulfing giants – so is the
aim of personal opportunity and freedom. The issue now is whether the
giant corporations should be privately or publicly owned.

I do not regard the present form of nationalisation as Socialism. I was at
Merthyr Tydfil in South Wales when the railways were nationalised. Engine
drivers wrote on the trucks, 'These are ours now'. No railwaymen feel that
now about the State-owned service. The boards of the nationalised industries
are as distant from the workers as the boards of privately owned monopolies;
the salaries of board members in contrast with the wages of the lowest paid
retain the gulf of Disraeli's two nations no less than in private industry.
Nationalisation may be a step towards Socialism, but Socialism means
industrial and consumers' democracy; a partnership between the workers
and the public whom they serve, requiring representation on the boards by
workers and consumers as well as by the State and workers' participation in
management from the shop floor upwards. The problem of participation is the
most urgent in our economic life; difficult, involving experimentation and
evolution, but essential to industrial democracy. Only when workers and
the public feel that industries are *theirs* shall we have the psychological basis
of Socialism.

The emergence of multi-national companies, anchored in the industrialised
West but expanding all over the world, makes it necessary for Socialism to
be international. The multi-national companies, despite their power of
exploitation, are not historically reactionary; the world today is so integrated
that the internationalisation of trade and industry is inevitable. The multi-
nationals are establishing the structure; the Socialist challenge will be to

adjust the structure to world needs rather than to the profit of financiers, and to apply democracy to its administration. This will involve enormous changes. There will have to be an international economic authority, responsible to the peoples and we shall have to become consciously internationalist. No modern Karl Marx has yet given his mind to this problem and I will not attempt an answer. I suggest only that an economic arm of the United Nations, as important as its political arm, is required to express international authority, and that community participation is required at all levels. This involves democratic allegiance to a revolutionised United Nations and a virile international Socialist awareness, both of which, alas, are still distant.

The Communist nations of Eastern Europe and China call themselves Socialist. I am ashamed to acknowledge that I know little about China, but what I do know suggests that it is more equalitarian than the Soviet Union and its Communist associates, though its foreign policy of opposition to détente is disastrous. The economic basis of the Communist nations may be socialist, but they do not represent Socialism to me. They claim that they have abolished classes, but they still retain a governing class and a class of technocrats whose standard of life is far higher than that of the masses. And worst, Communist states have an unacceptable absence of freedom of thought. I visited the Soviet Union once and was interviewed for newspapers. I cannot forget how, when I expressed certain views, an editor told me that he could not print them because they were contrary to government policy. My expectation is that liberty of expression will grow in Communist states as education extends and as the fear of intervention by capitalist governments decreases and the idea of détente develops. But the authoritarian character of Communism cannot be accepted by democratic Socialists.

Socialism to me means much more than this economic pattern. It should be a way of life. Sometimes I regret even the appeal to service; this so often implies patronage and 'do-goodism'. If one really believes in a universal life uniting us all, this means identity, acting for all as part of ourselves. I believe that Socialism will not be entirely convincing until Socialists themselves reject the privileges and aggrandisements of capitalism. They must stop sending their children to schools of the élite, thus giving them greater opportunities than the children of others, striving for high incomes when so many are poor, possessing second houses when so many are homeless, accepting directorships which involve responsibility for a system to which they are theoretically opposed – in a word, joining the exploiting nation in the two nations which capitalism imposes. I find inspiration in Nyerere's Socialist Charter in Tanzania which prohibits any member of his Government from accepting the privileges of capitalism or participating in its administration. I admit difficulties. I live in comfort whilst so many are comfortless. I live in a residential London suburb, far from the life of the mass of working-class people, and am conscious of this when I mix with rank-and-file members of the Labour Party in the industrial north. I associate with the richest in the land in the House of Lords. None of us is consistent.

People sometimes congratulate me on sticking to principles, but I have chosen the easier path. I have never wanted to be in government because not even a Labour Government will do things which I feel are fundamentally important. But this has allowed me uninhibited action without responsibility, with freedom to express principles more realistic in the future than the present. To be in a pressure-group is child's play compared with participation in administration tackling day-to-day problems which inevitably compel compromise. I have great admiration for Socialist idealists who undertake the often misunderstood task of guiding us in government, in circumstances which demand some immediate concession of principles, in order that we may advance to their realisation later. I have many friends among them. They have chosen the more difficult way and I respect them.

I have already written that I become more Left as I become older. I regard the problems for which even Labour Governments seek remedies within capitalism, such as problems of inflation, unemployment and poverty, incapable of solution without Socialism. Failure to apply Socialist principles may lead to Right reaction doomed in its turn to ever deepening failure. Then perhaps a real Socialist government could follow. The decisive confrontation should come within the next decade.

The realisation of Socialism is more than an economic transformation. It implies an ethical transformation. The apologists for capitalism applaud personal incentive. They encourage success through inequality, individual and group aggrandisement, profit-making, riches as a measure of life's achievement. This incentive for oneself and one's family is a strong instinct but is it the best? The Socialist alternative is identity with the community, working for it, and having as a reward an equitable share of what is achieved. This requires a revolution in psychology to accompany the economic change. This is why Socialism must be a religion. We may build the economic structure, but without the new ethic the soul of Socialism will be absent.

A second concern for me is liberty. Perhaps because of my Nonconformist ancestors, perhaps because of my early experience of imprisonment, personal liberty has been a passion. I revolt whenever I hear of political prisoners, of men imprisoned without trial, of tortures to extract information or confession, of suppression of freedom of thought and expression. Often I agree with the victims and that gives more strength to my protests, but even when I disagree I believe the right to voice opinions is fundamental. Truth will be reached only when all can speak; dissidence is the condition of progress.

Sometimes I despair of the world when everywhere, in Britain's Northern Ireland with torture acknowledged, in Soviet Russia with its Siberian labour camps, in South Africa, in Spain, Chile, Cambodia, Latin America, Indonesia, in parts of independent Africa and my loved India, in all continents free expressions of thought and speech is denied. Yet there is something more basic – the greatest oppressor of personal fulfilment is poverty. The hungry millions in Asia, Africa and Southern America care little about freedom of thought and speech. The stomach takes priority over the brain. I reject entirely the charge that democratic Socialism is the enemy of personal freedom. It is a condition of human living which will simultaneously liberate the body and the mind.

Perhaps again because of ancestors and my own association with Africa and Asia I am devoted to racial equality. I have no sense whatever of colour in human relationships. Races have different pigmentation, but all are amazingly alike in human attributes and all can reach the greatest heights of physical, mental and spiritual development; the extent to which colour divides men is the extent to which they are inhuman. Apartheid in South Africa may be the extreme form of racial intolerance, but it exists in some degree everywhere. One has ground for hope: in principle, racial discrimination is widely rejected; the doubt lies in practice. In the industrialised West the non-white sections of the population are too often treated as second-class citizens, living in ghettoes, restricted to low-paid jobs and suffering worst from unemployment. This is true of Negroes in America, Commonwealth immigrants in Britain and Algerians in France. The danger is that among them, particularly among the frustrated school-leavers, hatred of whites will grow. Only if social and economic equality can be secured will this century see the end of racial intolerance.

Above all, I desire peace. The world today is being destroyed by violence, within nations and between nations. Physical cruelty, hi-jacking, terrorism and bombing are a part of our life. The problem is the ease with which weapons of death can be made by a lunatic fringe in basement or attic. No security can prevent it; only as social harmony and evident justice are developed can we hope to contain it.

The greater danger is the obsession of all governments with armaments: the nuclear provision for human suicide, the trade in arms from the industrialised countries to the underdeveloped, the fantastic contradiction, even under a Labour Government in Britain, of having simultaneously a Minister for Disarmament and a Minister to trade in armaments. Unless we stop all this the human race will be annihilated. How to stop? By using every possible means to bring about cooperation between nations, but also by the creation of a moral revulsion against war. I do not believe this is impossible. The vast majority of people do not want war. The greatest need in the world is a movement across frontiers by people everywhere who will say 'enough'. A voice may yet arise so powerful that men and women everywhere will respond by demanding an end to the blasphemy which governments commit against creation. Must we have another and worse Hiroshima before we awake?

I began this confession of faith by acknowledging that my life is unfulfilled personally. It is unfulfilled politically as well. Friends sometimes say that I must feel satisfied because the political liberation of colonial territories to which I have devoted much of my life has been nearly completed. This view was put to me, astonishingly, by a political opponent. I have referred before to John Page who stood against me at Slough. His father was Sir Arthur Page, the distinguished Chief Justice of Burma. I was stunned when John sent me this assessment of my political life written by his father: 'I think Fenner Brockway is the most successful politician of his generation. Only he has been able to see the realisation during his lifetime of everything for which he has fought – though I disagree with all those aims.' I quote this to deny it. The tribute is generous, but it misunderstands: colonial liberation has been only a small part of my purpose. Besides, it has been achieved not by any individual, but by events – the democratic upsurge following the war against Fascism and the strength of the nationalist movements. Sir Arthur would have been surprised to hear that I have been more disappointed than enthused by the consequences of colonial liberation. It has been progress but only relatively, new oppressors sometimes taking over from the old, exploitation persisting from outside.

My ideals have been no less than those I have described above – freedom, equality, peace and Socialism and these are far from fulfilled. There has been some advance. Colonial liberation has not been without its encouraging transformations, and it provides the opportunity for more. In Indo-China military imperialism has been defeated. There is a new determination to grapple with the problem of the gulf between rich and poor nations, and there is a greater will for peace, despite ideological conflicts. In Britain we have left behind the extreme destitution of seventy and even forty years ago; and Socialist principles are increasingly accepted in recognition that the interests of workers come before personal profit and that there is justice in a participating industrial democracy.

Sometimes, however, I doubt whether mankind has progressed overall in my lifetime. The one consolation I find is that there are more reasonably sane people in this mad world than there have ever been. Are there enough, and have they the will and the skill to change the evil reality to the possible good?

At times I wonder, and yet something within me compels the conviction that over the years, perhaps over generations, mankind will progressively realise the aims which have inspired so many. Why do they arise in us if Destiny is to deny them? When tempted to despair I remember that the acorn becomes the oak. The human race is still in its childhood or perhaps adolescence. The day of adult reason and love will surely come. Politically no less than personally I am unfulfilled, but I am confident that tomorrow the purpose of yesterday and today will reach fulfilment. Towards Tomorrow.

INDEX